BUFFALO BILL
Last of the Great Scouts

BUFFALO BILL
Last of the Great Scouts

THE LIFE STORY OF
COL. WILLIAM F. CODY
"BUFFALO BILL"

AS TOLD BY HIS SISTER
HELEN CODY WETMORE

UNIVERSITY OF NEBRASKA PRESS
LINCOLN AND LONDON

Library of Congress Catalog Card number 65–13258
Manufactured in the United States of America
International Standard Book Number 0–8032–5215–3

Originally published under the title:
Last of the Great Scouts.

First Bison Book printing: April, 1965

Most recent printing shown by first digit below:

10

*Bison Book edition reproduced from the 1899 edition
published by the Duluth Press Publishing Company.*

TO THE MEMORY OF A MOTHER
WHOSE CHRISTIAN
CHARACTER STILL LIVES A HALLOWED
INFLUENCE

INTRODUCTION

The American legend that is Buffalo Bill Cody was formed from three main sources; the man, the Wild West Show, and the printed word. The man was an authentic, likeable, and even modest western hero, cited by his army superiors for his bravery and resourcefulness, and willing and able to capitalize upon his prairie exploits for financial gain. The show was so good that it almost lived up to its billings; it was an exhibition of real Indians, cowboys, sharpshooters and wild derring-do that captivated Europeans and Americans, kings and democrats. Every other "Western" was and is, in a sense, an imitation of Buffalo Bill's Wild West. The printed word has been in the form of novels, autobiographies, articles, and biographies. Cody books have been numerous and exaggerated. Perhaps none have contributed more to the Buffalo Bill legend than *Last of the Great Scouts, the Life Story of Col. William F. Cody "Buffalo Bill"* as told by his sister Helen Cody Wetmore.

Helen Cody was the fourth of five daughters of the Isaac Cody family. Her brother, Bill, was four years older and she idolized him. Her admiration did not diminish when he became the famous Buffalo Bill. Helen's second marriage was to Hugh Wetmore, editor of the Duluth *Press*. The generous Cody helped the Wetmores financially. Helen wrote *Last of the Great Scouts* and it was first published by the Duluth Press in 1899. The book was widely sold and read and was good advertising for the Wild West Show. On the mornings of the pre-show parade a wagonload of *Last of the Great Scouts* would tour the city with a salesman and an Indian. The Indian would dance and the salesman sell books at a dollar a copy

INTRODUCTION

with a fifty cent show ticket added to the bargain. Several editions were printed, one illustrated by Remington. In 1918 Grosset and Dunlap issued a reprint boasting a foreword by the famous Zane Grey.

Although Mrs. Wetmore stated that she told "a plain unvarnished tale" and that "embarrassed by riches of fact I have had no thought of fiction," the book treats fact lightly. Its obvious exaggerations and inventions not only helped to establish the Buffalo Bill legend but they also gave ammunition to the debunkers of Cody. It was easy to prove the book to be laced with fiction and it followed that its hero was a fraud. The living hero did not care because he was in show business and knew the value of publicity.

The frontier scout and hunter had become a showman. One of his contemporaries on the Nebraska frontier at Fort McPherson, a talented girl named Ena Raymonds, recorded the change in her diary with a mixture of insight and poor prophecy. They met for the first time in the summer of 1872. He had returned to the fort from a scouting trip and invited her to a shooting match. Later, she saw him "dashing around first one place and then another" preparing for a hunt. She recorded that his baby boy, Kit Carson Cody, was a handsome child with great promise of a future. Neither she nor Cody could know that the boy would die within four years. When Bill went East on his first theatrical tour, Ena read the reviews and noted that one termed him ill at ease and "at loss of what to do with his hands." Ena commented to her diary "poor Cody! . . . He is out of his sphere. I have seen him the very personification of grace and beauty; but it was not in the crowded city . . . but dashing over the free wild prairie and riding his horse as though he and the noble animal were bounding with one life and one motion! Well 'there is money in it' that golden fact renders every other consideration insignificant . . . Such fame is not lasting."

Ena was wrong. Cody's fame was made lasting because he

became more than a scout and Indian fighter; he became legend. As such he brought excitement and enjoyment to thousands, young and old. A part of the unsophisticated, simple pleasure they knew may be recaptured by an uncritical reading of *Last of the Great Scouts.*

DONALD F. DANKER
Nebraska State Historical Society

CONTENTS.

GENEALOGY OF BUFFALO BILL.

The following genealogical sketch was compiled in 1897. The crest is copied from John Rooney's "Genealogical History of Irish Families."

It is not generally known that genuine royal blood courses in Colonel Cody's veins. He is a lineal descendant of Milesius, king of Spain, that famous monarch whose three sons, Heber, Heremon, and Ir, founded the first dynasty in Ireland, about the beginning of the Christian era. The Cody family comes through the line of Heremon. The original name was Tireach, which signifies "The Rocks." Muiredach Tireach, one of the first of this line, and son of Fiacha Straivetine, was crowned king of Ireland, Anno Domini 320. Another of the line became king of Connaught, Anno Domini 701. The possessions of the Sept were located in the present counties of Clare, Galway, and Mayo. The names Connaught-Gallway, after centuries, gradually contracted to Connallway, Connellway, Connelly, Conly, Cory, Coddy, Coidy, and Cody, and is clearly shown by ancient indentures still traceable among existing records. On the maternal side, Colonel Cody can, without difficulty, follow his lineage to the best blood of England. Several of the Cody family emigrated to America in 1747, settling in Maryland, Pennsylvania, and Virginia. The name is frequently mentioned in Revolutionary history. Colonel Cody is a member of the Cody family of Revolutionary fame. Like the other Spanish-Irish families, the Codys have their proof of ancestry in the form of a crest, the one which Colonel Cody is entitled to use being printed herewith. The lion signifies Spanish origin. It is the same figure that forms a part of the royal coat-of-arms of Spain to this day—Castile and Leon. The arm and cross denote that the descent is through the line of Heremon, whose posterity were among the first to follow the cross, as a symbol of their adherence to the Christian faith.

PREFACE.

In presenting this volume to the public the writer has a twofold purpose. For a number of years there has been an increasing demand for an authentic biography of "Buffalo Bill," and in response, many books of varying value have been submitted; yet no one of them has borne the hall-mark of veracious history. Naturally, there were incidents in Colonel Cody's life—more especially in the earlier years — that could be given only by those with whom he had grown up from childhood. For many incidents of his later life I am indebted to his own and others' accounts. I desire to acknowledge obligation to General P. H. Sheridan, Colonel Inman, Colonel Ingraham, and my brother for valuable assistance furnished by Sheridan's Memoirs, "The Santa Fé Trail," "The Great Salt Lake Trail," "Buffalo Bill's Autobiography," and "Stories from the Life of Buffalo Bill."

A second reason that prompted the writing of my brother's life-story is purely personal. The sobriquet of "Buffalo Bill" has conveyed to many people an impression of his personality that is far removed from the facts. They have pictured in fancy a rough frontier character, without tenderness and true nobility. But in very truth has the poet sung:

"The bravest are the tenderest—
The loving are the daring."

The public knows my brother as boy Indian-slayer, a champion buffalo-hunter, a brave soldier, a daring scout, an intrepid frontiersman, and a famous exhibitor. It is only fair to him that a glimpse be given of the parts he played behind the scenes—devotion to a widowed mother, that pushed the boy so early upon a stage of ceaseless action, continued care and tenderness displayed in later years, and the generous thoughtfulness of manhood's prime.

Thus a part of my pleasant task has been to enable the public to see my brother through his sister's eyes—eyes that have seen truly if kindly. If I have been tempted into praise where simple narrative might to the reader seem all that was required, if I have seemed to exaggerate in any of my history's details, I may say that I am not conscious of having set down more than "a plain, unvarnished tale." Embarrassed with riches of fact, I have had no thought of fiction.

H. C. W.

CODYVIEW, DULUTH, MINNESOTA,
February 26, 1899.

LAST OF THE GREAT SCOUTS.

CHAPTER I.

THE OLD HOMESTEAD IN IOWA.

A PLEASANT, roomy farm-house, set in the sunlight against a background of cool, green wood and mottled meadow— this is the picture that my earliest memories frame for me. To this home my parents, Isaac and Mary Cody, had moved soon after their marriage.

The place was known as the Scott farm, and was situated in Scott County, Iowa, near the historic little town of Le Clair, where, but a few years before, a village of the Fox Indians had been located; where Black Hawk and his thousand warriors had assembled for their last war-dance; where the marquee of General Scott was erected, and the treaty with the Sacs and Foxes drawn up; and where, in obedience to the Sac chief's terms, Antoine Le Clair, the famous half-breed Indian scholar and interpreter, had built his cabin, and given to the place his name.   Here, in this atmosphere of pioneer struggle and Indian warfare—in the farm-house in the dancing sunshine, with the background of wood and meadow — my brother, William Frederick Cody, was born, on the 26th day of February, 1846.

Of the good, old-fashioned sort was our family, numbering five daughters and two sons — Martha, Samuel, Julia, William, Eliza, Helen, and May.   Samuel, a lad of unusual beauty of face and nature, was killed through an unhappy accident before he was yet fourteen.

He was riding "Betsy Baker," a mare well known among old settlers in Iowa as one of speed and pedigree, yet displaying at times a most malevolent temper, accompanied by Will, who, though only seven years of age, yet sat his pony with the ease and grace that distinguished the veteran rider of the future. Presently Betsy Baker became fractious, and sought to throw her rider. In vain did she rear and plunge; he kept his saddle. Then, seemingly, she gave up the fight, and Samuel cried, in boyish exultation:

"Ah, Betsy Baker, you didn't quite come it that time!"

His last words! As if she knew her rider was a careless victor off his guard, the mare reared suddenly and flung herself upon her back, crushing the daring boy beneath her.

Though to us younger children our brother Samuel was but a shadowy memory, in him had centered our parents' fondest hopes and aims. These, naturally, were transferred to the younger, now the only son, and the hope that mother, especially, held for him was strangely stimulated by the remembrance of the mystic divination of a soothsayer in the years agone. My mother was a woman of too much intelligence and force of character to nourish an average superstition; but prophecies fulfilled will temper, though they may not shake, the smiling unbelief of the most hard-headed skeptic. Mother's moderate skepticism was not proof against the strange fulfillment of one prophecy, which fell out in this wise:

To a Southern city, which my mother visited when a girl, there came a celebrated fortune-teller, and led by curiosity, my mother and my aunt one day made two of the crowd that thronged the sibyl's drawing-rooms.

Both received with laughing incredulity the prophecy that my aunt and the two children with her would be dead in a fortnight; but the dread augury was fulfilled to the letter. All three were stricken with yellow fever, and died within less than the time set. This startling confirmation of the soothsayer's divining powers not unnaturally affected my mother's belief in that part of the prophecy relating to herself that "she would meet her future husband on the steamboat by which she expected to return home; that she would be married to him in a year, and bear three sons, of whom only the second would live, but that the name of this son would be known all over the world, and would one day be that of the President of the United States." The first part of this prophecy was verified, and Samuel's death was another link in the curious chain of circumstances. Was it, then, strange that mother looked with unusual hope upon her second son?

That 'tis good fortune for a boy to be only brother to five sisters is open to question. The older girls petted Will; the younger regarded him as a superior being; while to all it seemed so fit and proper that the promise of the stars concerning his future should be fulfilled that never for a moment did we weaken in our belief that great things were in store for our only brother. We looked for the prophecy's complete fulfillment, and with childish veneration regarded Will as one destined to sit in the executive's chair.

My mother, always somewhat delicate, was so affected in health by the shock of Samuel's death that a change of scene was advised. The California gold craze was then at its height, and father caught the fever, though in a mild form; for he had prospered as a farmer, and we not only had a comfortable home, but were in easy circumstances.

Influenced in part by a desire to improve mother's health, and in part, no doubt, by the golden day-dreams that lured so many Argonauts Pacificward, he disposed of his farm, and bade us prepare for a Western journey. Before his plans were completed he fell in with certain disappointed gold-seekers returning from the Coast, and impressed by their representations, decided in favor of Kansas instead of California.

Father had very extravagant ideas regarding vehicles and horses, and such a passion for equestrian display, that we often found ourselves with a stable full of thoroughbreds and an empty cupboard. For our Western migration we had, in addition to three prairie-schooners, a large family carriage, drawn by a span of fine horses in silver-mounted harness. This carriage had been made to order in the East, upholstered in the finest leather, polished and varnished as though for a royal progress. Mother and we girls found it more comfortable riding than the springless prairie-schooners.

Brother Will constituted himself an armed escort, and rode proudly alongside on his pony, his gun slung across the pommel of his saddle, and the dog Turk bringing up the rear.

To him this Western trip thrilled with possible Indian skirmishes and other stirring adventures, though of the real dangers that lay in our path he did not dream. For him, therefore, the first week of our travels held no great interest, for we were constantly chancing upon settlers and farm-houses, in which the night might be passed; but with every mile the settlers grew fewer and farther between, until one day Will whispered to us, in great glee: "I heard father tell mother that he expected we should have to camp to-night. Now we'll have some fun!"

Will's hope was well founded. Shortly before nightfall we reached a stream that demanded a ferry-boat for its crossing, and as the nearest dwelling was a dozen miles away, it was decided that we should camp by the streamside. The family was first sent across the ferry, and upon the eight-year-old lad of the house father placed the responsibility of selecting the ground on which to pitch the tents.

My brother's career forcibly illustrates the fact that environment plays as large a part as heredity in shaping character. Perhaps his love for the free life of the plains is a heritage derived from some long-gone ancestor; but there can be no doubt that to the earlier experiences of which I am writing he owed his ability as a scout. The faculty for obtaining water, striking trails, and finding desirable camping-grounds in him seemed almost instinct.

The tents being pitched upon a satisfactory site, Will called to Turk, the dog, and rifle in hand, set forth in search of game for supper. He was successful beyond his fondest hopes. He had looked only for small game, but scarcely had he put the camp behind him when Turk gave a signaling yelp, and out of the bushes bounded a magnificent deer. Nearly every hunter will confess to "buck fever" at sight of his first deer, so it is not strange that a boy of Will's age should have stood immovable, staring dazedly at the graceful animal until it vanished from sight. Turk gave chase, but soon trotted back, and barked reproachfully at his young master. But Will presently had an opportunity to recover Turk's good opinion, for the dog, after darting away, with another signaling yelp fetched another fine stag within gun range. This time the young hunter, mastering his nerves, took aim with steady hand, and brought down his first deer.

On the following Sabbath we were encamped by another deep, swift-running stream. After being wearied and overheated by a rabbit chase, Turk attempted to swim across this little river, but was chilled, and would have perished had not Will rushed to the rescue. The ferryman saw the boy struggling with the dog in the water, and started after him with his boat. But Will reached the bank without assistance.

"I've hearn of dogs saving children, but this is the first time I ever hearn of a child saving a dog from drowning," ejaculated the ferryman. "How old be you?"

"Eight, going on nine," answered Will.

"You're a big boy for your age," said the man. "But it's a wonder you didn't sink with that load; he's a big old fellow," referring to Turk, who, standing on three feet, was vigorously shaking the water from his coat. Will at once knelt down beside him, and taking the uplifted foot in his hands, remarked: "He must have sprained one of his legs when he fell over that log; he doesn't whine like your common curs when they get hurt."

"He's blooded stock, then," said the man. "What kind of dog do you call him?"

"He's an Ulm dog," said Will.

"I never heard tell of that kind of dog before."

"Did you ever hear of a tiger-mastiff, German mastiff, boar-hound, great Dane? Turk's all of them together."

"Well," said the ferryman, "you're a pretty smart little fellow, and got lots of grit. You ought to make your mark in the world. But right now you had better get into some dry clothes." And on the invitation of the ferryman, Will and the limping dog got into the boat, and were taken back to camp.

Turk played so conspicuous and important a part in

our early lives that he deserves a brief description. He was a large and powerful animal of the breed of dogs anciently used in Germany in hunting the wild boars. Later the dogs were imported into England, where they were particularly valued by people desiring a strong, brave watch-dog. When specially trained, they are more fierce and active than the English mastiff. Naturally they are not as fond of the water as the spaniel, the stag-hound, or the Newfoundland, though they are the king of dogs on land. Not alone Will, but the rest of the family, regarded Turk as the best of his kind, and he well deserved the veneration he inspired. His fidelity and almost human intelligence were time and again the means of saving life and property; ever faithful, loyal, and ready to lay down his life, if need be, in our service.

Outlaws and desperadoes were always to be met with on Western trails in those rugged days, and more than once Turk's constant vigilance warned father in time to prevent attacks from suspicious night prowlers. The attachment which had grown up between Turk and his young master was but the natural love of boys for their dogs intensified. Will at that time estimated dogs as in later years he did men, the qualities which he found to admire in Turk being vigilance, strength, courage, and constancy. With men, as with dogs, he is not lavishly demonstrative; rarely pats them on the back. But deeds of merit do not escape his notice or want his appreciation. The patience, unselfishness, and true nobility observed in this faithful canine friend of his boyhood days have many times proved to be lacking in creatures endowed with a soul; yet he has never lost faith in mankind, or in the ultimate destiny of his race. This I conceive to be a characteristic of all great men.

This trip was memorable for all of us, perhaps especially

so for brother Will, for it comprehended not only his first deer, but his first negro.

As we drew near the Missouri line we came upon a comfortable farm-house, at which father made inquiry concerning a lodging for the night. A widow lived there, and the information that father was brother to Elijah Cody, of Platte County, Missouri, won us a cordial welcome and the hospitality of her home.

We were yet in the road, waiting father's report, when our startled vision and childish imagination took in a seeming apparition, which glided from the bushes by the way-side.

It proved a full-blooded African, with thick lips, woolly hair, enormous feet, and scant attire. To all except mother this was a new revelation of humanity, and we stared in wild-eyed wonder; even Turk was surprised into silence. At this point father rejoined us, to share in mother's amusement, and to break the spell for us by pleasantly addressing the negro, who returned a respectful answer, accompanied by an ample grin. He was a slave on the widow's plantation.

Reassured by the grin, Will offered his hand, and tasted the joy of being addressed as "Massa" in the talk that followed. It was with difficulty that we prevailed upon "Massa" to come to supper.

After a refreshing night's sleep we went on our way, and in a few days reached my uncle's home. A rest was welcome, as the journey had been long and toilsome, despite the fact that it had been enlivened by many interesting incidents, and was thoroughly enjoyed by all of the family.

CHAPTER II.

WILL'S FIRST INDIAN.

MY uncle's home was in Weston, Platte County, Missouri, at that time the large city of the West. As father desired to get settled again as soon as possible, he left us at Weston, and crossed the Missouri River on a prospecting tour, accompanied by Will and a guide. More than one day went by in the quest for a desirable location, and one morning Will, wearied in the reconnoissance, was left asleep at the night's camping-place, while father and the guide rode away for the day's exploring.

When Will opened his eyes they fell upon the most interesting object that the world just then could offer him—an Indian!

The "noble red man," as he has been poetically termed by people who have but known him from afar, was in the act of mounting Will's horse, while near by stood his own, a miserable, scrawny beast.

Will's boyish dreams were now a reality; he looked upon his first Indian. Here, too, was a "buck"—not a graceful, vanishing deer, but a dirty redskin, who seemingly was in some hurry to be gone. Without a trace of "buck fever," Will jumped up, rifle in hand, and demanded:

"Here, what are you doing with my horse?"

The Indian regarded the lad with contemptuous composure.

"Me swap horses with paleface boy," said he.

9

The red man was fully armed, and Will did not know whether his father and the guide were within call or not; but to suffer the Indian to ride away with Uncle Elijah's fine horse was to forfeit his father's confidence and shake his mother's and sisters' belief in the family hero; so he put a bold face upon the matter, and remarked carelessly, as if discussing a genuine transaction:

"No; I won't swap."

"Paleface boy fool!" returned the Indian, serenely.

Now this was scarcely the main point at issue, so Will contented himself with replying, quietly but firmly:

"You cannot take my horse."

The Indian condescended to temporize. "Paleface horse no good," said he.

"Good enough for me," replied Will, smiling despite the gravity of the situation. The Indian shone rather as a liar than a judge of horseflesh. "Good enough for me; so you can take your old rack of bones and go."

Much to Will's surprise, the red man dropped the rein, flung himself upon his own pony, and made off. And down fell "Lo the poor Indian" from the exalted niche that he had filled in Will's esteem, for while it was bad in a copper hero to steal horses, it was worse to flee from a boy not yet in his teens. But a few moments later Lo went back to his lofty pedestal, for Will heard the guide's voice, and realized that it was the sight of a man, and not the threats of a boy, that had sent the Indian about his business—if he had any.

The guide had returned to escort Will to the spot which father, after a search of nearly a week, had discovered, and where he had decided to locate our home. It was in Salt Creek Valley, a fertile blue-grass region, sheltered by an amphitheater range of hills. The old Salt Lake trail traversed this valley. There were at this time two great highways of Western travel, the Santa Fé and the Salt Lake trails; later the Oregon trail came into prominence. Of these the oldest and most historic was the Santa Fé trail, the route followed by explorers three hundred years ago. It had been used by Indian tribes from time, to white men, immemorial. At the beginning of this century it was first used as an artery of commerce. Over it Zebulon Pike made his well-known Western trip, and from it radiated his explorations. The trail lay some distance south of Leavenworth. It ran westward, dipping slightly to the south until the Arkansas River was reached; then, following the course of this stream to Bent's Fort, it crossed the river and turned sharply to the south. It went through Raton Pass, and below Las Vegas it turned west to Santa Fé.

Exploration along the line of the Salt Lake trail began also with this century. It became a beaten highway at the time of the Mormon exodus from Nauvoo to their present place of abode. The trail crossed the Missouri River at Leavenworth, and ran northerly to the Platte, touching that stream at Fort Kearny. With a few variations it paralleled the Platte to its junction with the Sweetwater, and left this river valley to run through South Pass to big Sandy Creek, turning south to follow this little stream. At Fort Bridger it turned westward again, passed Echo Cañon, and a few miles farther on ran into Salt Lake City. Over this trail journeyed thousands of gold-hunters toward California, hopeful and high-spirited on the westerly way, disappointed and depressed, the large majority of them, on the back track. Freighting outfits, cattle trains, emigrants—nearly all the western travel—followed this track across the new land. A man named Rively, with the gift of grasping the advantage of location, had obtained permission to establish a trading-post on this trail three miles beyond the Missouri, and as proximity to this depot of supplies was a manifest convenience, father's selection of a claim only two miles distant was a wise one.

The Kansas-Nebraska Bill, which provided for the organizing of those two territories and opened them for settlement, was passed in May, 1854. This bill directly opposed the Missouri Compromise, which restricted slavery to all territory south of 36° 30″ north latitude. A clause in the new bill provided that the settlers should decide for themselves whether the new territories were to be free or slave states. Already hundreds of settlers were camped upon the banks of the Missouri, waiting the passage of the bill before entering and acquiring possession of the land. Across the curtain of the night ran a broad ribbon of dancing camp-fires, stretching for miles along the bank of the river.

None too soon had father fixed upon his claim. The act allowing settlers to enter was passed in less than a week afterward. Besides the pioneers intending actual settlement, a great rush was made into the territories by members of both political parties. These became the gladiators, with Kansas the arena, for a bitter, bloody contest between those desiring and those opposing the extension of slave territory.

Having already decided upon his location, father was among the first, after the bill was passed, to file a claim and procure the necessary papers, and shortly afterward he had a transient abiding-place prepared for us. Whatever mother may have thought of the one-roomed cabin, whose chinks let in the sun by day and the moon and stars by night, and whose carpet was nature's greenest velvet, life in it was a perennial picnic for the children. Meantime father was at work on our permanent home, and before the summer fled we were domiciled in a large double-log house— rough and primitive, but solid and comfort-breeding.

This same autumn held an episode so deeply graven in my memory that time has not blurred a line of it. Jane, our faithful maid of all work, who went with us to our Western home, had little time to play the governess. Household duties claimed her every waking hour, as mother was delicate, and the family a large one; so Turk officiated as both guardian and playmate of the children

One golden September day Eliza and I set out after wild flowers, accompanied by Turk and mother's caution not to stray too far, as wild beasts, 'twas said, lurked in the neighboring forest; but the prettiest flowers were always just beyond, and we wandered afield until we reached a fringe of timber half a mile from the house, where we tarried under the trees. Meantime mother grew alarmed, and Will was dispatched after the absent tots.

Turk, as we recalled, had sought to put a check upon our wanderings, and when we entered the woods his rest-lessness increased. Suddenly he began to paw up the carpet of dry leaves, and a few moments later the shrill scream of a panther echoed through the forest aisles.

Eliza was barely six years old, and I was not yet four. We clung to each other in voiceless terror. Then from afar came a familiar whistle—Will's call to his dog. That heartened us, babes as we were, for was not our brother our reliance in every emergency? Rescue was at hand; but Turk continued tearing up the leaves, after signaling his master with a loud bark. Then, pulling at our dresses, he indicated the refuge he had dug for us. Here we lay down, and the dog covered us with the leaves, dragging to the heap, as a further screen, a large dead branch. Then, with the heart of a lion, he put himself on guard.

From our leafy covert we could see the panther's tawny form come gliding through the brush. He saw Turk, and crouched for a spring. This came as an arrow, but Turk dodged it; and then, with a scream such as I never heard from dog before or since, our defender hurled himself upon the foe.

Turk was powerful, and his courage was flawless, but he was no match for the panther. In a few moments the faithful dog lay stunned and bleeding from one stroke of the forest-rover's steel-shod paw. The cruel beast had scented other prey, and dismissing Turk, he paced to and fro, seeking to locate us. We scarcely dared to breathe, and every throb of our frightened little hearts was a prayer that Will would come to us in time.

At last the panther's roving eyes rested upon our inadequate hiding-place, and as he crouched for the deadly leap we hid our faces.

But Turk had arisen. Wounded as he was, he yet made one last heroic effort to save us by again directing the panther's attention to himself.

The helpless, hopeless ordeal of agony was broken by a rifle's sharp report. The panther fell, shot through the heart, and out from the screen of leaves rushed two hysterical little girls, with pallid faces drowned in tears, who clung about a brother's neck and were shielded in his arms.

Will, himself but a child, caressed and soothed us in a most paternal fashion; and when the storm of sobs was passed we turned to Turk. Happily his injuries were not fatal, and he whined feebly when his master reached him.

"Bravo! Good dog!" cried Will. "You saved them, Turk! You saved them!" And kneeling beside our faithful friend, he put his arms about the shaggy neck.

Dear old Turk! If there be a land beyond the sky for such as thou, may the snuggest corner and best of bones be thy reward!

CHAPTER III.

THE SHADOW OF PARTISAN STRIFE.

OWING to the conditions, already spoken of, under which Kansas was settled, all classes were represented in its population. Honest, thrifty farmers and well-to-do traders leavened a lump of shiftless ne'er-do-wells, lawless adventurers, and vagabonds of all sorts and conditions. If father at times questioned the wisdom of coming to this new and untried land, he kept his own counsel, and set a brave face against the future.

He had been prominent in political circles in Iowa, and had filled positions of public trust; but he had no wish to become involved in the partisan strife that raged in Kansas. He was a Free Soil man, and there were but two others in that section who did not believe in slavery. For a year he kept his political views to himself; but it became rumored about that he was an able public speaker, and the pro-slavery men naturally ascribed to him the same opinions as those held by his brother Elijah, a pronounced pro-slavery man; so they regarded father as a promising leader in their cause. He had avoided the issue, and had skillfully contrived to escape declaring for one side or the other, but on the scroll of his destiny it was written that he should be one of the first victims offered on the sacrificial altar of the struggle for human liberty.

The post-trader's was a popular rendezvous for all the settlers round. It was a day in the summer of '55 that father visited the store, accompanied, as usual, by Will and Turk. Among the crowd, which was noisy and excited, he noted a number of desperadoes in the pro-slavery faction, and noted, too, that Uncle Elijah and our two Free Soil neighbors, Mr. Hathaway and Mr. Lawrence, were present.

Father's appearance was greeted by a clamor for a speech. To speak before that audience was to take his life in his hands; yet in spite of his excuses he was forced to the chair.

It was written! There was no escape! Father walked steadily to the dry-goods box which served as a rostrum. As he passed Mr. Hathaway, the good old man plucked him by the sleeve and begged him to serve out platitudes to the crowd, and to screen his real sentiments.

But father was not a man that dealt in platitudes.

"Friends," said he, quietly, as he faced his audience and drew himself to his full height —"friends, you are mistaken in your man. I am sorry to disappoint you. I have no wish to quarrel with you. But you have forced me to speak, and I can do no less than declare my real convictions. I am, and always have been, opposed to slavery. It is an institution that not only degrades the slave, but brutalizes the slave-holder, and I pledge you my word that I shall use my best endeavors—yes, that I shall lay down my life, if need be—to keep this curse from finding lodgment upon Kansas soil. It is enough that the fairest portions of our land are already infected with this blight. May it spread no farther. All my energy and my ability shall swell the effort to bring in Kansas as a Free Soil state."

Up to this point the crowd had been so dumfounded by his temerity that they kept an astonished silence. Now the storm broke. The rumble of angry voices swelled into a roar of fury. An angry mob surrounded the speaker. Several desperadoes leaped forward with deadly intent, and one, Charles Dunn by name, drove his knife to the hilt into the body of the brave man who dared thus openly to avow his principles.

As father fell, Will sprang to him, and turning to the murderous assailant, cried out in boyhood's fury:

"You have killed my father! When I'm a man I'll kill you!"

The crowd slunk away, believing father dead. The deed appalled them; they were not yet hardened to the lawlessness that was so soon to put the state to blush.

Mr. Hathaway and Will then carried father to a hiding-place in the long grass by the wayside. The crowd dispersed so slowly that dusk came on before the coast was clear. At length, supported by Will, father dragged his way homeward, marking his tortured progress with a trail of blood.

This path was afterward referred to in the early history of Kansas as "The Cody Bloody Trail."

It was such wild scenes as these that left their impress on the youth and fashioned the Cody of later years—cool in emergency, fertile in resource, swift in decision, dashing and intrepid when the time for action came.

Our troubles were but begun. Father's convalescence was long and tedious; he never recovered fully. His enemies believed him dead, and for a while we kept the secret guarded; but as soon as he was able to be about persecution began.

About a month after the tragedy at Rively's, Will ran in one evening with the warning that a band of horsemen were approaching. Suspecting trouble, mother put some of her own clothes about father, gave him a pail, and bade him hide in the cornfield. He walked boldly from the house, and sheltered by the gathering dusk, succeeded in passing the horsemen unchallenged. The latter rode up to the house and dismounted.

"Where's Cody?" asked the leader. He was informed that father was not at home.

"Lucky for him!" was the frankly brutal rejoinder. "We'll make sure work of the killing next time."

Disappointed in their main intention, the marauders revenged themselves in their own peculiar way by looting the house of every article that took their fancy; then they sat down with the announced purpose of waiting the return of their prospective victim.

Fearing the effect of the night air upon father, though it was yet summer, mother made a sign to Will, who slipped from the room, and guided by Turk, carried blankets to the cornfield, returning before his absence had been remarked. The ruffians soon tired of waiting, and rode away, after warning mother of the brave deed they purposed to perform. Father came in for the night, returning to his covert with the dawn.

In expectation of some such raid, we had secreted a good stock of provisions; but as soon as the day was up Will was dispatched to Rively's store to reconnoiter, under pretext of buying groceries. Keeping eyes and ears open, he learned that father's enemies were on the watch for him; so the cornfield must remain his screen. After several days, the exposure and anxiety told on his strength. He decided to leave home and go to Fort Leavenworth, four miles distant. When night fell he returned to the house, packed a few needed articles, and bade us farewell.

Will urged that he ride Prince, but he regarded his journey as safer afoot. It was a sad parting. None of us knew whether we should ever again see our father.

"I hope," he said to mother, "that these clouds will soon pass away, and that we may have a happy home once more." Then, placing his hands on Will's head, "You will have to be the man of the house until my return," he said. "But I know I can trust my boy to watch over his mother and sisters."

With such responsibilities placed upon his shoulders, such confidence reposed in him, small wonder that Will should grow a man in thought and feeling before he grew to be one in years.

Father reached Fort Leavenworth in safety, but the quarrel between the pro-slavery party and the Free Soilers waxed more bitter, and he decided that security lay farther on; so he took passage on an up-river boat to Doniphan, twenty miles distant. This was then a mere landing-place, but he found a small band of men in camp cooking supper. They were part of Colonel Jim Lane's command, some three hundred strong, on their way West from Indiana.

Colonel Lane was an interesting character. He had been a friend to Elijah Lovejoy, who was killed, in 1836, for maintaining an anti-slavery newspaper in Illinois. The Kansas contest speedily developed the fact that the actual settlers sent from the North by the emigrant-aid societies would enable the Free State party to outnumber the ruffians sent in by the Southerners; and when the pro-slavery men were driven to substituting bullets for ballots, Colonel Lane recruited a band of hardy men to protect the anti-slavery settlers, and incidentally to avenge the murder of Lovejoy.

The meeting of father and Lane's men was a meeting of friends, and he chose to cast his lot with theirs. Shortly afterward he took part in "The Battle of Hickory Point," in which the pro-slavery men were defeated with heavy loss; and thenceforward the name of Jim Lane was a terror to the lawless and a wall of protection to our family.

The storm and stress of battle had drawn heavily on what little strength was left to father, and relying for safety upon the proximity of Colonel Lane and his men, he returned to us secretly by night, and was at once prostrated on a bed of sickness.

This proved a serious strain upon our delicate mother, for during father's absence a little brother had been added to our home, and not only had she, in addition to the care of Baby Charlie, the nursing of a sick man, but she was constantly harassed by apprehensions for his safety as well.

CHAPTER IV.

PERSECUTION CONTINUES.

MOTHER'S fears were well grounded. A few days after father had returned home, a man named Sharpe, who disgraced the small office of justice of the peace, rode up to our house, very much the worse for liquor, and informed mother that his errand was to "search the house for that abolition husband of yours." The intoxicated ruffian then demanded something to eat. While mother, with a show of hospitality, was preparing supper for him, the amiable Mr. Sharpe killed time in sharpening his bowie-knife on the sole of his shoe.

"That," said he to Will, who stood watching him, "that's to cut the heart out of that Free State father of yours!" And he tested the edge with brutally suggestive care.

Will's comment was to take down his rifle and place himself on the staircase leading up to father's room. There was trouble in that quarter for Mr. Sharpe, if he attempted to ascend those stairs.

But the justice, as mother surmised, had no notion that father was at home, else he would not have come alone. He ate heartily of the supper, which Will hoped would choke him, and passing from drowsiness to drunken slumber, soon tumbled from his chair. This so confused him that he forgot his pretended errand, and shambled out of the house. He was not so drunk that he could not tell a good bit of horseflesh, and he straightway took a fancy to Prince, the pet pony of the family. An unwritten plank in the platform of the pro-slavery men was that the Free Soil party had no rights they were bound to respect, and Sharpe remarked to Will, with a malicious grin:

"That's a nice pony of yours, sonny. Guess I'll take him along with me." And he proceeded to exchange the saddle from the back of his own horse to that of Prince.

"You old coward!" muttered Will, bursting with wrath. "I'll get even with you some day."

The justice was a tall, burly fellow, and he cut so ridic- ulous a figure as he rode away on Prince's back, his heels almost touching the ground, that Will laughed outright as he thought of a plan to save his pony.

A shrill whistle brought Turk to the scene, and receiv- ing his cue, the dog proceeded to give Sharpe a very bad five minutes. He would nip at one of the dangling legs, spring back out of reach of the whip with a triumphant bark, then repeat the performance with the other leg. This little comedy had a delighted spectator in Will, who had followed at a safe distance. Just as Sharpe made one extra effort to reach Turk, the boy whistled a signal to Prince, who responded with a bound that dumped his rider in the dust. Here Turk stood over him and showed his teeth.

"Call off your dog, bub!" the justice shouted to Will, "and you may keep your little sheep, for he's no good, anyway."

"That's a bargain!" cried Will, restored to good humor; and helping the vanquished foe upon his own steed, he assured him that he need not fear Turk so long as he kept his word. Sharpe departed, but we were far from being rid of him.

About a fortnight later we were enjoying an evening with father, who was now able to come downstairs. He was seated in a big arm-chair before the open fire, with his family gathered round him, by his side our frail, beautiful mother, with Baby Charlie on her knee, Martha and Julia, with their sewing, and Will, back of mother's chair, tenderly smoothing the hair from her brow, while he related spiritedly some new escapade of Turk. Suddenly he checked his narrative, listened for a space, and announced:

"There are some men riding on the road toward the house. We'd better be ready for trouble."

Mother, equal to every emergency, hurriedly disposed her slender forces for defense. Martha and Julia were directed to help father to bed; that done, to repair to the unfurnished front room above stairs; Will was instructed to call the hired man and Jane, who was almost as large and quite as strong as the average man; and the three were armed and given their cue. They were all handy with their weapons, but mother sought to win by strategy, if possible. She bade the older girls don heavy boots, and gave them further instructions. By this time the horsemen had reached the gate. Their leader was the redoubtable Justice Sharpe. He rode up to the door, and rapped with the but of his riding-whip. Mother threw up the window overhead.

"Who's there? and what do you want?" she demanded.

"We want that old abolition husband of yours, and, dead or alive, we mean to have him!"

"All right, Mr. Sharpe," was the steady answer. "I'll ask Colonel Lane and his men to wait on you."

The hired man, who had served in the Mexican War, here gave a sharp word of command, which was responded to by trampling of heavy boots upon the bare floor. Then, calling a halt, the pretended Colonel Lane advanced to the window, and shouted to the horsemen:

"Set foot inside that gate and my men will fire on you!"

Sharpe, an arrant coward, had retreated at the first sound of a man's voice, and after a short parley with his nonplused companions, he led them away—outwitted by a woman.

As a sort of consolation prize, Sharpe again made off with Prince; but Will's sorrow in the morning was short-lived, for the sagacious little creature slipped his halter and came flying home before the forenoon was half spent.

After this experience, father decided that, for our sakes as well as for his own, he must again leave home, and as soon as he recovered a measure of his strength he went to Grasshopper Falls, thirty-five miles west of Leavenworth. Here he erected a sawmill, and hoped that he had put so many miles between him and his enemies that he might be allowed to pursue a peaceful occupation. He made us occasional visits, so timing his journey that he reached home after nightfall, and left again before the sun was up.

One day when we were looking forward to one of these visits, our good friend Mr. Hathaway made his appearance about eleven o'clock.

"It is too bad to be the bearer of ill tidings," said he, "but the news of your husband's expected visit has been noised about in some way, and another plot to kill him is afoot. Some of his enemies are camped at Big Stranger's Creek, and intend to shoot him as he passes there."

Then followed a long and anxious consultation, which ended without any plan of rescue.

All of which had been overheard by Will, who was confined to his bed with an attack of ague. In him, he decided, lay the only hope for father's safety; so, dressing, he presented his fever-flushed face to mother. As he held out a handkerchief, "Tie it tight around my head, mother," said he; "then it won't ache so hard."

A remonstrance against his getting out of bed brought out the fact that he contemplated riding to Grasshopper Falls!

He was almost too weak to stand, a storm threatened, and thirty miles lay between him and father; yet he was not to be dissuaded from his undertaking. So Julia and Martha saddled Prince and helped the ague-racked courier to his saddle.

The plunge into the open air and the excitement of the start encouraged Will to believe that he could hold out. As he settled down to his long, hard ride he reflected that it was not yet noon, and that father would not set out until late in the day. Prince seemed to discern that something extraordinary was afoot, and swung along at a swift, steady gait.

Big Stranger's Creek cut the road half-way to the Falls, and Will approached it before the afternoon was half gone. The lowering sky darkened the highway, and he hoped to pass the ambush unrecognized; but as he came up to the stream he made out a camp and campers, one of whom called out carelessly to him as he passed:

"Are you all right on the goose?"—the cant phrase of the pro-slavery men.

"Never rode a goose in my life, gentlemen," was the reply.

"That's Cody's boy!" shouted another voice; and the word "Halt!" rang out just as Will had galloped safely past the camp.

Will's answer was to drive the spurs into Prince

and dart ahead, followed by a rain of bullets. He was now well out of range, and the pony still strong and fleet.

The chase was on, and in the thrill of it Will forgot his weakness. A new strength came with the rush of air and the ring of hoofs, and "I'll reach the Falls in time!" was his heartening thought, as pursurer and pursued sped through the forests, clattered over bridges, and galloped up hill and down.

Then broke the long-impending storm, and the hard road became the bed of a muddy stream. The pursuit was abandoned, and this stimulus removed, Will felt the chills and weakness coming on again. He was drenched to the skin, and it was an effort to keep his saddle, but he set his teeth firmly in his resolve to accomplish his heroic purpose.

At last! A welcome light gleamed between the crystal bars of the rain. His mission was accomplished.

His ride had been longer by ten miles than that famous gallop of the friend of his after years—Phil Sheridan. Like Sheridan, he reached the goal in time, for father was just mounting his horse.

But the ride proved too much for his strength, and Will collapsed. Father started with him, a few days later, for Topeka, which was headquarters for the Free State party.

Father acquainted mother of their safety, and explained that he had gone to Topeka because he feared his life was no longer safe at Grasshopper Falls.

Party strife in Kansas was now at its height. Thousands came into the territory from adjacent slave states simply to vote, and the pro-slavery party elected a legislature, whose first meeting was held at Le Compton. This election the Free Soilers declared illegal, because of fraudulent voting, and assembling at Topeka in the winter of 1855-56, they framed a constitution excluding slavery, and organized a rival government. Of this first Free-Soil Legislature father was a member.

Thenceforth war was the order of the day, and in the fall of 1856 a military governor was appointed, with full authority to maintain law and order in Kansas.

Recognizing the good work effected by the emigrant-aid societies, and realizing that in a still larger Northern emigration to Kansas lay the only hope of its admission as a free state, father went to Ohio in the following spring, to labor for the salvation of the territory he had chosen for his home. Here his natural gift of oratory had free play, and as the result of his work on the stump he brought back to Kansas sixty families, the most of whom settled in the vicinity of Grasshopper Falls, now Valley Falls.

This meant busy times for us, for with that magnificent disregard for practical matters that characterizes many men of otherwise great gifts, father had invited each separate family to make headquarters at his home until other arrangements could be perfected. As a result, our house overflowed, while the land about us was dotted with tents; but these melted away, as one by one the families selected claims and put up cabins.

Among the other settlers was Judge Delahay, who, with his family, located at Leavenworth, and began the publishing of the first abolition newspaper in Kansas. The appointing of the military governor was the means of restoring comparative tranquillity; but hundreds of outrages were committed, and the judge and his newspaper came in for a share of suffering. The printing-office was broken into, and the type and press thrown into the Missouri River. Undaunted, the judge procured a new press, and the paper continued.

A semi-quiet now reigned in the territory; father resumed work at the sawmill, and we looked forward to a peaceful home and the joy of being once more permanently united. But it was not to be. The knife wound had injured father's lung. With care and nursing it might have healed, but constant suffering attended on the life that persecution had led him, and in the spring of '57 he again came home, and took to his bed for the last time.

All that could be was done, but nothing availed. After a very short illness he passed away—one of the first martyrs in the cause of freedom in Kansas.

The land of his adoption became his last, long resting-place. His remains now lie on Pilot Knob, which overlooks the beautiful city of Leavenworth. His death was regretted even by his enemies, who could not help but grant a tribute of respect to a man who had been upright, just, and generous to friend and foe.

CHAPTER V.

THE "BOY EXTRA."

AT this sorrowful period mother was herself almost at death's door with consumption, but far from sinking under the blow, she faced the new conditions with a steadfast calm, realizing that should she, too, be taken, her children would be left without a protector, and at the mercy of the enemies whose malignity had brought their father to an untimely end. Her indomitable will opposed her bodily weakness. "I will not die," she told herself, "until the welfare of my children is assured." She was needed, for our persecution continued.

Hardly was the funeral over when a trumped-up claim for a thousand dollars, for lumber and supplies, was entered against our estate. Mother knew the claim was fictitious, as all the bills had been settled, but the business had been transacted through the agency of Uncle Elijah, and father had neglected to secure the receipts. In those bitter, troublous days it too often happened that brother turned against brother, and Elijah retained his fealty to his party at the expense of his dead brother's family.

This fresh affliction but added fuel to the flame of mother's energy. Our home was paid for, but father's business had been made so broken and irregular that our financial resources were of the slenderest, and should this unjust claim for a thousand dollars be allowed, we would be homeless.

The result of mother's study of the situation was, "If I had the ready money, I should fight the claim."

"You fight the claim, and I'll get the money," Will replied.

Mother smiled, but Will continued:

"Russell, Majors & Waddell will give me work. Jim Willis says I am capable of filling the position of 'extra.' If you'll go with me and ask Mr. Majors for a job, I'm sure he'll give me one."

Russell, Majors & Waddell were overland freighters and contractors, with headquarters at Leavenworth. To Will's suggestion mother entered a demurrer, but finally yielded before his insistence. Mr. Majors had known father, and was more than willing to aid us, but Will's youth was an objection not lightly overridden.

"What can a boy of your age do?" he asked, kindly.

"I can ride, shoot, and herd cattle," said Will; "but I'd rather be an 'extra' on one of your trains.'

"But that is a man's work, and is dangerous besides." Mr. Majors hesitated. "But I'll let you try it one trip, and if you do a man's work, I'll give you a man's pay."

So Will's name was put on the company roll, and he signed a pledge that illustrates better than a description the character and disposition of Mr. Majors.

"I, William F. Cody," it read, "do hereby solemnly swear, before the great and living God, that during my engagement with, and while I am in the employ of, Russell, Majors & Waddell, I will, under no circumstances, use profane language, that I will not quarrel or fight with any other employee of the firm, and that in every respect I will conduct myself honestly, be faithful to my duties, and so direct all my acts as to win the confidence of my employers. So help me God!"

Mr. Majors employed many wild and reckless men, but the language of the pledge penetrated to the better nature of them all. They endeavored, with varying success, to live up to its conditions, although most of them held that driving a bull-team constituted extenuating circumstances for an occasional expletive.

The pledge lightened mother's heart; she knew that Will would keep his word; she felt, too, that a man that required such a pledge of his employees was worthy of their confidence and esteem.

The train was to start in a day, and all of us were busy with the preparations for Will's two months' trip. The moment of parting came, and it was a trying ordeal for mother, so recently bereaved of husband. Will sought to soothe her, but the younger sisters had better success, for with tears in our eyes we crowded about him, imploring him to "run if he saw any Indians."

'Tis but a step from tears to smiles; the situation was relieved, and Will launched his life bark amid adieus of hope and confidence and love. His fortitude lasted only till he was out of sight of the house; but youth is elastic, the plains lay before him, and mother and sisters were to be helped; so he presented a cheerful face to his employers.

That night the bed of the "boy extra" was a blanket under a wagon; but he slept soundly, and was ready when the train started with the dawn.

The "bull-train" took its name from the fact that each of the thirty-five wagons making up a full train was hauled by several yoke of oxen, driven by one man, known as a bullwhacker. This functionary's whip cracked like a rifle, and could be heard about as far. The wagons resembled the ordinary prairie-schooner, but were larger and more strongly built; they were protected from the weather by a

double covering of heavy canvas, and had a freight capacity
of seven thousand pounds.

Besides the bullwhackers there were cavallard drivers
(who cared for the loose cattle), night herders, and sundry
extra hands, all under the charge of a chief wagon-master,
termed the wagon-boss, his lieutenants being the boss of
the cattle train and the assistant wagon-master.   The men
were disposed in messes, each providing its own wood and
water, doing its own cooking, and washing up its own tin
dinner service, while one man in each division stood guard.
Special duties were assigned to the "extras," and Will's
was to ride up and down the train delivering orders.   This
suited his fancy to a dot, for the oxen were snail-gaited,
and to plod at their heels was dull work.   Kipling tells us
it is quite impossible to "hustle the East"; it were as easy,
as Will discovered, to hustle a bull-train.

From the outset the "boy extra" was a favorite with
the men.   They liked his pluck in undertaking such work,
and when it was seen that he took pride in executing orders
promptly, he became a favorite with the bosses as well.
In part his work was play to him; he welcomed an order as
a break in the monotony of the daily march, and hailed the
opportunity of a gallop on a good horse.

The world of Will's fancy was bounded by the hazy
rim where plain and sky converge, and when the first day's
journey was done, and he had staked out and cared for his
horse, he watched with fascinated eyes the strange and
striking picture limned against the black hills and the
sweeping stretch of darkening prairie.   Everything was
animation; the bullwhackers unhitching and disposing of
their teams, the herders staking out the cattle, and—not
the least interesting—the mess cooks preparing the evening
meal at the crackling camp-fires, with the huge, canvas-

covered wagons encircling them like ghostly sentinels; the ponies and oxen blinking stupidly as the flames stampeded the shadows in which they were enveloped; and more weird than all, the buckskin-clad bullwhackers, squatted around the fire, their beards glowing red in its light, their faces drawn in strange black and yellow lines, while the spiked grasses shot tall and sword-like over them.

It was wonderful—that first night of the "boy extra."

But Will discovered that life on the plains is not all a supper under the stars when the sparks fly upward; it has its hardships and privations. There were days, as the wagons dragged their slow lengths along, when the clouds obscured the sky and the wind whistled dismally; days when torrents fell and swelled the streams that must be crossed, and when the mud lay ankle-deep; days when the cattle stampeded, and the round-up meant long, extra hours of heavy work; and, hardest but most needed work of all, the eternal vigil 'gainst an Indian attack.

Will did not share the anxiety of his companions. To him a brush with Indians would prove that boyhood's dreams sometimes come true, and in imagination he anticipated the glory of a first encounter with the "noble red man," after the fashion of the heroes in the hair-lifting Western tales he had read. He was soon to learn, as many another has learned, that the Indian of real life is vastly different from the Indian of fiction. He refuses to "bite the dust" at sight of a paleface, and a dozen of them have been known to hold their own against as many white men.

Some twenty miles west of Fort Kearny a halt was made for dinner at the bank of a creek that emptied into the Platte River. No signs of Indians had been observed, and there was no thought of special danger. Nevertheless, three men were constantly on guard. Many of the

THE BOY EXTRA'S FIRST NIGHT IN CAMP.

trainmen were asleep under the wagons while waiting dinner, and Will was watching the maneuvers of the cook in
his mess.   Suddenly a score of shots rang out from the
direction of a neighboring thicket, succeeded by a chorus
of savage yells.

Will saw the three men on the lookout drop in their
tracks, and saw the Indians divide, one wing stampeding
the cattle, the other charging down upon the camp.

The trainmen were old frontiersmen, and although taken
wholly by surprise, they lined up swiftly in battle array
behind the wagons, with the bosses, Bill and Frank Mc-
Carthy, at their head, and the "boy extra" under the
direction of the wagon-master.

A well-placed volley of rifle-balls checked the Indians,
and they wheeled and rode away, after sending in a scattering cloud of arrows, which wounded several of the trainmen.   The decision of a hasty council of war was, that a
defensive stand would be useless, as the Indians outnumbered the whites ten to one, and red reinforcements were
constantly coming up, until it seemed to Will as if the
prairie were alive with them.   The only hope of safety lay
in the shelter of the creek's high bank, so a run was made
for it.   The Indians charged again, with the usual accompaniment of whoops, yells, and flying arrows; but the
trainmen had reached the creek, and from behind its natural
breastwork maintained a rifle fire that drove the foe back
out of range.

To follow the creek and river to Fort Kearny was not
accounted much of a chance for escape, but it was the only
avenue that lay open; so, with a parting volley to deceive
the besiegers into thinking that the fort was still held, the
perilous and difficult journey was begun.

The Indians quickly penetrated the ruse, and another

charge had to be repulsed. Besides the tiresome work of wading, there were wounded men to help along, and a ceaseless watch to keep against another rush of the reds. It was a trying ordeal for a man, doubly so for a boy like Will; but he was encouraged to coolness and endurance by a few words from Frank McCarthy, who remarked, admiringly, "Well, Billy, you didn't scare worth a cent."

After a few miles of wading the little party issued out upon the Platte River. By this time the wounded men were so exhausted that a halt was called to improvise a raft. On this the sufferers were placed, and three or four men detailed to shove it before them. In consideration of his youth, Will was urged to get upon the raft, but he declined, saying that he was not wounded, and that if the stream got too deep for him to wade, he could swim. This was more than some of the men could do, and they, too, had to be assisted over the deep places.

Thus wore the long and weary hours away, and though the men, who knew how hard a trip it was, often asked, "How goes it, Billy?" he uttered no word of complaint.

But half a day's wading, without rest or food, gradually weighted his heels, and little by little he lagged behind his companions. The moon came out and silvered tree and river, but the silent, plodding band had no eyes for the glory of the landscape.

Will had fallen behind some twenty rods, but in a moment fatigue was forgotten, the blood jumped in his veins, for just ahead of him the moonlight fell upon the feathered head-dress of an Indian chief, who was peering over the bank. Motionless, he watched the head, shoulders, and body of the brave come into view. The Indian supposed the entire party ahead, and Will made no move until the savage bent his bow.

Then he realized, with a thumping heart, that death must come to one of his comrades or the Indian.

Even in direst necessity it is a fearful thing to deliberately take a human life, but Will had no time for hesitation. There was a shot, and the Indian rolled down the bank into the river.

His expiring yell was answered by others. The reds were not far away. Frank McCarthy, missing Will, stationed guards, and ran back to look for him. He found the lad hauling the dead warrior ashore, and seizing his hand, cried out: "Well done, my boy; you've killed your first Indian, and done it like a man!"

Will wanted to stop and bury the body, but being assured that it was not only an uncustomary courtesy, but in this case quite impossible, he hastened on. As they came up with the waiting group McCarthy called out:

"Pards, little Billy has killed his first redskin!"

The announcement was greeted with cheers, which grated on Will's ears, for his heart was sick, and the cheers seemed strangely out of place.

Little time, however, was afforded for sentiment of any sort. Enraged at the death of their scout, the Indians made a final charge, which was repulsed, like the others, and after this Bill McCarthy took the lead, with Frank at the rear, to prevent further straggling of the forces.

It was a haggard-faced band that came up to Fort Kearny with the dawn. The wounded men were left at the post, while the others returned to the wrecked bull-train under escort of a body of troops. They hoped to make some salvage, but the cattle had either been driven away or had joined one of the numerous herds of buffalo; the wagons and their freight had been burned, and there was nothing to do but bury the three pickets, whose scalped and mutilated bodies were stretched where they had fallen.

Then the troops and trainmen parted company, the former to undertake a bootless quest for the red marauders, the latter to return to Leavenworth, their occupation gone. The government held itself responsible for the depredations of its wards, and the loss of the wagons and cattle was assumed at Washington.

CHAPTER VI.

FAMILY DEFENDER AND HOUSEHOLD TEASE.

THE fame to which Byron woke one historic morning was no more unexpected to him than that which now greeted Will. The trainmen had not been over-modest in their accounts of his pluck; and when a newspaper reporter lent the magic of his imagination to the plain narrative, it became quite a story, headed in display type, "The Boy Indian Slayer."

But Will was speedily concerned with other than his own affairs, for as soon as his position with the freighters was assured, mother engaged a lawyer to fight the claim against our estate. This legal light was John C. Douglass, then unknown, unhonored, and unsung, but talented and enterprising notwithstanding. He had just settled in Leavenworth, and he could scarcely have found a better case with which to storm the heights of fame—the dead father, the sick mother, the helpless children, and relentless persecution, in one scale; in the other, an eleven-year-old boy doing a man's work to earn the money needed to combat the family's enemies. Douglass put his whole strength into the case.

He knew as well as we that our cause was weak; it hung by a single thread—a missing witness, Mr. Barnhart. This man had acted as bookkeeper when the bills were paid, but he had been sent away, and the prosecution—or persecution—had thus far succeeded in keeping his where-

abouts a secret. To every place where he was likely to be
Lawyer Douglass had written; but we were as much in the
dark as ever when the morning for the trial of the suit
arrived.

The case had excited much interest, and the court-room
was crowded, many persons having been drawn thither by
a curiosity to look upon "The Boy Indian Slayer." There
was a cheerful unanimity of opinion upon the utter hope-
lessness of the Cody side of the case. Not only were
prominent and wealthy men arrayed against us, but our
young and inexperienced lawyer faced the heaviest legal
guns of the Leavenworth bar. Our only witnesses were a
frail woman and a girl of eighteen, though by their side,
with his head held high, was the family protector, our
brave young brother. Against us were might and malignity;
upon our side, right and the high courage with which
Christianity steels the soul of a believer. Mother had
faith that the invisible forces of the universe were fighting
for our cause.

She and Martha swore to the fact that all the bills had
been settled; and after the opposition had rested its case,
Lawyer Douglass arose for the defense. His was a magnificent plea for the rights of the widow and the orphan, and
was conceded to be one of the finest speeches ever heard
in a Kansas court-room; but though all were moved by
our counsel's eloquence—some unto tears by the pathos of
it—though the justice of our cause was freely admitted
throughout the court-room, our best friends feared the
verdict.

But the climax was as stunning to our enemies as it
was unexpected. As Lawyer Douglass finished his last
ringing period, the missing witness, Mr. Barnhart, hurried
into the court-room. He had started for Leavenworth

upon the first intimation that his presence there was needed, and had reached it just in time. He took the stand, swore to his certain knowledge that the bills in question had been paid, and the jury, without leaving their seats, returned a verdict for the defense.

Then rose cheer upon cheer, as our friends crowded about us and offered their congratulations. Our home was saved, and Lawyer Douglass had won a reputation for eloquence and sterling worth that stood undimmed through all his long and prosperous career.

The next ripple on the current of our lives was sister Martha's wedding day. Possessed of remarkable beauty, she had become a belle, and as young ladies were scarce in Kansas at that time, she was the toast of all our country round. But her choice had fallen on a man unworthy of her. Of his antecedents we knew nothing; of his present life little more, save that he was fair in appearance and seemingly prosperous. In the sanction of the union Will stood aloof. Joined to a native intuition were the sharpened faculties of a lad that lived beyond his years. Almost unerring in his insight, he disliked the object of our sister's choice so thoroughly that he refused to be a witness of the nuptials. This dislike we attributed to jealousy, as brother and sister worshiped each other, but the sequel proved a sad corroboration of his views.

Nature seemed to join her protest to Will's silent antagonism. A terrific thunder-storm came up with the noon hour of the wedding. So deep and sullen were the clouds that we were obliged to light the candles. When the wedding pair took their places before Hymen's altar, a crash of thunder rocked the house and set the casements rattling.

The couple had their home awaiting them in Leavenworth, and departed almost immediately after the ceremony.

The cares and responsibilities laid upon our brother's shoulders did not quench his boyish spirits and love of fun. Not Buffalo Bill's! He gave us a jack-o'-lantern scare once upon a time, which I don't believe any of us will ever forget. We had never seen that weird species of pumpkin, and Will embroidered a blood-and-thunder narrative.

"The pumpkins all rise up out of the ground," said he, "on fire, with the devil's eyes, and their mouths open, like blood-red lions, and grab you, and go under the earth. You better look out!"

"That ain't so!" all of us little girls cried; "you know it's a fib. Ain't it, mother?" and we ran as usual to mother.

"Will, you mustn't tell the children such tales. Of course they're just fibs," said mother.

"So there!" we cried, in triumph. But Will had a "so there" answer for us a few nights later. We were coming home late one evening, and found the gate guarded by mad-looking yellow things, all afire, and grinning hideously like real live men in the moon dropped down from the sky.

"Jack-o'-lanterns!" screamed Eliza, grabbing May by the hand, and starting to run. I began to say my prayers, of course, and cry for mother. All at once the heads moved! Even Turk's tail shot between his legs, and he howled in fright. We saw the devil's eyes, the blood-red lion's mouths, and all the rest, and set up such a chorus of wild yells that the whole household rushed to our rescue. While we were panting out our story, we heard Will snickering behind the door.

THE FIRST REHEARSAL OF THE "WILD WEST."

"So there, smarties! You'll believe what I tell you next time. You bet—ter—had!"

But he liked best to invade our play-room and "work magic" on our dolls. Mother had set aside one apartment in our large log house for a play-room, and here each one of our doll families dwelt in peace and harmony, when Will wasn't around. But there was tragedy whenever he came near. He would scalp the mother dolls, and tie their babies to the bedposts, and would storm into their pasteboard-box houses at night, after we had fixed them all in order, and put the families to standing on their heads. He was a dreadful tease. It was in this play-room that the germ of his Wild West took life. He formed us into a regular little company—Turk and the baby, too—and would start us in marching order for the woods. He made us stick horses and wooden tomahawks, spears, and horsehair strings, so that we could be cowboys, Indians, bullwhackers, and cavalrymen. All the scenes of his first freighting trip were acted out in the woods of Salt Creek Valley. We had stages, robbers, "hold-ups," and most ferocious Indian battles.

Will was always the "principal scalper," however, and we had few of our feathers left after he was on the warpath. We were so little we couldn't reach his feathers. He always wore two long shiny ones, which had been the special pride of our black rooster, and when he threw a piece of an old blanket gotten from the Leavenworth barracks around his shoulders, we considered him a very fine general indeed.

All of us were obedient to the letter on "show days," and scarcely ever said "Now, stop," or "I'll tell mother on you!" But during one of these exciting performances Will came to a short stop.

"I believe I'll run a show when I get to be a man," said he.

"That fortune lady said you'd got to be President of the United States," said Eliza.

"How could ze presiman won a show?" asked May.

"How could that old fortune-teller know what I'm going to be?" Will would answer, disdainfully. "I rather guess I can have a show, in spite of all the fortune-tellers in the country. I'll tell you right now, girls, I don't propose to be President, but I do mean to have a show!"

Such temerity in disputing one's destiny was appalling; and though our ideas of destiny were rather vague, we could grasp one dreadful fact: Will had refused to be President of the United States! So we ran crying to mother, and burying our faces in her lap, sobbed out: "Oh, mother! Will says he ain't going to be President. Don't he have to be?"

Still, in spite of Will's fine scorn of fortune-tellers, the prophecy concerning his future must have been sometimes in his mind. This was shown in an episode that the writer is in duty bound, as a veracious chronicler, to set down.

Our neighbor, Mr. Hathaway, had a son, Eugene, of about Will's age, and the two were fast friends. One day, when Will was visiting at Eugene's house, the boys introduced themselves to a barrel of hard cider. Temperance sentiment had not progressed far enough to bring hard cider under the ban, and Mr. Hathaway had lately pressed out a quantity of the old-fashioned beverage. The boys, supposing it a harmless drink, took all they desired—much more than they could carry. They were in a deplorable condition when Mr. Hathaway found them; and much distressed, the good old man put Eugene to bed and brought Will home.

The family hero returned to us with a flourish of trumpets. He stood up in the wagon and sang and shouted; and when Mr. Hathaway reproved him, "Don't talk to me," was his lofty rejoinder. "You forget that I am to be President of the United States."

There is compensation for everything. Will never touched cider again; and never again could he lord it over his still admiring but no longer docile sisters. If he undertook to boss or tease us more than to our fancy, we would subdue him with an imitation of his grandiloquent, "You forget that I am to be President of the United States." Indeed, so severe was this retaliation that we seldom saw him the rest of the day.

But he got even with us when "preacher day" came around.

Like "Little Breeches'" father, Will never did go in much on religion, and when the ministers assembled for "quarterly meeting" at our house, we never knew what to expect from him. Mother was a Methodist, and as our log house was larger than the others in the valley, it fell to our lot to entertain the preachers often. We kept our preparations on the quiet when Will was home, but he always managed to find out what was up, and then trouble began. His first move was to "sick" Turk on the yellow-legged chickens. They were our best ones, and the only thing we had for the ministers to eat. Then Will would come stalking in:

"Say, mother, just saw all the yellow-legged chickens a-scooting up the road. Methodist preachers must be in the wind, for the old hens are flying like sixty!"

"Now, Will, you call Turk off, and round up those chickens right away."

"Catch meself!" And Will would dance around and tease so he nearly drove us all distracted. It was with the greatest difficulty that mother could finally prevail upon him to round up the chickens. That done, he would tie up the pump-handle, milk the cows dry, strew the path to the gate with burrs and thistles, and stick up a sign, "Thorney is the path and stickery the way that leedith unto the kingdom of heaven. Amen!"

Then when mother had put a nice clean valance, freshly starched and ruffled, around the big four-poster bed in the sitting-room, Will would daub it up with smearcase, and just before the preachers arrived, sneak in under it, and wait for prayers.

Mother always desired us to file in quietly, but we couldn't pass the bed without our legs being pinched; so we "hollered," but were afraid to tell mother the reason before the ministers. We had to bear it, but we snickered ourselves when the man Will called "Elder Green Persimmon," because when he prayed his mouth went inside out, came mincing into the room, and as he passed the valance and got a pinch, jerked out a sour-grape sneeze:

"Mercy on us! I thought I was bitten by that fierce dog of yours, Mrs. Cody; but it must have been a burr."

Then the "experiences" would begin. Will always listened quietly, until the folks began telling how wicked they had been before they got religion; then he would burst in with a vigorous "Amen!"

The elders did not know Will's voice; so they would get warmed up by degree as the amens came thicker and faster. When he had worked them all up to a red-hot pitch, Will would start that awful snort of his that always made us double up with giggles, and with a loud cockle-doodle-doo! would bolt from the bed like a lightning flash and make for the window.

So "preacher day," as Will always called it, became the torment of our lives.

To tell the truth, Will always was teasing us, but if he crooked his finger at us we would bawl. We bawled and squalled from morning till night. Yet we fairly worshiped him, and cried harder when he went away than when he was home.

CHAPTER VII.

INDIAN ENCOUNTER AND SCHOOL-DAY INCIDENTS.

WILL was not long at home. The Mormons, who were settled in Utah, rebelled when the government, objecting to the quality of justice meted out by Brigham Young, sent a federal judge to the territory. Troops, under the command of General Albert Sidney Johnston, were dispatched to quell the insurrection, and Russell, Majors & Waddell contracted to transport stores and beef cattle to the army massing against the Mormons in the fall of 1857. The train was a large one, better prepared against such an attack as routed the McCarthy brothers earlier in the summer; yet its fate was the same.

Will was assigned to duty as "extra" under Lew Simpson, an experienced wagon-master, and was subject to his orders only. There was the double danger of Mormons and Indians, so the pay was good. Forty dollars a month in gold looked like a large sum to an eleven-year-old.

Will's second departure was quite as tragic as the first. We girls, as before, were loud in our wailings, and offered to forgive him the depredations in the doll-house and all his teasings, if only he would not go away and be scalped by the Indians. Mother said little, but her anxious look, as she recalled the perils of the former trip, spoke volumes. He carried with him the memory of the open-mouthed admiration of little Charlie, to whom "Brother Will" was the greatest hero in the world. Turk's grief at the parting

was not a whit less than ours, and the faithful old fellow
seemed to realize that in Will's absence the duty of the
family protector devolved on him; so he made no attempt
to follow Will beyond the gate.

The train made good progress, and more than half the
journey to Fort Bridger was accomplished without a set-
back. When the Rockies were reached, a noon halt was
made near Green River, and here the men were surrounded
and overcome by a large force of Danites, the "Avenging
Angels" of the Mormon Church, who had "stolen the
livery of the court of heaven to serve the devil in." These
were responsible for the atrocious Mountain Meadow Massacre, in June of this same year, though the wily "Saints"
had planned to place the odium of an unprovoked murder
of innocent women and children upon the Indians, who
had enough to answer for, and in this instance were but
the tools of the Mormon Church. Brigham Young repudi-
ated his accomplice, and allowed John D. Lee to become
the scapegoat. The dying statement of this man is as
pathetic as Cardinal Wolsey's arraignment of Henry VIII.

"A victim must be had," said he, "and I am that victim. For thirty years I studied to make Brigham Young's
will my law. See now what I have come to this day.
I have been sacrificed in a cowardly, dastardly manner.
I do not fear death. I cannot go to a worse place than I
am now in."

John D. Lee deserved his fate, but Brigham Young was
none the less a coward.

The Danites spared the lives of the trainmen, but they
made sad havoc of the supplies. These they knew to be
intended for the use of the army opposed to Brigham
Young. They carried off all the stores they could handle,
drove with them or stampeded the cattle, and burned the

wagons. The trainmen were permitted to retain one wagon and team, with just enough supplies to last them to army headquarters.

It was a disheartened, discomfited band that reached Fort Bridger. The information that two other trains had been destroyed added to their discouragement, for that meant that they, in common with the other trainmen and the soldiers at the fort, must subsist on short rations for the winter. There were nearly four hundred of these trainmen, and it was so late in the season that they had no choice but to remain where they were until spring opened.

It was an irksome winter. The men at the fort hauled their firewood two miles; as the provisions dwindled, one by one the oxen were slaughtered, and when this food supply was exhausted, starvation reared its gaunt form. Happily the freighters got word of the situation, and a relief team reached the fort before the spring was fairly opened.

As soon as practicable the return journey was undertaken. At Fort Laramie two large trains were put in charge of Lew Simpson, as brigade wagon-master, and Will was installed as courier between the two caravans, which traveled twenty miles apart—plenty of elbow room for camping and foraging.

One morning, Simpson, George Woods, and Will, who were in the rear train, set out for the forward one, mounted upon mules, and armed, as the trainmen always were, with rifle, knife, and a brace of revolvers. About half of the twenty miles had been told off when the trio saw a band of Indians emerge from a clump of trees half a mile away and sweep toward them. Flight with the mules was useless; resistance promised hardly more success, as the Indians numbered a full half-hundred; but surrender was death and mutilation.

"Shoot the mules, boys!" ordered Simpson, and five minutes later two men and a boy looked grimly over a still palpitating barricade.

The defense was simple; rifles at range, revolvers for close quarters, knives at the last. The chief, easily distinguished by his feathered head-dress, was assigned to Will. Already his close shooting was the pride of the frontiersmen. Simpson's coolness steadied the lad, who realized that the situation was desperate.

The Indians came on with the rush and scream of the March wind. "Fire!" said Simpson, and three ponies galloped riderless as the smoke curled from three rifle barrels.

Dismayed by the fall of their chief, the redskins wheeled and rode out of range. Will gave a sigh of relief.

"Load up again, Billy!" smiled Simpson. "They'll soon be back."

"They've only three or four rifles," said Woods. There had been little lead in the cloud of arrows.

"Here they come!" warned Simpson, and the trio ran their rifles out over the dead mules.

Three more riderless ponies; but the Indians kept on, supposing they had drawn the total fire of the whites. A revolver fusillade undeceived them, and the charging column wavered and broke for cover.

Simpson patted Will on the shoulder as they reloaded. "You're a game one, Billy!" said he.

"You bet he is," echoed Woods, coolly drawing an arrow from his shoulder. "How is that, Lew—poisoned?"

Will waited breathless for the decision, and his relief was as great as Woods's when Simpson, after a critical scrutiny, answered "No."

The wound was hastily dressed, and the little company

gave an undivided attention to the foe, who were circling around their quarry, hanging to the off sides of their ponies and firing under them. With a touch of the grim humor that plain life breeds, Will declared that the mules were veritable pincushions, so full of arrows were they stuck.

The besieged maintained a return fire, dropping pony after pony, and occasionally a rider. This proved expensive sport to the Indians, and the whole party finally withdrew from range.

There was a long breathing spell, which the trio improved by strengthening their defense, digging up the dirt with their knives and piling it upon the mules. It was tedious work, but preferable to inactivity and cramped quarters.

Two hours went by, and the plan of the enemy was disclosed. A light breeze arose, and the Indians fired the prairie. Luckily the grass near the trail was short, and though the heat was intense and the smoke stifling, the barricade held off the flame. Simpson had kept a close watch, and presently gave the order to fire. A volley went through the smoke and blaze, and the yell that followed proved that it was not wasted. This last ruse failing, the Indians settled down to their favorite game—waiting.

A thin line of them circled out of range; ponies were picketed and tents pitched; night fell, and the stars shot out.

As Woods was wounded, he was excused from guard duty, Will and Simpson keeping watch in turn. Will took the first vigil, and, tired though he was, experienced no difficulty in keeping awake, but he went soundly to sleep the moment he was relieved. He was wakened by a dream that Turk was barking to him, and vaguely alarmed, he sat up to find Simpson sleeping across his rifle.

The midnight hush was unbroken, and the darkness lay thick upon the plain, but shapes blacker than night hovered near, and Will laid his hand on Simpson's shoulder.

The latter was instantly alive, and Woods was wakened. A faint click went away on the night breeze, and a moment later three jets of flame carried warning to the up-creeping foe that the whites were both alive and on the alert.

There was no more sleep within the barricade. The dawn grew into day, and anxious eyes scanned the trail for reinforcements—coming surely, but on what heavy and slow-turning wheels!

Noon came and passed. The anxious eyes questioned one another. Had the rear train been overcome by a larger band of savages? But suddenly half a dozen of the Indians were seen to spring up with gestures of excitement, and spread the alarm around the circle.

"They hear the cracking of the bull-whips," said Simpson.

The Indians who had seen the first team pass, and had assumed that Simpson and his companions were straggling members of it, did not expect another train so soon. There was "mounting in hot haste," and the Indians rode away in one bunch for the distant foothills, just as the first ox-team broke into view.

And never was there fairer picture to more appreciative eyes than those same lumbering, clumsy animals, and never sweeter music than the harsh staccato of the bull-whips.

When hunger was appeased, and Woods's wound properly dressed, Will, for the second time, found himself a hero among the plainsmen. His nerve and coolness were dwelt upon by Simpson, and to the dream that waked him in season was ascribed the continued life on earth of the

little company. Will, however, was disposed to allow
Turk the full credit for the service.

The remainder of the trip was devoid of special incident, and as Will neared home he hurried on in advance of
the train. His heart beat high as he thought of the dear
faces awaiting him, unconscious that he was so near.

But the home toward which he was hastening with beating heart and winged heels was shadowed by a great grief.
Sister Martha's married life, though brief, had amply justified her brother's estimate of the man into whose hands she
had given her life. She was taken suddenly ill, and it was
not until several months later that Will learned that the
cause of her sickness was the knowledge that had come to
her of the faithless nature of her husband. The revelation
was made through the visit of one of Mr. C——'s creditors,
who, angered at a refusal to liquidate a debt, accused Mr.
C—— of being a bigamist, and threatened to set the law
upon him. The blow was fatal to one of Martha's pure
and affectionate nature, already crushed by neglect and
cruelty. All that night she was delirious, and her one
thought was "Willie," and the danger he was in—not
alone the physical danger, but the moral and spiritual
peril that she feared lay in association with rough and
reckless men. She moaned and tossed, and uttered inco-
herent cries; but as the morning broke the storm went
down, and the anxious watchers fancied that she slept.
Suddenly she sat up, the light of reason again shining
in her eyes, and with a joyous cry, "Tell mother Willie's
saved! Willie's saved!" she fell back on her pillow, and
her spirit passed away. On her face was the peace that
the world can neither give nor take away. The veil of the
Unknown had been drawn aside for a space. She had
"sent her soul through the Invisible," and it had found

the light that lit the last weary steps through the Valley of the Shadow.

Mr. C—— had moved from Leavenworth to Johnson County, twenty-five miles away, and as there were neither telegraph nor mail facilities, he had the body sent home, himself accompanying it. Thus our first knowledge of Martha's sickness came when her lifeless clay was borne across our threshold, the threshold that, less than a year before, she had crossed a bright and bonny bride. Dazed by the shock, we longed for Will's return before we must lay his idolized sister forever in her narrow cell.

All of the family, Mr. C—— included, were gathered in the sitting-room, sad and silent, when Turk suddenly raised his head, listened a second, and bounded out of doors.

"Will is coming!" cried mother, and we all ran to the door. Turk was racing up the long hill, at the top of which was a moving speck that the dog knew to be his master. His keen ears had caught the familiar whistle half a mile away.

When Turk had manifested his joy at the meeting, he prepared Will for the bereavement that awaited him; he put his head down and emitted a long and repeated wail. Will's first thought was for mother, and he fairly ran down the hill. The girls met him some distance from the house, and sobbed out the sad news.

And when he had listened, the lad that had passed unflinching through two Indian fights, broke down, and sobbed with the rest of us.

"Did that rascal, C——, have anything to do with her death?" he asked, when the first passion of grief was over.

Julia, who knew no better at the time, replied that Mr. C—— was the kindest of husbands, and was crushed with sorrow at his loss; but spite of the assurance, Will, when he reached the house, had neither look nor word for him. He just put his arms about mother's neck, and mingled his grief with her words of sympathy and love.

Martha was shortly after laid by father's side, and as we stood weeping in that awful moment when the last spadeful of earth completes the sepulture, Will, no longer master of himself, stepped up before Mr. C——:

"Murderer," he said, "one day you shall answer to me for the death of her who lies there!"

When Will next presented himself at Mr. Majors's office, he was told that his services had been wholly satisfactory, and that he could have work at any time he desired. This was gratifying, but a sweeter pleasure was to lay his winter's wages in mother's lap. Through his help, and her business ability, our pecuniary affairs were in good condition. We were comfortably situated, and as Salt Creek Valley now boasted of a schoolhouse, mother wished Will to enter school. He was so young when he came West that his school-days had been few; nor was the prospect of adding to their number alluring. After the excitement of life on the plains, going to school was dull work; but Will realized that there was a world beyond the prairie's horizon, and he entered school, determined to do honest work.

Our first teacher was of the good, old-fashioned sort. He taught because he had to live. He had no love for his work, and knew nothing of children. The one motto he lived up to was, "Spare the rod and spoil the child." As Will was a regular Tartar in the schoolroom, he, more than all the other scholars, made him put his smarting theory into practice. Almost every afternoon was attended with the dramatic attempt to switch Will. The schoolroom was separated into two grand divisions, "the boys on teacher's side," and those "on the Cody side." The teacher would send his pets out to get switches, and part of our division—we girls, of course—would begin to weep; while those who had spunk would spit on their hands, clench their fists, and "dare 'em to bring them switches in!" Those were hot times in old Salt Creek Valley!

One morning Turk, too, was seized with educational ambition, and accompanied Will to school. We tried to drive him home, but he followed at a distance, and as we entered the schoolhouse, he emerged from the shrubbery by the roadside and crept under the building.

Alas for the scholars, and alas for the school! Another ambitious dog reposed beneath the temple of learning.

Will, about that time, was having a bad quarter of an hour. An examination into his knowledge, or lack of it, was under way, and he was hard pressed. Had he been asked how to strike a trail, locate water, or pitch a tent, his replies would have been full and accurate, but the teacher's queries seemed as foolish as the "Reeling and Writhing, Ambition, Distraction, Uglification, and Derision" of the Mock Turtle in "Alice in Wonderland."

Turk effected an unexpected rescue. Snarls were heard beneath the schoolhouse; then savage growls and yelps, while the floor resounded with the whacks of the canine combatants. With a whoop that would not have disgraced an Indian, Will was out of doors, shouting, "Eat him up, Turk! Eat him up!"

The owner of the opposing dog was one Steve Gobel. 'Twixt him and Will a good-sized feud existed. Steve was also on the scene, with a defiant, "Sic 'em, Nigger!" and the rest of the school followed in his wake.

Of the twisting, yelping bundle of dog-flesh that rolled

from under the schoolhouse it was difficult to say which was Turk and which Nigger. Eliza and I called to Turk, and wept because he would not hear. The teacher ordered the children back to their studies, but they were as deaf as Turk; whereat the enraged pedagogue hopped wildly about, flourishing a stick and whacking every boy that strayed within reach of it.

Nigger soon had enough of the fight, and striking his tail-colors, fled yelping from the battle-ground. His master, Steve Gobel, a large youth of nineteen or twenty years, pulled off his coat to avenge upon Will the dog's defeat, but the teacher effected a Solomon-like compromise by whipping both boys for bringing their dogs to school, after which the interrupted session was resumed.

But Gobel nursed his wrath, and displayed his enmity in a thousand small ways. Will paid no attention to him, but buckled down to his school work. Will was a born "lady's man," and when Miss Mary Hyatt complicated the feud 'twixt him and Steve, it hurried to its climax. Mary was older than Will, but she plainly showed her preference for him over Master Gobel. Steve had never distinguished himself in an Indian fight; he was not a hero, but just a plain boy.

Now, indeed, was Will's life unendurable; "patience had had its perfect work." He knew that a boy of twelve, however strong and sinewy, was not a match for an almost full-grown man; so, to balance matters, he secreted on his person an old bowie-knife. When next he met Steve, the latter climaxed his bullying tactics by striking the object of his resentment; but he was unprepared for the sudden leap that bore him backward to the earth. Size and strength told swiftly in the struggle that succeeded, but Will, with a dextrous thrust, put the point of the bowie into the fleshy part of Steve's lower leg, a spot where he knew the cut would not be serious.

The stricken bully shrieked that he was killed; the children gathered round, and screamed loudly at the sight of blood. "Will Cody has killed Steve Gobel!" was the wailing cry, and Will, though he knew Steve was but pinked, began to realize that frontier styles of combat were not esteemed in communities given up to the soberer pursuits of spelling, arithmetic, and history. Steve, he knew, was more frightened than hurt; but the picture of the prostrate, ensanguined youth, and the group of awe-stricken children, bore in upon his mind the truth that his act was an infraction of the civil code; that even in self-defense, he had no right to use a knife unless his life was threatened.

The irate pedagogue was hastening to the scene, and after one glance at him, Will incontinently fled. At the road he came upon a wagon train, and with a shout of joy recognized in the "boss" John Willis, a wagon-master employed by Russell, Majors & Waddell, and a great friend of the "boy extra." Will climbed up behind Willis on his horse, and related his escapade to a close and sympathetic listener.

"If you say so, Billy," was his comment, "I'll go over and lick the whole outfit, and stampede the school."

"No, let the school alone," replied Will; "but I guess I'll graduate, if you'll let me go along with you this trip."

Willis readily agreed, but insisted upon returning to the schoolhouse. "I'm not going," said he, "to let you be beaten by a bully of a boy, and a Yankee school-teacher, with a little learning, but not a bit of sand." His idea of equalizing forces was that he and "Little Billy" should fight against the pedagogue and Steve.

Will consented, and they rode back to the schoolhouse, on the door of which Willis pounded with his revolver butt, and when the door was opened he invited Gobel and the "grammar man" to come forth and do battle. But Steve had gone home, and the teacher, on seeing the two gladiators, fled, while the scholars, dismissing themselves, ran home in a fright.

That night mother received a note from the teacher.

He was not hired, he wrote, to teach desperadoes; therefore Will was dismissed. But Will had already dismissed himself, and had rejoined the larger school whose walls are the blue bowl called the sky. And long after was his name used by the pedagogue to conjure up obedience in his pupils; unless they kissed the rod, they, too, might go to the bad, and follow in Will Cody's erring footsteps.

Willis and Will had gone but a piece on the road when horsemen were seen approaching.

"Mr. Gobel and the officers are after me," said Will.

"Being after you and gittin' you are two different things," said the wagon-master. "Lie low, and I'll settle the men."

Mr. Gobel and his party rode up with the information that they had come to arrest Will; but they got no satisfaction from Willis. He would not allow them to search the wagons, and they finally rode away. That night, when the camp was pitched, the wagon-master gave Will a mule, and accompanied him home. We were rejoiced to see him, especially mother, who was much concerned over his escapade.

"Oh, Will, how could you do such a thing?" she said, sorrowfully. "It is a dreadful act to use a knife on any one."

Will disavowed any homicidal intentions; but his

explanations made little headway against mother's disapproval and her disappointment over the interruption of his school career. As it seemed the best thing to do, she consented to his going with the wagon train under the care of John Willis, and the remainder of the night was passed in preparations for the journey.

CHAPTER VIII.

DEATH AND BURIAL OF TURK.

THIS trip of Will's covered only two months, and was succeeded by another expedition, to the new post at Fort Wallace, at Cheyenne Pass.

Meanwhile mother had decided to improve the opportunity afforded by her geographical position, and under her supervision "The Valley Grove House" was going up.

The hotel commanded a magnificent prospect. Below lay the beautiful Salt Creek Valley. It derived its name from the saline properties of the little stream that rushed along its pebbly bed to empty its clear waters into the muddy Missouri. From the vantage-ground of our location Salt Creek looked like a silver thread, winding its way through the rich verdure of the valley. The region was dotted with fertile farms; from east to west ran the government road, known as the Old Salt Lake Trail, and back of us was Cody Hill, named for my father. Our house stood on the side hill, just above the military road, and between us and the hilltop lay the grove that gave the hotel its name. Government hill, which broke the eastern sky-line, hid Leavenworth and the Missouri River, culminating to the south in Pilot Knob, the eminence on which my father was buried, also beyond our view.

Mother's business sagacity was justified in the hotel venture. The trail began its half-mile ascent of Cody Hill just below our house, and at this point the expedient known as "doubling" was employed. Two teams hauled a wagon up the steep incline, the double team returning for the wagon left behind. Thus the progress of a wagon train, always slow, became a very snail's pace, and the hotel was insured a full quota of hungry trainmen.

Will found that his wages were of considerable aid to mother in the large expense incurred by the building of the hotel; and the winter drawing on, forbidding further freighting trips, he planned an expedition with a party of trappers. More money was to be made at this business during the winter than at any other time.

The trip was successful, and contained only one adventure spiced with danger, which, as was so often the case, Will twisted to his own advantage by coolness and presence of mind.

One morning, as he was making the round of his traps, three Indians appeared on the trail, each leading a pony laden with pelts. One had a gun; the others carried bows and arrows. The odds were three to one, and the brave with the gun was the most to be feared.

This Indian dropped his bridle-rein and threw up his rifle; but before it was at his shoulder Will had fired, and he fell forward on his face. His companions bent their bows, one arrow passing through Will's hat and another piercing his arm—the first wound he ever received. Will swung his cap about his head.

"This way! Here they are!" he shouted to an imaginary party of friends at his back. Then with his revolver he wounded another of the Indians, who, believing reinforcements were at hand, left their ponies and fled.

Will took the ponies on the double-quick back to camp, and the trappers decided to pull up stakes at once. It had been a profitable season, and the few more pelts to be had were not worth the risk of an attack by avenging Indians; so they packed their outfit, and proceeded to Fort Laramie. Will realized a handsome sum from the sale of his captured furs, besides those of the animals he had himself trapped.

At the fort were two men bound east, and impatient to set out, and Will, in his haste to reach home, joined forces with them. Rather than wait for an uncertain wagon train, they decided to chance the dangers of the road. They bought three ponies and a pack-mule for the camp outfit, and sallied forth in high spirits.

Although the youngest of the party, Will was the most experienced plainsman, and was constantly on the alert. They reached the Little Blue River without sign of Indians, but across the stream Will espied a band of them. The redskins were as keen of eye, and straightway exchanged the pleasures of the chase for the more exciting pursuit of human game. But they had the river to cross, and this gave the white men a good start. The pursuit was hot, and grew hotter, but the kindly darkness fell, and under cover of it the trio got safely away. That night they camped in a little ravine that afforded shelter from both Indians and weather.

A look over the ravine disclosed a cave that promised a snug harbor, and therein Will and one of his companions spread their blankets and fell asleep. The third man, whose duty it was to prepare the supper, kindled a fire just inside the cave, and returned outside for a supply of fuel. When he again entered the cave the whole interior was revealed by the bright firelight, and after one look he gave a yell of terror, dropped his firewood, and fled.

Will and the other chap were on their knees instantly,

groping for their rifles, in the belief that the Indians were upon them; but the sight that met their eyes was more terror-breeding than a thousand Indians. A dozen bleached and ghastly skeletons were gathered with them around the camp-fire, and seemed to nod and sway, and thrust their long-chilled bones toward the cheery blaze.

Ghastly as it was within the cave, Will found it more unpleasant in the open. The night was cold, and a storm threatened.

"Well," said he to his companions, "we know the worst that's in there now. Those old dead bones won't hurt us. Let's go back."

"Not if I know myself, sonny," returned one of the men decidedly, and the other heartily agreed with him, swearing that as it was, he should not be able to close his eyes for a week. So, after a hurried lunch upon the cold provisions, the party mounted their ponies and pushed on. The promised snowstorm materialized, and shortly became a young blizzard, and obliged to dismount and camp in the open prairie, they made a miserable night of it.

But it had an end, as all things have, and with the morning they resumed the trail, reaching Marysville, on the Big Blue, after many trials and privations.

From here the trail was easier, as the country was pretty well settled, and Will reached home without further adventure or misadventure. Here there was compensation for hardship in the joy of handing over to mother all his money, realizing that it would lighten her burdens—burdens borne that she might leave her children provided for when she could no longer repel the dread messenger, that in all those years seemed to hover so near that even our childish hearts felt its presence ere it actually crossed the threshold.

It was early in March when Will returned from his trapping expedition. Mother's business was flourishing, though she herself grew frailer with the passing of each day. The summer that came on was a sad one for us all, for it marked Turk's last days on earth. One evening he was lying in the yard, when a strange dog came up the road, bounded in, gave Turk a vicious bite, and went on. We dressed the wound, and thought little of it, until some horsemen rode up, with the inquiry, "Have you seen a dog pass here?"

We answered indignantly that a strange dog had passed, and had bitten our dog.

"Better look out for him, then," warned the men as they rode away. "The dog is mad."

Consternation seized us. It was dreadful to think of Turk going mad—he who had been our playmate from infancy, and who, through childhood's years, had grown more dear to us than many human beings could; but mother knew the matter was serious, and issued her commands. Turk must be shut up, and we must not even visit him for a certain space. And so we shut him up, hoping for the best; but it speedily became plain that the poison was working in his veins, and that the greatest kindness we could do him was to kill him.

That was a frightful alternative. Will utterly refused to shoot him, and the execution was delegated to the hired man, Will stipulating that none of his weapons should be used, and that he be allowed to get out of ear-shot.

Late that afternoon, just before sunset, we assembled in melancholy silence for the funeral. A grave had been dug on the highest point of the eastern extremity of Cody Hill, and decorated in black ribbons, we slowly filed up the steep path, carrying Turk's body on a pine board softened with moss. Will led the procession with his hat in his hand, and every now and then his fist went savagely at his eyes. When we reached the grave, we formed around it in a tearful circle, and Will, who always called me "the little preacher," told me to say the Lord's Prayer. The sun was setting, and the brilliant western clouds were shining round about us. There was a sighing in the treetops far below us, and the sounds in the valley were muffled and indistinct.

"Our Father which art in heaven," I whispered softly, as all the children bent their heads, "Hallowed be Thy name. Thy kingdom come, Thy will be done in earth as it is in heaven." I paused, and the other children said the rest in chorus. The next day Will procured a large block of red bloodstone, which abounds in that country, squared it off, carved the name of Turk upon it in large letters, and we placed it at the head of the grave.

To us there had been no incongruity in the funeral ceremonials and burial. Turk had given us all that dog could give; we, for our part, gave him Christian sepulture. Our sorrow was sincere. We had lost an honest, loyal friend. For many succeeding days his grave was garlanded with fresh flowers, placed there by loving hands. Vale Turk! Would that our friends of the higher evolution were all as stanch as thou!

THE BURIAL OF TURK.

Only a dog ! but the tears fall fast
   As we lay him to rest underneath the green sod,
Where bountiful nature, the sweet summer through,
   Will deck him with daisies and bright goldenrod.

The loving thought of a boyish heart
   Marks the old dog's grave with a bloodstone red ;
The name, carved in letters rough and rude,
   Keeps his memory green, though his life be sped.

For the daring young hero of wood and plain,
  Like all who are generous, strong, and brave,
Has a heart that is loyal and kind and true,
  And shames not to weep o'er his old friend's grave.

Only a dog, do you say ? but I deem
  A dog who with faithfulness fills his trust,
More worthy than many a man to be given
  A tribute of love, when but ashes and dust.

An unusually good teacher now presided at the school-house in our neighborhood, and Will was again persuaded into educational paths. He put in a hard winter's work; but with the coming of spring and its unrest, the swelling of buds and the springing of grass, the return of the birds and the twittering from myriad nests, the Spirits of the Plains beckoned to him, and he joined a party of gold-hunters on the long trail to Pike's Peak.

The gold excitement was at its apogee in 1860. By our house had passed the historic wagon bearing on its side the classic motto, "Pike's Peak or Bust!" Afterward, stranded by the wayside, a whole history of failure and disappointment, borne with grim humor, was told by the addition of the eloquent word, "Busted!"

For all his adventures, Will was only fourteen, and although tall for his age, he had not the physical strength that might have been expected from his hardy life. It was not strange that he should take the gold fever; less so that mother should dread to see him again leave home to face unknown perils; and it is not at all remarkable that upon reaching Auraria, now Denver, he should find that fortunes were not lying around much more promiscuously in a gold country than in any other.

Recent events have confirmed a belief that under the excitement of a gold craze men exercise less judgment than at any other time. Except in placer mining, which almost any one can learn, gold mining is a science. Now and again a nugget worth a fortune is picked up, but the average mortal can get a better livelihood, with half the work, in almost any other field of effort. To become rich a knowledge of ores and mining methods is indispensable.

But Will never reached the gold-fields. Almost the first person he met on the streets of Julesberg was George Chrisman, who had been chief wagon-master for Russell, Majors & Waddell. Will had become well acquainted with Chrisman on the various expeditions he had made for the firm.

This man was located at Julesberg as agent for the Pony Express line, which was in process of formation. This line was an enterprise of Russell, Majors & Waddell. Mr. Russell met in Washington the Senator from California. This gentleman knew that the Western firm of contractors was running a daily stagecoach from the Missouri River to Sacramento, and he urged upon Mr. Russell the desirability of operating a pony express line along the same route. There was already a line known as the "Butterfield Route," but this was circuitous; the fastest time ever made on it was twenty-one days.

Mr. Russell laid the matter before his partners. They were opposed to it, as they were sure it would be a losing venture; but the senior member urged the matter so strongly that they consented to try it, for the good of the country, with no expectation of profit. They utilized the stagecoach stations already established, and only about two months were required to put the Pony Express line in running order.

Riders received from a hundred and twenty to a hundred and twenty-five dollars a month, but they earned it.

In order to stand the life great physical strength and endurance were necessary; in addition, riders must be cool, brave, and resourceful. Their lives were in constant peril, and they were obliged to do double duty in case the comrade that was to relieve them had been disabled by outlaws or Indians.

Two hundred and fifty miles was the daily distance that must be made; this constituted an average of a little over ten miles an hour. In the exceedingly rough country this average could not be kept up; to balance it, there were a few places in the route where the rider was expected to cover twenty-five miles an hour.

In making such a run, it is hardly necessary to say that no extra weight was carried. Letters were written on the finest tissue paper; the charge was at the rate of five dollars for half an ounce. A hundred of these letters would make a bulk not much larger than an ordinary writing-tablet.

The mail-pouches were never to carry more than twenty pounds. They were leather bags, impervious to moisture; the letters, as a further protection, were wrapped in oiled silk. The pouches were locked, sealed, and strapped to the rider's side. They were not unlocked during the journey from St. Joseph to Sacramento.

The first trip was made in ten days; this was a saving of eleven days over the best time ever made by the "Butterfield Route." Sometimes the time was shortened to eight days; but an average trip was made in nine. The distance covered in this time was nineteen hundred and sixty-six miles.

President Buchanan's last presidential message was carried in December, 1860, in a few hours over eight days. President Lincoln's inaugural, the following March, was transmitted in seven days and seventeen hours. This was the quickest trip ever made.

The Pony Express line made its worth at once felt. It would have become a financial success but that a telegraph line was put into operation over the same stretch of territory, under the direction of Mr. Edward Creighton. The first message was sent over the wires the 24th of October, 1861. The Pony Express line had outlived its usefulness, and was at once discontinued. But it had accomplished its main purpose, which was to determine whether the route by which it went could be made a permanent track for travel the year through. The cars of the Union Pacific road now travel nearly the same old trails as those followed by the daring riders of frontier days.

Mr. Chrisman gave Will a cordial greeting. He explained the business of the express line to his young friend, and stated that the company had nearly perfected its arrangements. It was now buying ponies and putting them into good condition, preparatory to beginning operations. He added, jokingly:

"It's a pity you're not a few years older, Billy. I would give you a job as Pony Express rider. There's good pay in it."

Will was at once greatly taken with the idea, and begged so hard to be given a trial that Mr. Chrisman consented to give him work for a month. If the life proved too hard for him, he was to be laid off at the end of that time. He had a short run of forty-five miles; there were three relay stations, and he was expected to make fifteen miles an hour.

The 3d of April, 1860, Mr. Russell stood ready to receive the mail from a fast New York train at St. Joseph. He adjusted the letter-pouch on the pony in the presence of an excited crowd.   Besides the letters, several large New York papers printed special editions on tissue paper for this inaugural trip.   The crowd plucked hairs from the tail of the first animal to start on the novel journey, and preserved these hairs as talismans.   The rider mounted, the moment for starting came, the signal was given, and off he dashed.

At the same moment Sacramento witnessed a similar scene; the rider of that region started on the two thousand mile ride eastward as the other started westward.   All the way along the road the several other riders were ready for their initial gallop.

Will looked forward eagerly to the day when the express line should be set in motion, and when the hour came it found him ready, standing beside his horse, and waiting for the rider whom he was to relieve.   There was a clatter of hoofs, and a horseman dashed up and flung him the saddle-bags.   Will threw them upon the waiting pony, vaulted into the saddle, and was off like the wind.

The first relay station was reached on time, and Will changed with hardly a second's loss of time, while the panting, reeking animal he had ridden was left to the care of the stock-tender.   This was repeated at the end of the second fifteen miles, and the last station was reached a few minutes ahead of time.   The return trip was made in good order, and then Will wrote to us of his new position, and told us that he was in love with the life.

CHAPTER IX.

AFTER being pounded against a saddle three dashes daily for three months, to the tune of fifteen miles an hour, Will began to feel a little loose in his joints, and weary withal, but he was determined to "stick it out." Besides the daily pounding, the track of the Pony Express rider was strewn with perils. A wayfarer through that wild land was more likely to run across outlaws and Indians than to pass unmolested, and as it was known that packages of value were frequently dispatched by the Pony Express line, the route was punctuated by ambuscades.

Will had an eye out every trip for a hold-up, but three months went by before he added that novelty to his other experiences. One day, as he flew around a bend in a narrow pass, he confronted a huge revolver in the grasp of a man who manifestly meant business, and whose salutation was:

"Halt! Throw up your hands!"

Most people do, and Will's hands were raised reluctantly. The highwayman advanced, saying, not unkindly:

"I don't want to hurt you, boy, but I do want them bags."

Money packages were in the saddlebags, and Will was minded to save them if he could, so, as the outlaw reached for the booty, Will touched the pony with his foot, and the upshot was satisfactory to an unexpected degree. The

73

plunge upset the robber, and as the pony swept over him he got a vicious blow from one hoof. Will wheeled for a revolver duel, but the foe was prostrate, stunned, and bleeding at the head. Will disarmed the fellow, and pinioned his arms behind him, and then tied up his broken head. Will surmised that the prisoner must have a horse hidden hard by, and a bit of a search disclosed it. When he returned with the animal, its owner had opened his eyes and was beginning to remember a few things. Will helped him to mount, and out of pure kindness tied him on; then he straddled his own pony, and towed the dismal outfit along with him.

It was the first time that he had been behind on his run, but by way of excuse he offered to Mr. Chrisman a broken-headed and dejected gentleman tied to a horse's back; and Chrisman, with a grin, locked the excuse up for future reference.

A few days after this episode Will received a letter from Julia, telling him that mother was ill, and asking him to come home. He at once sought out Mr. Chrisman, and giving his reason, asked to be relieved.

"I'm sorry your mother is sick," was the answer, "but I'm glad something has occurred to make you quit this life. It's wearing you out, Billy, and you're too gritty to give it up without a good reason."

Will reached home to find mother slightly improved. For three weeks was he content to remain idly at home; then (it was November of 1860) his unquiet spirit bore him away on another trapping expedition, this time with a young friend named David Phillips.

They bought an ox-team and wagon to transport the traps, camp outfit, and provisions, and took along a large supply of ammunition, besides extra rifles. Their destination was the Republican River. It coursed more than a hundred miles from Leavenworth, but the country about it was reputed rich in beaver. Will acted as scout on the journey, going ahead to pick out trails, locate camping grounds, and look out for breakers. The information concerning the beaver proved correct; the game was indeed so plentiful that they concluded to pitch a permanent camp and see the winter out.

They chose a hollow in a sidehill, and enlarged it to the dimensions of a decent-sized room. A floor of logs was put in, and a chimney fashioned of stones, the open lower part doing double duty as cook-stove and heater; the bed was spread in the rear, and the wagon sheltered the entrance. A corral of poles was built for the oxen, and one corner of it protected by boughs. Altogether, they accounted their winter quarters thoroughly satisfactory and agreeable.

The boys had seen no Indians on their trip out, and were not concerned in that quarter, though they were too good plainsmen to relax their vigilance. There were other foes, as they discovered the first night in their new quarters. They were aroused by a commotion in the corral where the oxen were confined, and hurrying out with their rifles, they found a huge bear intent upon a feast of beef. The oxen were bellowing in terror, one of them dashing crazily about the inclosure, and the other so badly hurt that it could not get up.

Phillips, who was in the lead, fired first, but succeeded only in wounding the bear. Pain was now added to the savagery of hunger, and the infuriated monster rushed upon Phillips. Dave leaped back, but his foot slipped on a bit of ice, and he went down with a thud, his rifle flying from his hand as he struck.

But there was a cool young head and a steady hand behind him. A ball from Will's rifle entered the distended mouth of the onrushing bear and pierced the brain, and the huge mass fell lifeless almost across Dave's body.

Phillips's nerves loosened with a snap, and he laughed for very relief as he seized Will's hands.

"That's the time you saved my life, old fellow!" said he. "Perhaps I can do as much for you sometime."

"That's the first bear I ever killed," said Will, more interested in that topic than in the one Dave held forth on.

One of the oxen was found to be mortally hurt, and a bullet ended its misery. Will then took his first lesson in the gentle art of skinning a bear.

Dave's chance to square his account with Will came a fortnight later. They were chasing a bunch of elk, when Will fell, and discovered that he could not rise.

"I'm afraid I've broken my leg," said he, as Dave ran to him.

Phillips had once been a medical student, and he examined the leg with a professional eye. "You're right, Billy; the leg's broken," he reported.

Then he went to work to improvise splints and bind up the leg; and this done, he took Will on his back and bore him to the dugout. Here the leg was stripped, and set in carefully prepared splints, and the whole bound up securely.

The outlook was unpleasant, cheerfully as one might regard it. Living in the scoop of a sidehill when one is strong and able to get about and keep the blood coursing is one thing; living there pent up through a tedious winter is quite another. Dave meditated as he worked away at the pair of crutches.

"Tell you what I think I'd better do," said he. "The nearest settlement is some hundred miles away, and I can get there and back in twenty days. Suppose I make the trip, get a team for our wagon, and come back for you?"

The idea of being left alone and well-nigh helpless struck dismay to Will's heart, but there was no help for it, and he assented. Dave put matters into shipshape, piled wood in the dugout, cooked a quantity of food and put it where Will could reach it without rising, and fetched several days' supply of water. Mother, ever mindful of Will's education, had put some school-books in the wagon, and Dave placed these beside the food and water. When Phillips finally set out, driving the surviving ox before him, he left behind a very lonely and homesick boy.

During the first day of his confinement Will felt too desolate to eat, much less to read; but as he grew accustomed to solitude he derived real pleasure from the companionship of books. Perhaps in all his life he never extracted so much benefit from study as during that brief period of enforced idleness, when it was his sole means of making the dragging hours endurable. Dave, he knew, could not return in less than twenty days, and one daily task, never neglected, was to cut a notch in the stick that marked the humdrum passage of the days. Within the week he could hobble about on his crutches for a short distance; after that he felt more secure.

A fortnight passed. And one day, weary with his studies, he fell asleep over his books. Some one touched his shoulder, and looking up, he saw an Indian in war paint and feathers.

"How?" said Will, with a show of friendliness, though he knew the brave was on the war-path.

Half a score of bucks followed at the heels of the first, squeezing into the little dugout until there was barely room for them to sit down.

With a sinking heart Will watched them enter, but he plucked up spirit again when the last, a chief, pushed in, for in this warrior he recognized an Indian that he had once done a good turn.

Whatever Lo's faults, he never forgets a kindness any more than he forgets an injury. The chief, who went by the name of Rain-in-the-Face, at once recognized Will, and asked him what he was doing in that place. Will displayed his bandages, and related the mishap that had made them necessary, and refreshed the chief's memory of a certain occasion when a blanket and provisions had drifted his way. Rain-in-the-Face replied, with proper gravity, that he and his chums were out after scalps, and confessed to designs upon Will's, but in consideration of Auld Lang Syne he would spare the paleface boy.

Auld Lang Syne, however, did not save the blankets and provisions, and the bedizened crew stripped the dugout almost bare of supplies; but Will was thankful enough to see the back of the last of them.

Two days later a blizzard set in. Will took an inventory, and found that, economy considered, he had food for a week; but as the storm would surely delay Dave, he put himself on half rations.

Three weeks were now gone, and he looked for Dave momentarily; but as night followed day, and day grew into night again, he was given over to keen anxiety. Had Phillips lost his way? Had he failed to locate the snow-covered dugout? Had he perished in the storm? Had he fallen victim to Indians? These and like questions haunted the poor lad continually. Study became impossible, and he lost his appetite for what food there was left; but the tally on the stick was kept.

The twenty-ninth day dawned.   Starvation stalked into the dugout.   The wood, too, was nigh gone.   But great as was Will's physical suffering, his mental distress was greater.   He sat before a handful of fire, shivering and hungry, wretched and despondent.

Hark! Was that his name? Choking with emotion, unable to articulate, he listened intently. Yes; it was his name, and Dave's familiar voice, and with all his remaining energy he made an answering call.

His voice enabled Phillips to locate the dugout, and a passage was cleared through the snow. And when Will saw the door open, the tension on his nerves let go, and he wept—"like a girl," as he afterward told us.

"God bless you, Dave!" he cried, as he clasped his friend around the neck.

CHAPTER X.

ECHOES FROM SUMTER.

THE guns that opened on Fort Sumter set the country all ablaze. In Kansas, where blood had already been shed, the excitement reached an extraordinary pitch. Will desired to enlist, but mother would not listen to the idea.

My brother had never forgotten the vow made in the post-trader's, and now with the coming of war his opportunity seemed ripe and lawful; he could at least take up arms against father's old-time enemies, and at the same time serve his country. This aspect of the case was presented to mother in glowing colors, backed by most eloquent pleading; but she remained obdurate.

"You are too young to enlist, Willie," she said. "They would not accept you, and if they did, I could not endure it. I have only a little time to live; for my sake, then, wait till I am no more before you enter the army."

This request was not to be disregarded, and Will promised that he would not enlist while mother lived.

Kansas had long been the scene of bitter strife between the two parties, and though there was a preponderance of the Free-Soil element when it was admitted to the Union in 1861, we were fated to see some of the horrors of slavery. Suffering makes one wondrous kind; mother had suffered so much herself that the misery of others ever

vibrated a chord of sympathy in her breast, and our house
became a station on "the underground railway." Many
a fugitive slave did we shelter, many here received food
and clothing, and, aided by mother, a great number reached
safe harbors.

One old man, named Uncle Tom, became so much
attached to us that he refused to go on. We kept him as
help about the hotel. He was with us several months, and
we children grew very fond of him. Every evening when
supper was over, he sat before the kitchen fire and told a
breathless audience strange stories of the days of slavery.
And one evening, never to be forgotten, Uncle Tom was
sitting in his accustomed place, surrounded by his juvenile
listeners, when he suddenly sprang to his feet with a cry of
terror. Some men had entered the hotel sitting-room, and
the sound of their voices drove Uncle Tom to his own little
room, and under the bed.

"Mrs. Cody," said the unwelcome visitors, "we understand that you are harboring our runaway slaves. We
propose to search the premises; and if we find our property, you cannot object to our removing it."

Mother was sorely distressed for the unhappy Uncle
Tom, but she knew objection would be futile. She could
only hope that the old colored man had made good his
escape.

But no! Uncle Tom lay quaking under his bed, and
there his brutal master found him. It is not impossible
that there were slaveholders kind and humane, but the
bitter curse of slavery was the open door it left for brutal-
ity and inhumanity; and never shall I forget the barbarity
displayed by the owner of Uncle Tom before our horrified
eyes. The poor slave was so old that his hair was wholly
white; yet a rope was tied to it, and, despite our pleadings,

he was dragged from the house, every cry he uttered evoking only a savage kick from a heavy riding-boot. When he was out of sight, and his screams out of hearing, we wept bitterly on mother's loving breast.

Uncle Tom again escaped, and made his way to our house, but he reached it only to die. We sorrowed for the poor old slave, but thanked God that he had passed beyond the inhumanity of man.

Debarred from serving his country as a soldier, Will decided to do so in some other capacity, and accordingly took service with a United States freight caravan, transporting supplies to Fort Laramie. On this trip his frontier training and skill as a marksman were the means of saving a life.

In Western travel the perils from outlaws and Indians were so real that emigrants usually sought the protection of a large wagon-train. Several families of emigrants journeyed under the wing of the caravan to which Will was attached.

When in camp one day upon the bank of the Platte River, and the members of the company were busied with preparations for the night's rest and the next day's journey, Mamie Perkins, a little girl from one of the emigrant families, was sent to the river for a pail of water. A moment later a monster buffalo was seen rushing upon the camp. A chorus of yells and a fusillade from rifles and revolvers neither checked nor swerved him. Straight through the camp he swept, like a cyclone, leaping ropes and boxes, overturning wagons, and smashing things generally.

Mamie, the little water-bearer, had filled her pail and was returning in the track selected by the buffalo. Too terrified to move, she watched, with white face and parted lips, the maddened animal sweep toward her, head down and tail up, its hoofs beating a thunderous tattoo on the plain.

Will had been asleep, but the commotion brought him to his feet, and snatching up his rifle, he ran toward the little girl, aimed and fired at the buffalo. The huge animal lurched, staggered a few yards farther, then dropped within a dozen feet of the terrified child.

A shout of relief went up, and while a crowd of praising men gathered about the embryo buffalo-hunter, Mamie was taken to her mother. Will never relished hearing his praises sung, and as the camp was determined to pedestal him as a hero, he ran away and hid in his tent.

Upon reaching Fort Laramie, Will's first business was to look up Alf Slade, agent of the Pony Express line, whose headquarters were at Horseshoe Station, twenty miles from the fort. He carried a letter of recommendation from Mr. Russell, but Slade demurred.

"You're too young for a Pony Express rider," said he.

"I rode three months a year ago, sir, and I'm much stronger now," said Will.

"Oh, are you the boy rider that was on Chrisman's division?"

"Yes, sir."

"All right; I'll try you. If you can't stand it, I 'll give you something easier."

Will's run was from Red Buttes, on the North Platte, to Three Crossings, on the Sweetwater—seventy-six miles.

The wilderness was of the kind that is supposed to howl, and no person fond of excitement had reason to complain of lack of it. One day Will arrived at his last station to find that the rider on the next run had been mortally hurt by Indians. There being no one else to do it, he volunteered to ride the eighty-five miles for the wounded man. He accomplished it, and made his own return trip on time—a continuous ride of three hundred and twenty-two miles. There was no rest for the rider, but twenty-one horses were used on the run—the longest ever made by a Pony Express rider.

Shortly afterward Will fell in with California Joe, a remarkable frontier character. He was standing beside a group of bowlders that edged the trail when Will first clapped eyes on him, and the Pony Express man instantly reached for his revolver. The stranger as quickly dropped his rifle, and held up his hands in token of friendliness. Will drew rein, and ran an interested eye over the man, who was clad in buckskin.

California Joe, who was made famous in General Custer's book, entitled "Life on the Plains," was a man of wonderful physique, straight and stout as a pine. His red-brown hair hung in curls below his shoulders; he wore a full beard, and his keen, sparkling eyes were of the brightest hue. He came from an Eastern family, and possessed a good education, somewhat rusty from disuse.

"Hain't you the boy rider I has heard of—the youngest rider on the trail?" he queried, in the border dialect. Will made an affirmative answer, and gave his name.

"Waal," said Joe, "I guess you've got some money on this trip. I was strikin' fer the Big Horn, and I found them two stiffs up yonder layin' fer ye. We had a little misunderstandin', and now I has 'em to plant."

Will thanked him warmly, and begged him not to risk the perils of the Big Horn; but California Joe only laughed, and told him to push ahead.

When Will reached his station he related his adventure, and the stock-tender said it was "good by, California Joe."

But Will had conceived a better opinion of his new friend, and he predicted his safe return.

This confidence was justified by the appearance of California Joe, three months later, in the camp of the Pony Riders on the Overland trail. He received a cordial greeting, and was assured by the men that they had not expected to see him alive again. In return he told them his story, and a very interesting story it was.

"Some time ago," said he (I shall not attempt to reproduce his dialect), "a big gang of gold-hunters went into the Big Horn country. They never returned, and the general sent me to see if I could get any trace of them. The country is full of Indians, and I kept my eye skinned for them, but I wasn't looking for trouble from white men. I happened to leave my revolver where I ate dinner one day, and soon after discovering the loss I went back after the gun. Just as I picked it up I saw a white man on my trail. I smelled trouble, but turned and jogged along as if I hadn't seen anything. That night I doubled back over my trail until I came to the camp where the stranger belonged. As I expected, he was one of a party of three, but they had five horses. I'll bet odds, Pard Billy"—this to Will—"that the two pilgrims laying for you belonged to this outfit.

"They thought I'd found gold, and were going to follow me until I struck the mine, then do me up and take possession.

"The gold is there, too, lots of it. There's silver, iron, copper, and coal, too, but no one will look at them so long as gold is to be had; but those that go for gold will, many of them, leave their scalps behind.

"We kept the trail day after day; the men stuck right to me, the chap ahead keeping me in sight and marking out the trail for his pard.   When we got into the heart of the Indian country I had to use every caution; I steered clear of every smoke that showed a village or camp, and didn't use my rifle on game, depending on the rations I had with me.

"At last I came to a spot that showed signs of a battle. Skulls and bones were strewn around, and after a look about I was satisfied beyond doubt that white men had been of the company. The purpose of my trip was accomplished; I could safely report that the party of whites had been exterminated by Indians.

"The question now was, could I return without running into Indians?   The first thing was to give my white pursuers the slip.

"That night I crept down the bed of a small stream, passed their camp, and struck the trail a half mile or so below.

"It was the luckiest move I ever made.   I had ridden but a short distance when I heard the familiar war-whoop, and knew that the Indians had surprised my unpleasant acquaintances and taken their scalps.   I should have shared the same fate if I hadn't moved.

"But, boys, it is a grand and beautiful country, full of towering mountains, lovely valleys, and mighty trees."

About the middle of September the Indians became very troublesome along the Sweetwater. Will was ambushed one day, but fortunately he was mounted on one of the fleetest of the company's horses, and lying flat on the animal's back, he distanced the redskins.   At the relay station he found the stock-tender dead, and as the horses had been driven off, he was unable to get a fresh mount; so he rode the same horse to Plontz Station, twelve miles farther.

A few days later the station boss of the line hailed Will
with the information:

"There's Injun signs about; so keep your eyes open."

"I'm on the watch, boss," was Will's answer, as he
exchanged ponies and dashed away.

The trail ran through a grim wild.   It was darkened by
mountains, overhung with cliffs, and fringed with monster
pines.   The young rider's every sense had been sharpened
by frontier dangers.   Each dusky rock and tree was scanned
for signs of lurking foes as he clattered down the twilight
track.

One large bowlder lay in plain view far down the valley,
and for a second he saw a dark object appear above it.

He kept his course until within rifle-shot, and then
suddenly swerved away in an oblique line.   The ambush
had failed, and a puff of smoke issued from behind the
bowlder.   Two braves, in gorgeous war paint, sprang up,
and at the same time a score of whooping Indians rode out
of timber on the other side of the valley.

Before Will the mountains sloped to a narrow pass;
could he reach that he would be comparatively safe.   The
Indians at the bowlder were unmounted, and though they
were fleet of foot, he easily left them behind. The mounted
reds were those to be feared, and the chief rode a very
fleet pony.   As they neared the pass Will saw that it was
life against life.   He drew his revolver, and the chief, for
his part, fitted an arrow to his bow.

Will was a shade the quicker.   His revolver cracked,
and the warrior pitched dead from his saddle.   His fall was
the signal for a shower of arrows, one of which wounded
the pony slightly; but the station was reached on time.

The Indians were now in evidence all the time.
Between Split Rock and Three Crossings they robbed a

stage, killed the driver and two passengers, and wounded Lieutenant Flowers, the assistant division agent. They drove the stock from the stations, and continually harassed the Pony Express riders and stage-drivers. So bold did the reds become that the Pony riders were laid off for six weeks, though stages were to make occasional runs if the business were urgent. A force was organized to search for missing stock. There were forty men in the party—stage-drivers, express-riders, stock-tenders, and ranchmen; and they were captained by a plainsman named Wild Bill, who was a good friend of Will for many years.

He had not earned the sobriquet through lawlessness. It merely denoted his dashing and daring. Physically he was well-nigh faultless—tall, straight, and symmetrical, with broad shoulders and splendid chest. He was handsome of face, with a clear blue eye, firm and well-shaped mouth, aquiline nose, and brown, curling hair, worn long upon his shoulders. Born of a refined and cultured family, he, like Will, seemingly inherited from some remote ancestor his passion for the wild, free life of the plains.

At this time Wild Bill was a well-known scout, and in this capacity served the United States to good purpose during the war.

CHAPTER XI.

As Will was one of the laid-off riders, he was allowed to join the expedition against the Indian depredators, though he was the youngest member of the company.

The campaign was short and sharp. The Indian trail was followed to Powder River, and thence along the banks of the stream the party traveled to within forty miles of the spot where old Fort Reno now stands; from here the trail ran westerly, at the foot of the mountains, and was crossed by Crazy Woman's Fork, a tributary of the Powder.

Originally this branch stream went by the name of the Big Beard, because of a peculiar grass that fringed it. On its bank had stood a village of the Crow Indians, and here a half-breed trader had settled. He bought the red man's furs, and gave him in return bright-colored beads and pieces of calico, paints, and blankets. In a short time he had all the furs in the village; he packed them on ponies, and said good by to his Indian friends. They were sorry to see him go, but he told them he would soon return from the land of the paleface, bringing many gifts. Months passed; one day the Indian sentinels reported the approach of a strange object. The village was alarmed, for the Crows had never seen ox, horse, or wagon; but the excitement was allayed when it was found that the strange outfit was the property of the half-breed trader.

He had brought with him his wife, a white woman; she, too, was an object of much curiosity to the Indians.

The trader built a lodge of wood and stones, and exposed all his goods for sale. He had brought beads, ribbons, and brass rings as gifts for all the tribe.

One day the big chief visited the store; the trader led him into a back room, swore him to secrecy, and gave him a drink of black water. The chief felt strangely happy. Usually he was very dignified and stately; but under the influence of the strange liquid he sang and danced on the streets, and finally fell into a deep sleep, from which he could not be wakened. This performance was repeated day after day, until the Indians called a council of war. They said the trader had bewitched their chief, and it must be stopped, or they would kill the intruder. A warrior was sent to convey this intelligence to the trader; he laughed, took the warrior into the back room, swore him to secrecy, and gave him a drink of the black water. The young Indian, in his turn, went upon the street, and laughed and sang and danced, just as the chief had done. Surprised, his companions gathered around him and asked him what was the matter. "Oh, go to the trader and get some of the black water!" said he.

They asked for the strange beverage. The trader denied having any, and gave them a drink of ordinary water, which had no effect. When the young warrior awoke, they again questioned him. He said he must have been sick, and have spoken loosely.

After this the chief and warrior were both drunk every day, and all the tribe were sorely perplexed. Another council of war was held, and a young chief arose, saying that he had made a hole in the wall of the trader's house, and had watched; and it was true the trader gave their friends black water.   The half-breed and the two unhappy Indians were brought before the council, and the young chief repeated his accusation, saying that if it were not true, they might fight him.   The second victim of the black water yet denied the story, and said the young chief lied; but the trader had maneuvered into the position he desired, and he confessed.   They bade him bring the water, that they might taste it; but before he departed the young chief challenged to combat the warrior that had said he lied.   This warrior was the best spearsman of the tribe, and all expected the death of the young chief; but the black water had palsied the warrior's arm, his trembling hand could not fling true, he was pierced to the heart at the first thrust.   The tribe then repaired to the trader's lodge, and he gave them all a drink of the black water. They danced and sang, and then lay upon the ground and slept.

After two or three days the half-breed declined to provide black water free; if the warriors wanted it, they must pay for it.   At first he gave them a "sleep," as they called it, for one robe or skin, but as the stock of black water diminished, two, then three, then many robes were demanded.   At last he said he had none left except what he himself desired.   The Indians offered their ponies, until the trader had all the robes and all the ponies of the tribe.

Now, he said, he would go back to the land of the paleface and procure more of the black water.   Some of the warriors were willing he should do this; others asserted that he had plenty of black water left, and was going to trade with their enemy, the Sioux.   The devil had awakened in the tribe.   The trader's stores and packs were searched, but no black water was found.   'Twas hidden, then, said the Indians.   The trader must produce it, or they would kill him. Of course he could not do this. He had sowed the wind; he reaped the whirlwind. He was scalped before the eyes of his horrified wife, and his body mutilated and mangled. The poor woman attempted to escape; a warrior struck her with his tomahawk, and she fell as if dead. The Indians fired the lodge. As they did so, a Crow squaw saw that the white woman was not dead. She took the wounded creature to her own lodge, bound up her wounds, and nursed her back to strength. But the unfortunate woman's brain was crazed, and could not bear the sight of a warrior.

As soon as she could get around she ran away. The squaws went out to look for her, and found her crooning on the banks of the Big Beard. She would talk with the squaws, but if a warrior appeared, she hid herself till he was gone. The squaws took her food, and she lived in a covert on the bank of the stream for many months. One day a warrior, out hunting, chanced upon her. Thinking she was lost, he sought to catch her, to take her back to the village, as all Indian tribes have a veneration for the insane; but she fled into the hills, and was never seen afterward. The stream became known as the "Place of the Crazy Woman," or Crazy Woman's Fork, and has retained the name to this day.

At this point, to return to my narrative, the signs indicated that reinforcements had reached the orignal body of Indians. The plainsmen were now in the heart of the Indian country, the utmost caution was required, and a sharp lookout was maintained. When Clear Creek, another tributary of the Powder, was come up with, an Indian camp, some three miles distant, was discovered on the farther bank.

A council of war was held.   Never before had the white man followed the red so far into his domain, and 'twas plain the Indian was off his guard; not a scout was posted.

At Wild Bill's suggestion, the attack waited upon nightfall.   Veiled by darkness, the company was to surprise the Indian camp and stampede the horses.

The plan was carried out without a hitch.   The Indians outnumbered the white men three to one, but when the latter rushed cyclonically through the camp, no effort was made to repel them, and by the time the Indians had recovered from their surprise the plainsmen had driven off all the horses—those belonging to the reds as well as those that had been stolen.   A few shots were fired, but the whites rode scathless away, and unpursued.

The line of march was now taken up for Sweetwater Bridge, and here, four days later, the plainsmen brought up, with their own horses and about a hundred Indian ponies.

This successful sally repressed the hostilities for a space. The recovered horses were put back on the road, and the stage-drivers and express-riders resumed their interrupted activity.

"Billy," said Mr. Slade, who had taken a great fancy to Will—"Billy, this is a hard life, and you're too young to stand it.   You've done good service, and in consideration of it I'll make you a supernumerary.   You'll have to ride only when it's absolutely necessary."

There followed for Will a period of *dolce far niente;* days when he might lie on his back and watch the clouds drift across the sky; when he might have an eye to the beauty of the woodland and the sweep of the plain, without the nervous strain of studying every tree and knoll that might conceal a lurking redskin.   Winter closed in, and with it came the memories of the trapping season of 1860-61, when he had laid low his first and last bear. But there were other bears to be killed—the mountains were full of them; and one bracing morning he turned his horse's head toward the hills that lay down the Horseshoe Valley. Antelope and deer fed in the valley, the sage-hen and the jack-rabbit started up under his horse's hoofs, but such small game went by unnoticed.

Two o'clock passed without a sign of bear, save some tracks in the snow. The wintry air had put a keen edge on Will's appetite, and hitching his tired horse, he shot one of the lately scorned sage-hens, and broiled it over a fire that invited a longer stay than an industrious bear-hunter could afford. But nightfall found him and his quarry still many miles asunder, and as he did not relish the prospect of a chaffing from the men at the station, he cast about for a camping-place, finding one in an open spot on the bank of a little stream. Two more sage-hens were added to the larder, and he was preparing to kindle a fire when the whinnying of a horse caught his ear. He ran to his own horse to check the certain response, resaddled him, and disposed everything for flight, should it be necessary. Then, taking his rifle, he put forth on a reconnoissance.

He shortly came upon a bunch of horses, a dozen or more, around a crook of the stream. Above them, on the farther bank, shone a light. Drawing nearer, he saw that it came from a dugout, and he heard his own language spoken. Reassured, he walked boldly up to the door and rapped.

Silence—followed by a hurried whispering, and the demand:

"Who's there?"

"Friend and white man," answered Will.

The door opened reluctantly, and an ugly-looking customer bade him enter. The invitation was not responded to with alacrity, for eight such villainous-looking faces as the dugout held it would have been hard to match. Too late to retreat, there was nothing for it but a determined front, and let wit point the way of escape. Two of the men Will recognized as discharged teamsters from Lew Simpson's train, and from his knowledge of their long-standing weakness he assumed, correctly, that he had thrust his head into a den of horsethieves.

"Who's with you?" was the first query; and this answered, with sundry other information esteemed essential, "Where's your horse?" demanded the most striking portrait in the rogues' gallery.

"Down by the creek," said Will.

"All right, sonny; we'll go down and get him," was the obliging rejoinder.

"Oh, don't trouble yourself," said Will. "I'll fetch him and put up here over night, with your permission. I'll leave my gun here till I get back."

"That's right; leave your gun, you won't need it," said the leader of the gang, with a grin that was as near amiability as his rough, stern calling permitted him. "Jim and I will go down with you after the horse."

This offer compelled an acquiescence, Will consoling himself with the reflection that it is easier to escape from two men than from eight.

When the horse was reached, one of the outlaws obligingly volunteered to lead it.

"All right," said Will, carelessly. "I shot a couple of sage-hens here; I'll take them along. Lead away!"

He followed with the birds, the second horsethief bringing up the rear. As the dugout was neared he let fall one of the hens, and asked the chap following to pick it up, and as the obliging rear guard stopped, Will knocked him senseless with the butt of his revolver. The man ahead heard the blow, and turned, with his hand on his gun, but Will dropped him with a shot, leaped on his horse, and dashed off.

The sextet in the dugout sprang to arms, and came running down the bank, and likely getting the particulars of the escape from the ruffian by the sage-hen, who was probably only stunned for the moment, they buckled warmly to the chase. The mountain-side was steep and rough, and men on foot were better than on horseback; accordingly Will dismounted, and clapping his pony soundly on the flank, sent him clattering on down the declivity, and himself stepped aside behind a large pine. The pursuing party rushed past him, and when they were safely gone, he climbed back over the mountain, and made his way as best he could to the Horseshoe. It was a twenty-five mile plod, and he reached the station early in the morning, weary and footsore.

He woke the plainsmen, and related his adventure, and Mr. Slade at once organized a party to hunt out the bandits of the dugout. Twenty well-armed stock-tenders, stage-drivers, and ranchmen rode away at sunrise, and, notwithstanding his fatigue, Will accompanied them as guide.

But the ill-favored birds had flown; the dugout was deserted.

Will soon tired of this nondescript service, and gladly accepted a position as assistant wagon-master under Wild Bill, who had taken a contract to fetch a load of government freight from Rolla, Missouri.

He returned with a wagon-train to Springfield, in that

state, and thence came home on a visit. It was a brief one, however, for the air was too full of war for him to endure inaction. Contented only when at work, he continued to help on government freight contracts, until he received word that mother was dangerously ill. Then he resigned his position and hastened home.

CHAPTER XII.

THE MOTHER'S LAST ILLNESS.

IT was now the autumn of 1863, and Will was a well-grown young man, tall, strong, and athletic, though not yet quite eighteen years old. Our oldest sister, Julia, had been married, the spring preceding, to Mr. J. A. Goodman.

Mother had been growing weaker from day to day; being with her constantly, we had not remarked the change for the worse; but Will was much shocked by the transformation which a few months had wrought. Only an indomitable will power had enabled her to overcome the infirmities of the body, and now it seemed to us as if her flesh had been refined away, leaving only the sweet and beautiful spirit.

Will reached home none too soon, for only three weeks after his return the doctor told mother that only a few hours were left to her, and if she had any last messages, it were best that she communicate them at once. That evening the children were called in, one by one, to receive her blessing and farewell. Mother was an earnest Christian character, but at that time I alone of all the children appeared religiously disposed. Young as I was, the solemnity of the hour when she charged me with the spiritual welfare of the family has remained with me through all the years that have gone. Calling me to her side, she sought to impress upon my childish mind, not the sorrow of death, but the glory of the resurrection. Then, as if

she were setting forth upon a pleasant journey, she bade
me good by, and I kissed her for the last time in life.
When next I saw her face it was cold and quiet. The
beautiful soul had forsaken its dwelling-place of clay, and
passed on through the Invisible, to wait, a glorified spirit,
on the farther shore for the coming of the loved ones
whose life-story was as yet unfinished.

Julia and Will remained with her throughout the night.
Just before death there came to her a brief season of long-
lost animation, the last flicker of the torch before darkness.
She talked to them almost continuously until the dawn.
Into their hands was given the task of educating the others
of the family, and on their hearts and consciences the
charge was graven. Charlie, who was born during the
early Kansas troubles, had ever been a delicate child, and
he lay an especial burden on her mind.

"If," she said, "it be possible for the dead to call the
living, I shall call Charlie to me."

Within the space of a year, Charlie, too, was gone; and
who shall say that the yearning of a mother's heart for her
child was not stronger than the influences of the material
world?

Upon Will mother sought to impress the responsibilities of his destiny. She reminded him of the prediction
of the fortune-teller, that "his name would be known the
world over."

"But," said she, "only the names of them that are
upright, brave, temperate, and true can be honorably
known. Remember always that 'he that overcometh his
own soul is greater than he who taketh a city.' Already
you have shown great abilities, but remember that they
carry with them grave responsibilities. You have been a
good son to me. In the hour of need you have always

aided me, so that I can die now feeling that my children are not unprovided for. I have not wished you to enlist in the war, partly because I knew you were too young, partly because my life was drawing near its close. But now you are nearly eighteen, and if when I am gone your country needs you in the strife of which we in Kansas know the bitterness, I bid you go as soldier in behalf of the cause for which your father gave his life.''

She talked until sleep followed exhaustion. When she awoke she tried to raise herself in bed. Will sprang to aid her, and with the upward look of one that sees ineffable things, she passed away, resting in his arms.

Oh, the glory and the gladness
Of a life without a fear;
Of a death like nature fading
In the autumn of the year;
Of a sweet and dreamless slumber,
In a faith triumphant borne,
Till the bells of Easter wake her
On the resurrection morn!

Ah, for such a blessed falling
Into quiet sleep at last,
When the ripening grain is garnered,
And the toil and trial past;
When the red and gold of sunset
Slowly changes into gray;
Ah, for such a quiet passing,
Through the night into the day!

The morning of the 22d day of November, 1863, began the saddest day of our lives. We rode in a rough lumber wagon to Pilot Knob Cemetery, a long, cold, hard ride; but we wished our parents to be united in death as they had been in life, so buried mother in a grave next to father's.

The road leading from the cemetery forked a short distance outside of Leavenworth, one branch running to that city, the other winding homeward along Government Hill. When we were returning, and reached this fork, Will jumped out of the wagon.

"I can't go home when I know mother is no longer there," said he. "I am going to Leavenworth to see Eugene Hathaway. I shall stay with him to-night."

We pitied Will—he and mother had been so much to each other—and raised no objection, as we should have done had we known the real purpose of his visit.

The next morning, therefore, we were much surprised to see him and Eugene ride into the yard, both clothed in the blue uniforms of United States soldiers.   Overwhelmed with grief over mother's death, it seemed more than we could bear to see our big brother ride off to war.   We threatened to inform the recruiting officers that he was not yet eighteen; but he was too thoroughly in earnest to be moved by our objections.   The regiment in which he had enlisted was already ordered to the front, and he had come home to say good by.   He then rode away to the hard-ships, dangers, and privations of a soldier's life.   The joy of action balanced the account for him, while we were obliged to accept the usual lot of girlhood and woman-hood—the weary, anxious waiting, when the heart is torn with uncertainty and suspense over the fate of the loved ones who bear the brunt and burden of the day.

The order sending Will's regiment to the front was countermanded, and he remained for a time in Fort Leav-enworth.   His Western experiences were well known there, and probably for this reason he was selected as a bearer of military dispatches to Fort Larned.   Some of our old pro-slavery enemies, who were upon the point of join-ing the Confederate army, learned of Will's mission, which they thought afforded them an excellent chance to gratify their ancient grudge against the father by murdering the son. The killing could be justified on the plea of service rendered to their cause. Accordingly a plan was made to waylay Will and capture his dispatches at a creek he was obliged to ford.

He received warning of this plot. On such a mission the utmost vigilance was demanded at all times, and with an ambuscade ahead of him, he was alertness itself. His knowledge of Indian warfare stood him in good stead now. Not a tree, rock, or hillock escaped his keen glance. When he neared the creek at which the attack was expected, he left the road, and attempted to ford the stream four or five hundred yards above the common crossing, but found it so swollen by recent rains that he was unable to cross; so he cautiously picked his way back to the trail.

The assassins' camp was two or three hundred feet away from the creek. Darkness was coming on, and he took advantage of the shelter afforded by the bank, screening himself behind every clump of bushes. His enemies would look for his approach from the other direction, and he hoped to give them the slip and pass by unseen.

When he reached the point where he could see the little cabin where the men were probably hiding, he ran upon a thicket in which five saddle-horses were concealed.

"Five to one! I don't stand much show if they see me," he decided as he rode quietly and slowly along, his carbine in his hand ready for use.

"There he goes, boys! he's at the ford!" came a sudden shout from the camp, followed by the crack of a rifle. Two or three more shots rang out, and from the bound his horse gave Will knew one bullet had reached a mark. He rode into the water, then turned in his saddle and aimed like a flash at a man within range. The fellow staggered and fell, and Will put spurs to his horse, turning again only when the stream was crossed. The men were running toward the ford, firing as they came, and getting a warm return fire. As Will was already two or three hundred yards in advance, pursuers on foot were not to be feared, and he knew that before they could reach and mount their horses he would be beyond danger. Much depended on his horse. Would the gallant beast, wounded as he was, be able to long maintain the fierce pace he had set? Mile upon mile was put behind before the stricken creature fell. Will shouldered the saddle and bridle and continued on foot. He soon reached a ranch where a fresh mount might be procured, and was shortly at Fort Larned.

After a few hours' breathing-spell, he left for Fort Leavenworth with return dispatches. As he drew near the ford, he resumed his sharp lookout, though scarcely expecting trouble. The planners of the ambuscade had been so certain that five men could easily make away with one boy that there had been no effort at disguise, and Will had recognized several of them. He, for his part, felt certain that they would get out of that part of the country with all dispatch; but he employed none the less caution in crossing the creek, and his carbine was ready for business as he approached the camp.

The fall of his horse's hoofs evoked a faint call from one of the buildings. It was not repeated; instead there issued hollow moans.

It might be a trap; again, a fellow-creature might be at death's door. Will rode a bit nearer the cabin entrance.

"Who's there?" he called.

"Come in, for the love of God! I am dying here alone!" was the reply.

"Who are you?"

"Ed Norcross."

Will jumped from his horse. This was the man at whom he had fired. He entered the cabin.

"What is the matter?" he asked.

"I was wounded by a bullet," moaned Norcross, "and my comrades deserted me."

Will was now within range of the poor fellow lying on the floor.

"Will Cody!" he cried.

Will dropped on his knee beside the dying man, choking with the emotion that the memory of long years of friendship had raised.

"My poor Ed!" he murmured. "And it was my bullet that struck you."

"It was in defense of your own life, Will," said Norcross. "God knows, I don't blame you. Don't think too hard of me. I did everything I could to save you. It was I who sent you warning. I hoped you might find some other trail."

"I didn't shoot with the others," continued Norcross, after a short silence. "They deserted me. They said they would send help back, but they haven't."

Will filled the empty canteen lying on the floor, and rearranged the blanket that served as a pillow; then he offered to dress the neglected wound. But the gray of death was already upon the face of Norcross.

"Never mind, Will," he whispered; "it's not worth while. Just stay with me till I die."

It was not a long vigil. Will sat beside his old friend, moistening his pallid lips with water. In a very short time the end came. Will disposed the stiffening limbs, crossing the hands over the heart, and with a last backward look went out of the cabin.

It was his first experience in the bitterness and savagery of war, and he set a grave and downcast face against the remainder of his journey.

As he neared Leavenworth he met the friend who had conveyed the dead man's warning message, and to him he committed the task of bringing home the body. His heaviness of spirit was scarcely mitigated by the congratulations of the commander of Fort Leavenworth upon his pluck and resources, which had saved both his life and the dispatches.

There followed another period of inaction, always irritating to a lad of Will's restless temperament. Meantime, we at home were having our own experiences.

We were rejoiced in great measure when sister Julia decided that we had learned as much as might be hoped for in the country school, and must thereafter attend the winter and spring terms of the school at Leavenworth. The dresses she cut for us, however, still followed the country fashion, which has regard rather to wear than to appearance, and we had not been a day in the city school before we discovered that our apparel had stamped "provincial" upon us in plain, large characters. In addition to this, our brother-in-law, in his endeavor to administer the estate economically, bought each of us a pair of coarse calfskin shoes. To these we were quite unused, mother having accustomed us to serviceable but pretty ones. The author of our "extreme" mortification, totally ignorant of the shy and sensitive nature of girls, only laughed at our protests, and in justice to him it may be said that he really had no conception of the torture he inflicted upon us.

We turned to Will. In every emergency he was our first thought, and here was an emergency that taxed his powers to an extent we did not dream of. He made answer to our letter that he was no longer an opulent trainman, but drew only the slender income of a soldier, and even that pittance was in arrears. Disappointment was swallowed up in remorse. Had we reflected how keenly he must feel his inability to help us, we would not have sent him the letter, which, at worst, contained only a sly suggestion of a fine opportunity to relieve sisterly distress. All his life he had responded to our every demand; now allegiance was due his country first. But, as was always the way with him, he made the best of a bad matter, and we were much comforted by the receipt of the following letter:

"My Dear Sisters:
    "I am sorry that I cannot help you and furnish you with such clothes as you wish. At this writing I am so short of funds myself that if an entire Mississippi steamer could be bought for ten cents I couldn't purchase the smokestack. I will soon draw my pay, and I will send it, every cent, to you. So brave it out, girls, a little longer. In the mean time I will write to Al.   Lovingly,

                                    Will."

We were comforted, yes; but my last hope was gone, and I grew desperate. I had never worn the obnoxious shoes purchased by my guardian, and I proceeded to dispose of them forever. I struck what I regarded as a famous bargain with an accommodating Hebrew, and came into possession of a pair of shiny morocco shoes, worth perhaps a third of what mine had cost. One would say they were designed for shoes, and they certainly looked like shoes, but as certainly they were not wearable. Still they were of service, for the transaction convinced my guardian that the truest economy did not lie in the pur-

chasing of calfskin shoes for at least one of his charges.
A little later he received a letter from Will, presenting our
grievances and advocating our cause.   Will also sent us
the whole of his next month's pay as soon as he drew it.

In February, 1864, Sherman began his march through
Mississippi.   The Seventh Kansas regiment, known as
"Jennison's Jayhawkers," was reorganized at Fort Leavenworth as veterans, and sent to Memphis, Tenn., to join
General A. J. Smith's command, which was to operate
against General Forrest and cover the retreat of General
Sturgis, who had been so badly whipped by Forrest at
Cross-Roads.   Will was exceedingly desirous of engaging
in a great battle, and through some officers with whom he
was acquainted preferred a petition to be transferred to this
regiment.   The request was granted, and his delight knew
no bounds.   He wrote to us that his great desire was about
to be gratified, that he should soon know what a real battle
was like.

He was well versed in Indian warfare; now he was
ambitious to learn, from experience, the superiority of
civilized strife—rather, I should say, of strife between civilized people.

General Smith had acquainted himself with the record
made by the young scout of the plains, and shortly after
reaching Memphis he ordered Will to report to headquarters for special service.

"I am anxious," said the general, "to gain reliable
information concerning the enemy's movements and position.   This can only be done by entering the Confederate
camp.   You possess the needed qualities—nerve, coolness,
resource—and I believe you could do it."

"You mean," answered Will, quietly, "that you wish
me to go as a spy into the rebel camp."

"Exactly. But you must understand the risk you run. If you are captured, you will be hanged."

"I am ready to take the chances, sir," said Will; "ready to go at once, if you wish."

General Smith's stern face softened into a smile at the prompt response.

"I am sure, Cody," said he, kindly, "that if any one can go through safely, you will. Dodging Indians on the plains was good training for the work in hand, which demands quick intelligence and ceaseless vigilance. I never require such service of any one, but since you volunteer to go, take these maps of the country to your quarters and study them carefully. Return this evening for full instructions."

During the few days his regiment had been in camp, Will had been on one or two scouting expeditions, and was somewhat familiar with the immediate environments of the Union forces. The maps were unusually accurate, showing every lake, river, creek, and highway, and even the by-paths from plantation to plantation.

Only the day before, while on a reconnoissance, Will had captured a Confederate soldier, who proved to be an old acquaintance named Nat Golden. Will had served with Nat on one of Russell, Majors & Waddell's freight trains, and at one time had saved the young man's life, and thereby earned his enduring friendship. Nat was born in the East, became infected with Western fever, and ran away from home in order to become a plainsman.

"Well, this is too bad," said Will, when he recognized his old friend. "I would rather have captured a whole regiment than you. I don't like to take you in as a prisoner. What did you enlist on the wrong side for, anyway?"

"The fortunes of war, Billy, my boy," laughed Nat. "Friend shall be turned against friend, and brother against brother, you know. You wouldn't have had me for a prisoner, either, if my rifle hadn't snapped; but I'm glad it did, for I shouldn't want to be the one that shot you."

"Well, I don't want to see you strung up," said Will; "so hand me over those papers you have, and I will turn you in as an ordinary prisoner."

Nat's face paled as he asked, "Do you think I'm a spy, Billy?"

"I know it."

"Well," was the reply, "I've risked my life to obtain these papers, but I suppose they will be taken from me anyway; so I might as well give them up now, and save my neck."

Examination showed them to be accurate maps of the location and position of the Union army; and besides the maps, there were papers containing much valuable information concerning the number of soldiers and officers and their intended movements. Will had not destroyed these papers, and he now saw a way to use them to his own advantage. When he reported for final instructions, therefore, at General Smith's tent, in the evening, Will said to him:

"I gathered from a statement dropped by the prisoner captured yesterday, that a Confederate spy has succeeded in making out and carrying to the enemy a complete map of the position of our regiment, together with some idea of the projected plan of campaign."

"Ah," said the general; "I am glad that you have put me on my guard. I will at once change my position, so that the information will be of no value to them."

Then followed full instructions as to the duty required of the volunteer.

"When will you set out?" asked the general.

"To-night, sir. I have procured my uniform, and have everything prepared for an early start."

"Going to change your colors, eh?"

"Yes, for the time being, but not my principles."

The general looked at Will approvingly. "You will need all the wit, pluck, nerve, and caution of which you are possessed to come through this ordeal safely," said he. "I believe you can accomplish it, and I rely upon you fully. Good by, and success go with you!"

After a warm hand-clasp, Will returned to his tent, and lay down for a few hours' rest. By four o'clock he was in the saddle, riding toward the Confederate lines.

CHAPTER XIII.

IN THE SECRET–SERVICE.

IN common walks of life to play the spy is an ignoble rôle; yet the work has to be done, and there must be men to do it. There always are such men—nervy fellows who swing themselves into the saddle when their commander lifts his hand, and ride a mad race, with Death at the horse's flank every mile of the way. They are the unknown heroes of every war.

It was with a full realization of the dangers confronting him that Will cantered away from the Union lines, his borrowed uniform under his arm. As soon as he had put the outposts behind him, he dismounted and exchanged the blue clothes for the gray. Life on the plains had bronzed his face. For aught his complexion could tell, the ardent Southern sun might have kissed it to its present hue. Then, if ever, his face was his fortune in good part; but there was, too, a stout heart under his jacket, and the light of confidence in his eyes.

The dawn had come up when he sighted the Confederate outposts. What lay beyond only time could reveal; but with a last reassuring touch of the papers in his pocket, he spurred his horse up to the first of the outlying sentinels. Promptly the customary challenge greeted him:

"Halt! Who goes there?"

"Friend."

"Dismount, friend! Advance and give the countersign!"

'Haven't the countersign," said Will, dropping from his horse, "but I have important information for General Forrest.   Take me to him at once."

"Are you a Confederate soldier?"

"Not exactly.   But I have some valuable news about the Yanks, I reckon.   Better let me see the general."

"Thus far," he added to himself, "I have played the part.   The combination of 'Yank' and 'I reckon' ought to establish me as a promising candidate for Confederate honors."

His story was not only plausible, but plainly and fairly told; but caution is a child of war, and the sentinel knew his business.   The pseudo-Confederate was disarmed as a necessary preliminary, and marched between two guards to headquarters, many curious eyes (the camp being now astir) following the trio.

When Forrest heard the report, he ordered the prisoner brought before him.   One glance at the general's handsome but harsh face, and the young man steeled his nerves for the encounter.   There was no mercy in those cold, piercing eyes.   This first duel of wits was the one to be most dreaded.   Unless confidence were established, his after work must be done at a disadvantage.

The general's penetrating gaze searched the young face before him for several seconds.

"Well, sir," said he, "what do you want with me?"

Yankee-like, the reply was another question:

"You sent a man named Nat Golden into the Union lines, did you not, sir?"

"And if I did, what then?"

"He is an old friend of mine.   He tried for the Union camp to verify information that he had received, but before he started he left certain papers with me in case he should be captured.''

"Ah!" said Forrest, coldly. "And he was captured?"

"Yes, sir; but, as I happen to know, he wasn't hanged, for these weren't on him.''

As he spoke, Will took from his pocket the papers he had obtained from Golden, and passed them over with the remark, "Golden asked me to take them to you."

General Forrest was familiar with the hapless Golden's handwriting, and the documents were manifestly genuine. His suspicion was not aroused.

"These are important papers," said he, when he had run his eye over them. "They contain valuable information, but we may not be able to use it, as we are about to change our location. Do you know what these papers contain?"

"Every word," was the truthful reply. "I studied them, so that in case they were destroyed you would still have the information from me.''

"A wise thing to do," said Forrest, approvingly. "Are you a soldier?"

"I have not as yet joined the army, but I am pretty well acquainted with this section, and perhaps could serve you as a scout.''

"Um!" said the general, looking the now easy-minded young man over. "You wear our uniform."

"It's Golden's," was the second truthful answer. "He left it with me when he put on the blue."

"And what is your name?"

"Frederick Williams."

Pretty near the truth. Only a final "s" and a rearrangement of his given names.

"Very well," said the general, ending the audience; "you may remain in camp. If I need you, I'll send for you."

He summoned an orderly, and bade him make the volunteer scout comfortable at the couriers' camp. Will breathed a sigh of relief as he followed at the orderly's heels. The ordeal was successfully passed. The rest was action.

Two days went by. In them Will picked up valuable information here and there, drew maps, and was prepared to depart at the first favorable opportunity. It was about time, he figured, that General Forrest found some scouting work for him. That was a passport beyond the lines, and he promised himself the outposts should see the cleanest pair of heels that ever left unwelcome society in the rear. But evidently scouting was a drug in the general's market, for the close of another day found Will impatiently awaiting orders in the couriers' quarters. This sort of inactivity was harder on the nerves than more tangible perils, and he about made up his mind that when he left camp it would be without orders, but with a hatful of bullets singing after him. And he was quite sure that his exit lay that way when, strolling past headquarters, he clapped eyes on the very last person that he expected or wished to see—Nat Golden.

And Nat was talking to an adjutant-general!

There were just two things to do, knock Golden on the head, or cut and run. Nat would not betray him knowingly, but unwittingly was certain to do so the moment General Forrest questioned him. There could be no choice between the two courses open; it was cut and run, and as a preliminary Will cut for his tent. First concealing his papers, he saddled his horse and rode toward the outposts with a serene countenance.

The same sergeant that greeted him when he entered the lines chanced to be on duty, and of him Will asked an unimportant question concerning the outer-flung lines. Yet as he rode along he could not forbear throwing an apprehensive glance behind.

No pursuit was making, and the farthest picket-line was passed by a good fifty yards. Ahead was a stretch of timber.

Suddenly a dull tattoo of horses' hoofs caught his ear, and he turned to see a small cavalcade bearing down upon him at a gallop. He sank the spurs into his horse's side and plunged into the timber.

It was out of the frying-pan into the fire. He ran plump into a half-dozen Confederate cavalrymen, guarding two Union prisoners.

"Men, a Union spy is escaping!" shouted Will. "Scatter at once, and head him off. I'll look after your prisoners."

There was a ring of authority in the command; it came at least from a petty officer; and without thought of challenging it, the cavalrymen hurried right and left in search of the fugitive.

"Come," said Will, in a hurried but smiling whisper to the dejected pair of Union men. "I'm the spy! There!" cutting the ropes that bound their wrists. "Now ride for your lives!"

Off dashed the trio, and not a minute too soon. Will's halt had been brief, but it had been of advantage to his pursuers, who, with Nat Golden at their head, came on in full cry, not a hundred yards behind.

Here was a race with Death at the horse's flanks. The timber stopped a share of the singing bullets, but there were plenty that got by the trees, one of them finding lodg-

ment in the arm of one of the fleeing Union soldiers.
Capture meant certain death for Will; for his companions
it meant Andersonville or Libby, at the worst, which was
perhaps as bad as death; but Will would not leave them,
though his horse was fresh, and he could easily have distanced them.   Of course, if it became necessary, he was
prepared to cut their acquaintance, but for the present he
made one of the triplicate targets on which the galloping
marksmen were endeavoring to score a bull's-eye.

The edge of the wood was shortly reached, and
beyond—inspiring sight!—lay the outposts of the Union
army.   The pickets, at sight of the fugitives, sounded the
alarm, and a body of blue-coats responded.

Will would have gladly tarried for the skirmish that
ensued, but he esteemed it his first duty to deliver the
papers he had risked his life to obtain; so, leaving friend
and foe to settle the dispute as best they might, he put for
the clump of trees where he had hidden his uniform, and
exchanged it for the gray, that had served its purpose and
was no longer endurable.   Under his true colors he rode
into camp.

General Forrest almost immediately withdrew from that
neighborhood, and after the atrocious massacre at Fort
Pillow, on the 12th of April, left the state.   General Smith
was recalled, and Will was transferred, with the commission
of guide and scout for the Ninth Kansas Regiment.

The Indians were giving so much trouble along the line
of the old Santa Fé trail that troops were needed to protect
the stagecoaches, emigrants, and caravans traveling that
great highway.   Like nearly all our Indian wars, this
trouble was precipitated by the injustice of the white man's
government of certain of the native tribes.   In 1860
Colonel A. G. Boone, a worthy grandson of the immortal

Daniel, made a treaty with the Comanches, Kiowas, Cheyennes, and Arapahoes, and at their request he was made
agent.   During his wise, just, and humane administration
all of these savage nations were quiet, and held the kind-
liest feelings toward the whites.   Any one could cross the
plains without fear of molestation.   In 1861 a charge of
disloyalty was made against Colonel Boone by Judge
Wright, of Indiana, and he succeeded in having the right
man removed from the right place.   Russell, Majors &
Waddell, recognizing his influence over the Indians, gave
him fourteen hundred acres of land near Pueblo, Colorado.
Colonel Boone moved there, and the place was named
Booneville.   Fifty chieftains from the tribes referred to
visited Colonel Boone in the fall of 1862, and implored him
to return to them.   He told them that the President had
sent him away.   They offered to raise money, by selling
their horses, to send him to Washington, to tell the Great
Father what their agent was doing—that he stole their
goods and sold them back again; and they bade the colonel
say that there would be trouble unless some one were put
in the dishonest man's place.   With the innate logic for
which the Indian is noted, they declared that they had as
much right to steal from passing caravans as the agent had
to steal from them.

No notice was taken of so trifling a matter as an injustice to the Indian.   The administration had its hands more
than full in the attempt to right the wrongs of the negro.

In the fall of 1863 a caravan passed along the trail.   It
was a small one, but the Indians had been quiet for so long
a time that travelers were beginning to lose fear of them.
A band of warriors rode up to the wagon-train and asked
for something to eat.   The teamsters thought they would
be doing humanity a service if they killed a redskin, on the

ancient principle that "the only good Indian is a dead one." Accordingly, a friendly, inoffensive Indian was shot.

The bullet that reached his heart touched that of every warrior in these nations. Every man but one in the wagon-train was slain, the animals driven off, and the wagons burned.

The fires of discontent that had been smoldering for two years in the red man's breast now burst forth with volcanic fury. Hundreds of atrocious murders followed, with wholesale destruction of property.

The Ninth Kansas Regiment, under the command of Colonel Clark, was detailed to protect the old trail between Fort Lyon and Fort Larned, and as guide and scout Will felt wholly at home. He knew the Indian and his ways, and had no fear of him. His fine horse and glittering trappings were an innocent delight to him; and who will not pardon in him the touch of pride—say vanity—that thrilled him as he led his regiment down the Arkansas River?

During the summer there were sundry skirmishes with the Indians. The same old vigilance, learned in earlier days on the frontier, was in constant demand, and there was many a rough and rapid ride to drive the hostiles from the trail. Whatever Colonel Clark's men may have had to complain of, there was no lack of excitement, no dull days, in that summer.

In the autumn the Seventh Kansas was again ordered to the front, and at the request of its officers Will was detailed for duty with his old regiment. General Smith's orders were that he should go to Nashville. Rosecrans was then in command of the Union forces in Missouri. His army was very small, numbering only about 6,500 men, while the Confederate General Price was on the point of entering the state with 20,000. This superiority of numbers was so great that General Smith received an order countermanding the other, and remained in Missouri, joining forces with Rosecrans to oppose Price. Rosecrans's entire force still numbered only 11,000, and he deemed it prudent to concentrate his army around St. Louis. General Ewing's forces and a portion of General Smith's command occupied Pilot Knob. On Monday, the 24th of September, 1864, Price advanced against this position, but was repulsed with heavy losses. An adjacent fort in the neighborhood of Ironton was assaulted, but the Confederate forces again sustained a severe loss. This fort held a commanding lookout on Shepard Mountain, which the Confederates occupied, and their well-directed fire obliged General Ewing to fall back to Harrison Station, where he made a stand, and some sharp fighting followed. General Ewing again fell back, and succeeded in reaching General McNeill, at Rolla, with the main body of his troops.

This was Will's first serious battle, and it so chanced that he found himself opposed at one point by a body of Missouri troops numbering many of the men who had been his father's enemies and persecutors nine years before. In the heat of the conflict he recognized more than one of them, and with the recognition came the memory of his boyhood's vow to avenge his father's death. Three of those men fell in that battle; and whether or not it was he who laid them low, from that day on he accounted himself freed of his melancholy obligation.

After several hard-fought battles, Price withdrew from Missouri with the remnant of his command—seven thousand where there had been twenty.

During this campaign Will received honorable mention "for most conspicuous bravery and valuable service upon the field," and he was shortly brought into favorable notice in many quarters. The worth of the tried veterans was known, but none of the older men was in more demand than Will. His was seemingly a charmed life. Often was he detailed to bear dispatches across the battlefield, and though horses were shot under him—riddled by bullets or torn by shells—he himself went scathless.

During this campaign, too, he ran across his old friend of the plains, Wild Bill. Stopping at a farm-house one day to obtain a meal, he was not a little surprised to hear the salutation:

"Well, Billy, my boy, how are you?"

He looked around to see a hand outstretched from a coat-sleeve of Confederate gray, and as he knew Wild Bill to be a stanch Unionist, he surmised that he was engaged upon an enterprise similar to his own. There was an exchange of chaffing about gray uniforms and blue, but more serious talk followed.

"Take these papers, Billy," said Wild Bill, passing over a package. "Take 'em to General McNeill, and tell him I'm picking up too much good news to keep away from the Confederate camp."

"Don't take too many chances," cautioned Will, well knowing that the only chances the other would not take would be the sort that were not visible.

Colonel Hickok, to give him his real name, replied, with a laugh:

"Practice what you preach, my son. Your neck is of more value than mine. You have a future, but mine is mostly past. I'm getting old."

At this point the good woman of the house punctuated the colloquy with a savory meal, which the pair discussed with good appetite and easy conscience, in spite of their hostess's refusal to take pay from Confederate soldiers.

"As long as I have a crust in the house," said she, "you boys are welcome to it."

But the pretended Confederates paid her for her kindness in better currency than she was used to. They withheld information concerning a proposed visit of her husband and son, of which, during one spell of loquacity, she acquainted them. The bread she cast upon the waters returned to her speedily.

The two friends parted company, Will returning to the Union lines, and Colonel Hickok to the opposing camp.

A few days later, when the Confederate forces were closing up around the Union lines, and a battle was at hand, two horsemen were seen to dart out of the hostile camp and ride at full speed for the Northern lines. For a space the audacity of the escape seemed to paralyze the Confederates; but presently the bullets followed thick and fast, and one of the saddles was empty before the rescue party—of which Will was one—got fairly under way. As the survivor drew near, Will shouted:

"It's Wild Bill, the Union scout."

A cheer greeted the intrepid Colonel Hickok, and he rode into camp surrounded by a party of admirers. The information he brought proved of great value in the battle of Pilot Knob (already referred to), which almost immediately followed.

CHAPTER XIV.

A RESCUE AND A BETROTHAL.

AFTER the battle of Pilot Knob Will was assigned, through the influence of General Polk, to special service at military headquarters in St. Louis. Mrs. Polk had been one of mother's school friends, and the two had maintained a correspondence up to the time of mother's death. As soon as Mrs. Polk learned that the son of her old friend was in the Union army, she interested herself in obtaining a good position for him. But desk-work is not a Pony Express rush, and Will found the St. Louis detail about as much to his taste as clerking in a dry-goods store. His new duties naturally became intolerable, lacking the excitement and danger-scent which alone made his life worth while to him.

One event, however, relieved the dead-weight monotony of his existence; he met Louise Frederici, the girl who became his wife. The courtship has been written far and wide with blood-and-thunder pen, attended by lariat-throwing and runaway steeds. In reality it was a romantic affair.

More than once, while out for a morning canter, Will had remarked a young woman of attractive face and figure, who sat her horse with the grace of Diana Vernon. Now, few things catch Will's eye more quickly than fine horsemanship. He desired to establish an acquaintance with the young lady, but as none of his friends knew her, he found it impossible.

At length a chance came. Her bridle-rein broke one

morning; there was a runaway, a rescue, and then acquaintance was easy.

From war to love, or from love to war, is but a step,
and Will lost no time in taking it.   He was somewhat better than an apprentice to Dan Cupid.   If the reader
remembers, he went to school with Steve Gobel.   True,
his opportunities to enjoy feminine society had not been
many, which, perhaps, accounts for the promptness with
which he embraced them when they did arise.   He became
the accepted suitor of Miss Louise Frederici before the war
closed and his regiment was mustered out.

The spring of 1865 found him not yet twenty, and he
was sensible of the fact that before he could dance at his
own wedding he must place his worldly affairs upon a surer
financial basis than falls to the lot of a soldier; so, much as
he would have enjoyed remaining in St. Louis, fortune
pointed to wider fields, and he set forth in search of
remunerative and congenial employment.

First, there was the visit home, where the warmest of
welcomes awaited him.   During his absence the second sister, Eliza, had married a Mr. Myers, but the rest of us
were at the old place, and the eagerness with which we
awaited Will's home-coming was stimulated by the hope
that he would remain and take charge of the estate.   Before
we broached this subject, however, he informed us of his
engagement to Miss Frederici, which, far from awakening
jealousy, aroused our delight, Julia voicing the sentiment
of the family in the comment:

"When you're married, Will, you will have to stay at
home."

This led to the matter of his remaining with us to man-
age the estate—and to the upsetting of our plans.   The
pay of a soldier in the war was next to nothing, and as

Will had been unable to put any money by, he took the first chance that offered to better his fortunes.

This happened to be a job of driving horses from Leavenworth to Fort Kearny, and almost the first man he met after reaching the fort was an old plains friend, Bill Trotter.

"You're just the chap I've been looking for," said Trotter, when he learned that Will desired regular work. "I'm division station agent here, but stage-driving is dangerous work, as the route is infested with Indians and outlaws. Several drivers have been held up and killed lately, so it's not a very enticing job, but the pay's good, and you know the country. If any one can take the stage through, you can. Do you want the job?"

When a man is in love and the wedding-day has been dreamed of, if not set, life takes on an added sweetness, and to stake it against the marksmanship of Indian or outlaw is not, perhaps, the best use to which it may be put. Will had come safely through so many perils that it seemed folly to thrust his head into another batch of them, and thinking of Louise and the coming wedding-day, his first thought was no.

But it was the old story, and there was Trotter at his elbow expressing confidence in his ability as a frontiersman—an opinion Will fully shared, for a man knows what he can do. The pay was good, and the sooner earned the sooner would the wedding be, and Trotter received the answer he expected.

The stage line was another of the Western enterprises projected by Russell, Majors & Waddell. When gold was discovered on Pike's Peak there was no method of traversing the great Western plain except by plodding ox-team, mule-pack, or stagecoach. A semi-monthly stage line ran from St. Joseph to Salt Lake City, but it was poorly equipped and very tedious, oftentimes twenty-one days being required to make the trip. The senior member of the firm, in partnership with John S. Jones, of Missouri, established a new line between the Missouri River and Denver, at that time a straggling mining hamlet. One thousand Kentucky mules were bought, with a sufficient number of coaches to insure a daily run each way. The trip was made in six days, which necessitated travel at the rate of a hundred miles a day.

The first stage reached Denver on May 17, 1859. It was accounted a remarkable achievement, and the line was pronounced a great success. In one way it was; but the expense of equipping it had been enormous, and the new line could not meet its obligations. To save the credit of their senior partner, Russell, Majors & Waddell were obliged to come to the rescue. They bought up all the outstanding obligations, and also the rival stage line between St. Joseph and Salt Lake City. They consolidated the two, and thereby hoped to put the Overland stage route on a paying basis. St. Joseph now became the starting-point of the united lines. From there the road went to Fort Kearny, and followed the old Salt Lake trail, already described in these pages. After leaving Salt Lake it passed through Camp Floyd, Ruby Valley, Carson City, Placerville, and Folsom, and ended in Sacramento.

The distance from St. Joseph to Sacramento by this old stage route was nearly nineteen hundred miles. The time required by mail contracts and the government schedule was nineteen days. The trip was frequently made in fifteen, but there were so many causes for detention that the limit was more often reached.

Each two hundred and fifty miles of road was designated a "division," and was in charge of an agent, who had great authority in his own jurisdiction. He was commonly a man of more than ordinary intelligence, and all matters pertaining to his division were entirely under his control. He hired and discharged employés, purchased horses, mules, harness, and food, and attended to their distribution at the different stations. He superintended the erection of all buildings, had charge of the water supply, and he was the paymaster.

There was also a man known as the conductor, whose route was almost coincident with that of the agent. He sat with the driver, and often rode the whole two hundred and fifty miles of his division without any rest or sleep, except what he could catch sitting on the top of the flying coach.

The coach itself was a roomy, swaying vehicle, swung on thorough-braces instead of springs. It always had a six-horse or six-mule team to draw it, and the speed was nerve-breaking. Passengers were allowed twenty-five pounds of baggage, and that, with the mail, express, and the passengers themselves, was in charge of the conductor.

The Overland stagecoaches were operated at a loss until 1862. In March of that year Russell, Majors & Waddell transferred the whole outfit to Ben Holliday. Here was a typical frontiersman, of great individuality and character. At the time he took charge of the route the United States mail was given to it. This put the line on a sound financial basis, as the government spent $800,000 yearly in transporting the mail to San Francisco.

Will reported for duty the morning after his talk with Trotter, and when he mounted the stage-box and gathered the reins over the six spirited horses, the passengers were assured of an expert driver.

His run was from Fort Kearny to Plum Creek. The country was sharply familiar. It was the scene of his first encounter with Indians. A long and lonely ride it was, and a dismal one when the weather turned cold; but it meant a hundred and fifty dollars a month, and each pay day brought him nearer to St. Louis.

Indian signs there had been right along, but they were only signs until one bleak day in November. He pulled out of Plum Creek with a sharp warning ringing in his ears. Indians were on the war-path, and trouble was more likely than not ahead. Lieutenant Flowers, assistant division agent, was on the box with him, and within the coach were six well-armed passengers.

Half the run had been covered, when Will's experienced eye detected the promised red men. Before him lay a stream which must be forded. The creek was densely fringed with underbrush, and along this the Indians were skulking, expecting to cut the stage off at the only possible crossing.

Perhaps this is a good place to say a word concerning the seemingly extraordinary fortune that has stood by Will in his adventures. Not only have his own many escapes been of the hairbreadth sort, but he has arrived on the scene of danger at just the right moment to rescue others from extinction. Of course, an element of luck has entered into these affairs, but for the most part they simply proved the old saying that an ounce of prevention is better than a pound of cure. Will had studied the plains as an astronomer studies the heavens. The slightest disarrangement of the natural order of things caught his eye. With the astronomer, it is a comet or an asteroid appearing upon a field whose every object has long since been placed and studied; with Will, it was a feathered headdress where there should have been but tree, or rock, or grass; a moving figure where nature should have been inanimate.

When seen, those things were calculated as the astronomer calculates the motion of the objects that he studies. A planet will arrive at a given place at a certain time; an Indian will reach a ford in a stream in about so many minutes. If there be time to cross before him, it is a matter of hard driving; if the odds are with the Indian, that is another matter.

A less experienced observer than Will would not have seen the skulking redskins; a less skilled frontiersman would not have apprehended their design; a less expert driver would not have taken the running chance for life; a less accurate marksman would not have picked off an Indian with a rifle while shooting from the top of a swinging, jerking stagecoach.

Will did not hesitate. A warning shout to the passengers, and the whip was laid on, and off went the horses full speed. Seeing that they had been discovered, the Indians came out into the open, and ran their ponies for the ford, but the stage was there full five hundred yards before them. It was characteristic of their driver that the horses were suffered to pause at the creek long enough to get a swallow of water; then, refreshed, they were off at full speed again.

The coach, creaking in every joint, rocked like a captive balloon, the unhappy passengers were hurled from one side of the vehicle to the other, flung into one another's laps, and occasionally, when some uncommon obstacle sought to check the flying coach, their heads collided with its roof. The Indians menaced them without, cracked skulls seemed their fate within.

Will plied the whip relentlessly, and so nobly did the

powerful horses respond that the Indians gained but slowly on them. There were some fifty redskins in the band, but Will assumed that if he could reach the relay station, the two stock-tenders there, with himself, Lieutenant Flowers, and the passengers, would be more than a match for the marauders.

When the pursuers drew within fair rifle range, Will handed the reins to the lieutenant, swung round in his seat, and fired at the chief.

"There," shouted one of the passengers, "that fellow with the feathers is shot!" and another fusillade from the coach interior drove holes in the air.

The relay station was now hard by, and attracted by the firing, the stock-tenders came forth to take a hand in the engagement. Disheartened by the fall of their chief, the Indians weakened at the sign of reinforcements, and gave up the pursuit.

Lieutenant Flowers and two of the passengers were wounded, but Will could not repress a smile at the excited assurance of one of his fares that they (the passengers) had "killed one Indian and driven the rest back." The stock-tenders smiled also, but said nothing. It would have been too bad to spoil such a good story.

The gravest fears for the safety of the coach had been expressed when it was known that the reds were on the war-path; it was not thought possible that it could get through unharmed, and troops were sent out to scour the country. These, while too late to render service in the adventure just related, did good work during the remainder of the winter. The Indians were thoroughly subdued, and Will saw no more of them.

There was no other adventure of special note until February. Just before Will started on his run, Trotter took him to one side and advised him that a small fortune was going by the coach that day, and extra vigilance was urged, as the existence of the treasure might have become known.

"I'll do the best I can," said Will; and he had scarcely driven away when he suspected the two ill-favored passengers he carried. The sudden calling away of the conductor, whereby he was left alone, was a suspicious circumstance. He properly decided that it would be wiser for him to hold up his passengers than to let them hold up him, and he proceeded to take time by the forelock. He stopped the coach, jumped down, and examined the harness as if something was wrong; then he stepped to the coach door and asked his passengers to hand him a rope that was inside. As they complied, they looked into the barrels of two cocked revolvers.

"Hands up!" said Will.

"What's the matter with you?" demanded one of the pair, as their arms were raised.

"Thought I'd come in first—that's all," was the answer.

The other was not without appreciation of humor.

"You're a cute one, youngster," said he, "but you'll find more'n your match down the road, or I miss my guess."

"I'll look after that when I get to it," said Will. "Will you oblige me by tying your friend's hands? Thank you. Now throw out your guns. That all? All right. Let me see your hands."

When both outlaws had been securely trussed up and proven to be disarmed, the journey was resumed. The remark dropped by one of the pair was evidence that they were part of the gang. He must reach the relay station before the attack. If he could do that, he had a plan for farther on.

The relay station was not far away, and was safely reached. The prisoners were turned over to the stock-tenders, and then Will disposed of the treasure against future molestation. He cut open one of the cushions of the coach, taking out part of the filling, and in the cavity thus made stored everything of value, including his own watch and pocketbook; then the filling was replaced and the hole smoothed to a natural appearance.

If there were more in the gang, he looked for them at the ford where the Indians had sought to cut him off, and he was not disappointed. As he drew near the growth of willows that bordered the road, half a dozen men with menacing rifles stepped out.

"Halt, or you're a dead man!" was the conventional salutation, in this case graciously received.

"Well, what do you want?" asked Will.

"The boodle you carry.   Fork it over!"

"Gentlemen," said Will, smiling, "this is a case where it takes a thief to catch a thief."

"What's that?" cried one of the outlaws, his feelings outraged by the frank description.

"Not that I'm the thief," continued Will, "but your pals were one too many for you this time."

"Did they rob you?" howled the gang in chorus, shocked by such depravity on the part of their comrades.

"If there's anything left in the coach worth having, don't hesitate to take it," offered Will, pleasantly.

"Where's your strong-box?" demanded the outlaws, loath to believe there was no honor among thieves.

Will drew it forth and exposed its melancholy empti-ness. The profanity that ensued was positively shocking.

"Where did they hold you up?" demanded the leader of the gang.

"Eight or nine miles back.   You'll find some straw in the road.   You can have that, too."

"Were there horses to meet them?"

"On foot the last I saw them."

"Then we can catch 'em, boys," shouted the leader, hope upspringing in his breast.   "Come, let's be off!"

They started for the willows on the jump, and presently returned, spurring their horses.

"Give them my regards!" shouted Will.   But only the thud! thud! of horsehoofs answered him.   Retribution was sweeping like a hawk upon its prey.

Will pushed along to the end of his run, and handed over his trust undisturbed.   Fearing that his ruse might have been discovered, he put the "extra vigilance" urged by Trotter into the return trip, but the trail was deserted. He picked up the prisoners at the relay station and carried them to Fort Kearny.   If their companions were to discover the sorry trick played upon them, they would have demanded his life as a sacrifice.

At the end of this exciting trip he found a letter from Miss Frederici awaiting him.   She urged him to give up the wild life he was leading, return East, and find another calling.   This was precisely what Will himself had in mind, and persuasion was not needed.   In his reply he asked that the wedding-day be set, and then he handed Trotter his resignation from the lofty perch of a stage-driver.

"I don't like to let you go," objected Trotter.

"But," said Will, "I took the job only in order to save enough money to get married on."

"In that case," said Trotter, "I have nothing to do but wish you joy."

CHAPTER XV.

WILL AS A BENEDICT.

WHEN Will reached home, he found another letter from Miss Frederici, who, agreeably to his request, had fixed the wedding-day, March 6, 1866.

The wedding ceremony was quietly performed at the home of the bride, and the large number of friends that witnessed it united in declaring that no handsomer couple ever bowed for Hymen's benediction.

The bridal journey was a trip to Leavenworth on a Missouri steamer. At that time there was much travel by these boats, and their equipment was first-class. They were sumptuously fitted out, the table was excellent, and except when sectional animosities disturbed the serenity of their decks, a trip on one of them was a very pleasant excursion.

The young benedict soon discovered, however, that in war times the "trail of the serpent" is liable to be over all things; even a wedding journey is not exempt from the baneful influence of sectional animosity. A party of excursionists on board the steamer manifested so extreme an interest in the bridal couple that Louise retired to a stateroom to escape their rudeness. After her withdrawal, Will entered into conversation with a gentleman from Indiana, who had been very polite to him, and asked him if he knew the reason for the insolence of the excursion party. The gentleman hesitated a moment, and then answered:

"To tell the truth, Mr. Cody, these men are Missourians, and say they recognize you as one of Jennison's Jayhawkers; that you were an enemy of the South, and are, therefore, an enemy of theirs."

Will answered, steadily: "I was a soldier during the war, and a scout in the Union army, but I had some experience of Southern chivalry before that time." And he related to the Indianian some of the incidents of the early Kansas border warfare, in which he and his father had played so prominent a part.

The next day the insolent behavior was continued. Will was much inclined to resent it, but his wife pleaded so earnestly with him to take no notice of it that he ignored it.

In the afternoon, when the boat landed at a lonely spot to wood up, the Missourians seemed greatly excited, and all gathered on the guards and anxiously scanned the river-bank.

The roustabouts were just about to make the boat fast, when a party of armed horsemen dashed out of the woods and galloped toward the landing. The captain thought the boat was to be attacked, and hastily gave orders to back out, calling the crew on board at the same time. These orders the negroes lost no time in obeying, as they often suffered severely at the hands of these reckless marauders. The leader of the horsemen rode rapidly up, firing at random. As he neared the steamer he called out, "Where is that Kansas Jayhawker? We have come for him." The other men caught sight of Will, and one of them cried, "We know you, Bill Cody." But they were too late. Already the steamer was backing away from the shore, dragging her gang-plank through the water; the negro roustabouts were too much terrified to pull it in. When the attacking party saw their plans were frustrated, and that they were balked of their prey, they gave vent to their disappointment in yells of rage. A random volley was fired at the retreating steamer, but it soon got out of range, and continued on its way up the river.

Will had prepared himself for the worst; he stood, revolver in hand, at the head of the steps, ready to dispute the way with his foes.

There was also a party of old soldiers on board, six or eight in number; they were dressed in civilians' garb, and Will knew nothing of them; but when they heard of their comrade's predicament, they hastily prepared to back up the young scout. Happily the danger was averted, and their services were not called into requisition. The remainder of the trip was made without unpleasant incident.

It was afterward learned that as soon as the Missourians became aware of the presence of the Union scout on board, they telegraphed ahead to the James and Younger brothers that Will was aboard the boat, and asked to have a party meet it at this secluded landing, and capture and carry off the young soldier. Will feared that Louise might be somewhat disheartened by such an occurrence on the bridal trip, but the welcome accorded the young couple on their arrival at Leavenworth was flattering enough to make amends for all unpleasant incidents. The young wife found that her husband numbered his friends by the score in his own home, and in the grand reception tendered them he was the lion of the hour.

Entreated by Louise to abandon the plains and pursue a vocation along more peaceful paths, Will conceived the idea of taking up the business in which mother had won financial success—that of landlord. The house she had built was purchased after her death by Dr. Crook, a surgeon in the Seventh Kansas Regiment. It was now for rent, which fact no doubt decided Will in his choice of an occupation. It was good to live again under the roof that had sheltered his mother in her last days; it was good to see the young wife amid the old scenes. So Will turned boniface, and invited May and me to make our home with him.

There was a baby in Julia's home, and it had so wound itself around May's heartstrings that she could not be enticed away; but there was never anybody who could supplant Will in my heart; so I gladly accepted his invitation.

Thoreau has somewhere drawn a sympathetic portrait of the Landlord, who is supposed to radiate hospitality as the sun throws off heat—as its own reward—and who feeds and lodges men purely from a love of the creatures. Yet even such a landlord, if he is to continue long in business, must have an eye to profit, and make up in one corner what he parts with in another. Now, Will radiated hospitality, and his reputation as a lover of his fellowman got so widely abroad that travelers without money and without price would go miles out of their way to put up at his tavern. Socially, he was an irreproachable landlord; financially, his shortcomings were deplorable.

And then the life of an innkeeper, while not without its joys and opportunities to love one's fellowman, is somewhat prosaic, and our guests oftentimes remarked an absent, far-away expression in the eyes of Landlord Cody. He was thinking of the plains. Louise also remarked that expression, and the sympathy she felt for his yearnings was accentuated by an examination of the books of the hostelry at the close of the first six months' business. Half smiling, half tearful, she consented to his return to his Western life.

Will disposed of the house and settled his affairs, and when all the bills were paid, and Sister Lou and I cozily ensconced in a little home at Leavenworth, we found that Will's generous thought for our comfort through the winter had left him on the beach financially. He had planned a freighting trip on his own account, but the acquiring of a team, wagon, and the rest of the outfit presented a knotty problem when he counted over the few dollars left on hand.

For the first time I saw disappointment and discouragement written on his face, and I was sorely distressed, for he had never denied me a desire that he could gratify, and it was partly on my account that he was not in better financial condition. I was not yet sixteen; it would be two years more before I could have a say as to the disposition of my own money, yet something must be done at once.

I decided to lay the matter before Lawyer Douglass. Surely he could suggest some plan whereby I might assist my brother. I had a half-matured plan of my own, but I was assured that Will would not listen to it.

Mr. Douglass had been the legal adviser of the family since he won our first lawsuit, years before. We considered the problem from every side, and the lawyer suggested that Mr. Buckley, an old friend of the famliy, had a team and wagon for sale; they were strong and serviceable, and just the thing that Will would likely want. I was a minor, but if Mr. Buckley was willing to accept me as security for the property, there would be no difficulty in making the transfer.

Mr. Buckley proved entirely agreeable to the proposi tion. Will could have the outfit in return for his note with my indorsement.

That disposed of, the question of freight to put into the wagon arose. I thought of another old friend of the family, M. E. Albright, a wholesale grocer in Leavenworth. Would he trust Will for a load of supplies? He would.

Thus everything was arranged satisfactorily, and I hastened home to not the easiest task—to prevail upon Will to accept assistance at the hands of the little sister who, not so long ago, had employed his aid in the matter of a pair of shoes.

But Will could really do nothing save accept, and proud and happy, he sallied forth one day as an individual freighter, though not a very formidable rival of Russell, Majors & Waddell.

Alas for enterprises started on borrowed capital! How many of them end in disaster, leaving their projectors not only penniless, but in debt. Our young frontiersman, whose life had been spent in protecting the property of others, was powerless to save his own. Wagon, horses, and freight were all captured by Indians, and their owner barely escaped with his life. From a safe covert he watched the redskins plunge him into bankruptcy. It took him several years to recover, and he has often remarked that the responsibility of his first business venture on borrowed capital aged him prematurely.

The nearest station to the scene of this disaster was Junction City, and thither he tramped, in the hope of retrieving his fortunes. There he met Colonel Hickok, and in the pleasure of the greeting forgot his business ruin for a space. The story of his marriage and his stirring adventures as a landlord and lover of his fellowman were first to be related, and when these were commented upon, and his old friend had learned, too, of the wreck of the freighting enterprise, there came the usual inquiry:

"And now, do you know of a job with some money in it?"

"There isn't exactly a fortune in it," said Wild Bill, "but I'm scouting for Uncle Sam at Fort Ellsworth. The commandant needs more scouts, and I can vouch for you as a good one."

"All right," said Will, always quick in decision; "I'll go along with you, and apply for a job at once."

He was pleased to have Colonel Hickok's recommendation, but it turned out that he did not need it, as his own reputation had preceded him. The commandant of the fort was glad to add him to the force. The territory he had to scout over lay between Forts Ellsworth and Fletcher, and he alternated between those points throughout the winter.

It was at Fort Fletcher, in the spring of 1867, that he fell in with the dashing General Custer, and the friendship established between them was ended only by the death of the general at the head of his gallant three hundred.

This spring was an exceedingly wet one, and the fort, which lay upon the bank of Big Creek, was so damaged by floods that it was abandoned. A new fort was erected, some distance to the westward, on the south fork of the creek, and was named Fort Hayes.

Returning one day from an extended scouting trip, Will discovered signs indicating that Indians in considerable force were in the neighborhood. He at once pushed forward at all speed to report the news, when a second discovery took the wind out of his sails; the hostiles were between him and the fort.

At that moment a party of horsemen broke into view, and seeing they were white men, Will waited their approach. The little band proved to be General Custer and an escort of ten, en route from Fort Ellsworth to Fort Hayes.

Informed by Will that they were cut off by Indians, and that the only hope of escape lay in a rapid flank movement, Custer's reply was a terse:

"Lead on, scout, and we'll follow."

Will wheeled, clapped spurs to his horse, and dashed away, with the others close behind. All hands were sufficiently versed in Indian warfare to appreciate the seriousness of their position. They pursued a roundabout trail, and reached the fort without seeing a hostile, but learned from the reports of others that their escape had been a narrow one.

Custer was on his way to Larned, sixty miles distant, and he needed a guide. He requested that Will be assigned to the position, so pleased was he by the service already rendered.

"The very man I proposed to send with you, General," said the commandant, who knew well the keen desire of the Indians to get at "Yellow Hair," as they called Custer. "Cody knows this part of the country like a book; he is up to all the Indian games, and he is as full of resources as a nut is of meat."

At daybreak the start was made, and it was planned to cover the sixty miles before nightfall. Will was mounted on a mouse-colored mule, to which he was much attached, and in which he had every confidence. Custer, however, was disposed to regard the lowly steed in some disdain.

"Do you think, Cody, that mule can set the pace to reach Larned in a day?" he asked.

"When you get to Larned, General," smiled Will, "the mule and I will be with you."

Custer said no more for a while, but the pace he set was eloquent, and the mouse-colored mule had to run under "forced draught" to keep up with the procession.

It was a killing pace, too, for the horses, which did not possess the staying power of the mule. Will was half regretting that he had ridden the animal, and was wondering how he could crowd on another pound or two of steam, when, suddenly glancing at Custer, he caught a gleam of mischief in the general's eye. Plainly the latter was seeking to compel an acknowledgment of error, but Will only patted the mouse-colored flanks.

Fifteen miles were told off; Custer's thoroughbred horse was still in fine fettle, but the mule had got the second of its three or four winds, and was ready for a century run.

"Can you push along a little faster, General?" asked Will, slyly.

"If that mule of yours can stand it, go ahead," was the reply

To the general's surprise, the long-eared animal did go ahead, and when the party got into the hills, and the traveling grew heavy, it set a pace that seriously annoyed the general's thoroughbred.

Fifteen miles more were pounded out, and a halt was called for luncheon. The horses needed the rest, but the mouse-colored mule wore an impatient expression. Having got its third wind, it wanted to use it.

"Well, General," said Will, when they swung off on the trail again, "what do you think of my mount?"

Custer laughed. "It's not very handsome," said he, "but it seems to know what it's about, and so does the rider. You're a fine guide, Cody. Like the Indian, you seem to go by instinct, rather than by trails and landmarks."

The praise of Custer was sweeter to the young scout than that of any other officer on the plains would have been.

At just four o'clock the mouse-colored mule jogged into Fort Larned and waved a triumphant pair of ears. A short distance behind rode Custer, on a thoroughly tired thoroughbred, while the escort was strung along the trail for a mile back.

"Cody," laughed the general, "that remarkable quadruped of yours looks equal to a return trip. Our horses are pretty well fagged out, but we have made a quick trip and a good one. You brought us 'cross country straight as the crow flies, and that's the sort of service I appreciate. Any time you're in need of work, report to me. I'll see that you're kept busy."

It was Custer's intention to remain at Fort Larned for some time, and Will, knowing that he was needed at Hayes, tarried only for supper and a short rest before starting back.

When night fell, he proceeded warily. On the way out he had directed Custer's attention to signs denoting the near-by presence of a small band of mounted Indians.

Suddenly a distant light flashed into view, but before he could check his mule it had vanished. He rode back a few paces, and the light reappeared. Evidently it was visible through some narrow space, and the matter called for investigation. Will dismounted, hitched his mule, and went forward.

After he had covered half a mile, he found himself between two sandhills, the pass leading into a little hollow, within which were a large number of Indians camped around the fire whose light he had followed. The ponies were in the background.

Will's position was somewhat ticklish, as, without a doubt, an Indian sentinel was posted in the pass; yet it was his duty, as he understood it, to obtain a measurably accurate estimate of the number of warriors in the band. Himself a very Indian in stealth, he drew nearer the camp-fire, when suddenly there rang out upon the night air—not a rifle-shot, but the unearthly braying of his mule.

Even in the daylight, amid scenes of peace and tranquillity, the voice of a mule falls short of the not enchanting music of the bagpipe. At night in the wilderness, when every nerve is keyed up to the snapping-point, the sound is simply appalling.

Will was startled, naturally, but the Indians were thrown into dire confusion. They smothered the camp-fires and scattered for cover, while a sentinel sprang up from behind a rock not twenty feet from Will, and was off like a deer.

The scout held his ground till he had made a good guess at the number of Indians in the party; then he ran for his mule, whose voice, raised in seeming protest, guided him unerringly.

As he neared the animal he saw that two mounted Indians had laid hold of it, and were trying to induce it to follow them; but the mule, true to tradition and its master, stubbornly refused to budge a foot.

It was a comical tableau, but Will realized that it was but a step from farce to tragedy. A rifle-shot dropped one of the Indians, and the other darted off into the darkness.

Another bray from the mule, this time a pæan of triumph, as Will jumped into the saddle, with an arrow from the bow of the wounded Indian through his coat-sleeve. He declined to return the fire of the wounded wretch, and rode away into the timber, while all around the sound of Indians in pursuit came to his ears.

"Now, my mouse-colored friend," said Will, "if you win this race your name is Custer."

The mule seemed to understand; at all events, it settled down to work that combined the speed of a racer with the endurance of a buffalo. The Indians shortly abandoned the pursuit, as they could not see their game.

Will reached Fort Hayes in the early morning, to report the safe arrival of Custer at Larned and the discovery of the Indian band, which he estimated at two hundred braves. The mule received "honorable mention" in his report, and was brevetted a thoroughbred.

The colonel prepared to dispatch troops against the Indians, and requested Will to guide the expedition, if he were sufficiently rested, adding, with a smile:

"You may ride your mule if you like."

"No, thank you," laughed Will. "It isn't safe, sir, to hunt Indians with an animal that carries a brass-band attachment."

Captain George A. Armes, of the Tenth Cavalry, was to command the expedition, which comprised a troop of colored cavalry and a howitzer. As the command lined up for the start, a courier on a foam-splashed horse rode up with the news that the workmen on the Kansas Pacific Railroad had been attacked by Indians, six of them killed, and over a hundred horses and mules and a quantity of stores stolen.

The troops rode away, the colored boys panting for a chance at the redskins, and Captain Armes more than willing to gratify them.

At nightfall the command made camp near the Saline River, at which point it was expected to find the Indians. Before dawn they were in the saddle again, riding straight across country, regardless of trails, until the river was come up with.

Will's judgment was again verified by the discovery of a large camp of hostiles on the opposite bank of the stream. The warriors were as quick of eye, and as they greatly outnumbered the soldiers, and were emboldened by the success of their late exploit, they did not wait the attack, but came charging across the river.

They were nearly a mile distant, and Captain Armes had time to plant the howitzer on a little rise of ground. Twenty men were left to handle it. The rest of the command advanced to the combat.

They were just at the point of attack when a fierce yelling was heard in the rear, and the captain discovered that his retreat to the gun was cut off by another band of reds, and that he was between two fires. His only course was to repulse the enemy in front. If this were done, and the colored gunners did not flee before the overwhelming numbers, he might unite his forces by another charge.

The warriors came on with their usual impetuosity, whooping and screaming, but they met such a raking fire from the disciplined troops that they fell back in disorder. Just then the men at the howitzer opened fire. The effect of this field-piece on the children of the plains was magical—almost ludicrous. A veritable stampede followed.

"Follow me!" shouted Captain Armes, galloping in pursuit; but in their eagerness to give chase the troops fell into such disorder that a bugle-blast recalled them before any further damage was done the flying foe. The Indians kept right along, however; they were pretty badly frightened.

Captain Armes was somewhat chagrined that he had no prisoners, but there was consolation in taking back nearly all the horses that had been stolen. These were found picketed at the camp across the river, where likely they had been forgotten by the Indians in their flight.

Shortly after this, Will tried his hand at land speculation. During one of his scouting trips to Fort Harker, he visited Ellsworth, a new settlement, three miles from the fort. There he met a man named Rose, who had a grading contract for the Kansas Pacific Railroad, near Fort Hayes. Rose had bought land at a point through which the railroad was to run, and proposed staking it out as a town, but he needed a partner in the enterprise.

The site was a good one. Big Creek was hard by, and it was near enough to the fort to afford settlers reasonable security against Indian raids. Will regarded the enterprise favorably. Besides the money sent home each month, he had put by a small sum, and this he invested in the partnership with Rose.

The town site was surveyed and staked off into lots; a cabin was erected, and stocked with such goods as are needed on the frontier, and the budding metropolis was weighted with the classic name of Rome.

As an encouragement to settlers, a lot was offered to any one that would agree to erect a building. The proprietors, of course, reserved the choicest lots.

Rome boomed. Two hundred cabins went up in less than sixty days. Mr. Rose and Will shook hands and complimented each other on their penetration and business sagacity. They were coming millionaires, they said. Alas! they were but babes in the woods.

One day Dr. W. E. Webb alighted in Rome. He was a gentleman of most amiable exterior, and when he entered the store of Rose & Cody they prepared to dispose of a large bill of goods. But Dr. Webb was not buying groceries. He chatted a while about the weather and Rome, and then suggested that the firm needed a third partner. But this was the last thing the prospective millionaires had in mind, and the suggestion of their visitor was mildly but firmly waived.

Dr. Webb was not a gentleman to insist upon a suggestion. He was locating towns for the Kansas Pacific Railroad, he said, and as Rome was well started, he disliked to interfere with it; but, really, the company must have a show.

Neither Mr. Rose nor Will had had experience with the power of a big corporation, and satisfied that they had the only good site for a town in that vicinity, they declared that the railroad could not help itself.

Dr. Webb smiled pleasantly, and not without compassion. "Look out for yourselves," said he, as he took his leave.

And within sight of Rome he located a new town. The citizens of Rome were given to understand that the railroad shops would be built at the new settlement, and that there was really nothing to prevent it becoming the metropolis of Kansas.

Rome became a wilderness. Its citizens stampeded to the new town, and Mr. Rose and Will revised their estimate of their penetration and business sagacity.

Meantime, the home in Leavenworth had been gladdened by the birth of a little daughter, whom her father named Arta. As it was impossible for Will to return for some months, it was planned that the mother, the baby, and I should make a visit to the St. Louis home. This was accomplished safely; and while the grandparents were enraptured with the baby, I was enjoying the delight of a first visit to a large city.

While the new town of Rome was regarded as an assured success by Will, he had journeyed to St. Louis after his wife and little one. They proceeded with him to the cozy cabin home he had fitted up, while I went back to Leavenworth.

After the fall of Rome the little frontier home was no longer the desirable residence that Will's dreams had pictured it, and as Rome passed into oblivion the little family returned to St. Louis.

CHAPTER XVI.

HOW THE SOBRIQUET OF "BUFFALO BILL" WAS WON.

IN frontier days a man had but to ask for work to get it. There was enough and to spare for every one. The work that paid best was the kind that suited Will, it mattered not how hard or dangerous it might be.

At the time Rome fell, the work on the Kansas Pacific Railroad was pushing forward at a rapid rate, and the junior member of the once prosperous firm of Rose & Cody saw a new field of activity open for him—that of buffalo-hunting. Twelve hundred men were employed on the railroad construction, and Goddard Brothers, who had undertaken to board the vast crew, were hard pressed to obtain fresh meat. To supply this indispensable, buffalo-hunters were employed, and as Will was known to be an expert buffalo-slayer, Goddard Brothers were glad to add him to their "commissary staff." His contract with them called for an average of twelve buffaloes daily, for which he was to receive five hundred dollars a month. It was "good pay," the desired feature, but the work was hard and hazardous. He must first scour the country for his game, with a good prospect always of finding Indians instead of buffalo; then, when the game was shot, he must oversee its cutting and dressing, and look after the wagons that transported it to the camp where the workmen messed. It was while working under this contract that he acquired the sobriquet of "Buffalo Bill." It clung to him ever after, and he wore it with more pride than he would have done the title of prince or grand duke. Probably there are thousands of people to-day who know him by that name only.

At the outset he procured a trained buffalo-hunting horse, which went by the unconventional name of "Brigham," and from the government he obtained an improved breech-loading needle-gun, which, in testimony of its murderous qualities, he named "Lucretia Borgia."

Buffaloes were usually plentiful enough, but there were times when the camp supply of meat ran short. During one of these dull spells, when the company was pressed for horses, Brigham was hitched to a scraper. One can imagine his indignation. A racer dragging a street-car would have no more just cause for rebellion than a buffalo-hunter tied to a work implement in the company of stupid horses that never had a thought above a plow, a hay-rake, or a scraper. Brigham expostulated, and in such plain language, that Will, laughing, was on the point of unhitching him, when a cry went up—the equivalent of a whaler's "There she blows!"—that a herd of buffaloes was coming over the hill.

Brigham and the scraper parted company instantly, and Will mounted him bareback, the saddle being at the camp, a mile away. Shouting an order to the men to follow him. with a wagon to take back the meat, he galloped toward the game.

There were other hunters that day. Five officers rode out from the neighboring fort, and joined Will while waiting for the buffaloes to come up. They were recent arrivals in that part of the country, and their shoulder-straps indicated that one was a captain and the others were lieutenants. They did not know "Buffalo Bill." They saw nothing but a good-looking young fellow, in the dress of a working man, astride a not handsome horse, which had a blind bridle and no saddle. It was not a formidable-looking hunting outfit, and the captain was disposed to be a trifle patronizing.

"Hello!" he called out. "I see you're after the same game we are."

"Yes, sir," returned Will. "Our camp's out of fresh meat."

The officer ran a critical eye over Brigham. "Do you expect to run down a buffalo with a horse like that?" said he.

"Why," said Will, innocently, "are buffaloes pretty speedy?"

"Speedy? It takes a fast horse to overhaul those animals on the open prairie."

"Does it?" said Will; and the officer did not see the twinkle in his eye. Nothing amuses a man more than to be instructed on a matter that he knows thoroughly, and concerning which his instructor knows nothing. Probably every one of the officers had yet to shoot his first buffalo.

"Come along with us," offered the captain, graciously. "We're going to kill a few for sport, and all we care for are the tongues and a chunk of the tenderloin; you can have the rest."

"Thank you," said Will. "I'll follow along."

There were eleven buffaloes in the herd, and the officers started after them as if they had a sure thing on the entire number. Will noticed that the game was pointed toward a creek, and understanding "the nature of the beast," started for the water, to head them off.

As the herd went past him, with the military quintet five hundred yards in the rear, he gave Brigham's blind bridle a twitch, and in a few jumps the trained hunter was at the side of the rear buffalo; Lucretia Borgia spoke, and the buffalo fell dead. Without even a bridle signal, Brigham was promptly at the side of the next buffalo, not ten feet away, and this, too, fell at the first shot. The maneuver was repeated until the last buffalo went down. Twelve shots had been fired; then Brigham, who never wasted his strength, stopped. The officers had not had even a shot at the game. Astonishment was written on their faces as they rode up.

"Gentlemen," said Will, courteously, as he dismounted, "allow me to present you with eleven tongues and as much of the tenderloin as you wish."

"By Jove!" exclaimed the captain, "I never saw anything like that before. Who are you, anyway?"

"Bill Cody's my name."

"Well, Bill Cody, you know how to kill buffalo, and that horse of yours has some good running points, after all."

"One or two," smiled Will.

Captain Graham—as his name proved to be—and his companions were a trifle sore over missing even the opportunity of a shot, but they professed to be more than repaid for their disappointment by witnessing a feat they had not supposed possible in a white man—hunting buffalo without a saddle, bridle, or reins. Will explained that Brigham knew more about the business than most two-legged hunters. All the rider was expected to do was to shoot the buffalo. If the first shot failed, Brigham allowed another; if this, too, failed, Brigham lost patience, and was as likely as not to drop the matter then and there.

It was this episode that fastened the name of "Buffalo Bill" upon Will, and learning of it, the friends of Billy Comstock, chief of scouts at Fort Wallace, filed a protest.

Comstock, they said, was Cody's superior as a buffalo-hunter. So a match was arranged to determine whether it should be "Buffalo Bill" Cody or "Buffalo Bill" Comstock.

The hunting-ground was fixed near Sheridan, Kansas, and quite a crowd of spectators was attracted by the news of the contest. Officers, soldiers, plainsmen, and railroad-men took a day off to see the sport, and one excursion party, including many ladies, among them Louise, came up from St. Louis.

Referees were appointed to follow each man and keep a tally of the buffaloes slain. Comstock was mounted on his favorite horse, and carried a Henry rifle of large caliber. Brigham and Lucretia went with Will. The two hunters rode side by side until the first herd was sighted and the word given, when off they dashed to the attack, separating to the right and left. In this first trial Will killed thirty-eight and Comstock twenty-three. They had ridden miles, and the carcasses of the dead buffaloes were strung all over the prairie. Luncheon was served at noon, and scarcely was it over when another herd was sighted, composed mainly of cows with their calves. The damage to this herd was eighteen and fourteen, in favor of Cody.

In those days the prairies were alive with buffaloes, and a third herd put in an appearance before the rifle-barrels were cooled. In order to give Brigham a share of the glory, Will pulled off saddle and bridle, and advanced bareback to the slaughter.

That closed the contest. Score, sixty-nine to forty-eight. Comstock's friends surrendered, and Cody was dubbed "Champion Buffalo Hunter of the Plains."

The heads of the buffaloes that fell in this hunt were mounted by the Kansas Pacific Company, and distributed about the country, as advertisements of the region the new road was traversing. Meanwhile, Will continued hunting for the Kansas Pacific contractors, and during the year and a half that he supplied them with fresh meat he killed four thousand two hundred and eighty buffaloes. But when the railroad reached Sheridan it was decided to build no farther at that time, and Will was obliged to look for other work.

The Indians had again become so troublesome that a general war threatened all along the border, and General P. H. Sheridan came West to personally direct operations. He took up his quarters at Fort Leavenworth, but the Indian depredations becoming more widespread, he transferred his quarters to Fort Hayes, then the terminus of the Kansas Pacific Railroad. Will was then in the employ of the quartermaster's department at Fort Larned, but was sent with an important dispatch to General Sheridan announcing that the Indians near Larned were preparing to decamp. The distance between Larned and Hayes was sixty-five miles, through a section infested with Indians, but Will tackled it, and reached the commanding General without mishap.

Shortly afterward it became necessary to send dispatches from Fort Hayes to Fort Dodge. Ninety-five miles of country lay between, and every mile of it was dangerous ground. Fort Dodge was surrounded by Indians, and three scouts had lately been killed while trying to get dispatches through, but Will's confidence in himself or his destiny was unshakable, and he volunteered to take the dispatches, as far, at least, as the Indians would let him.

"It is a dangerous undertaking," said General Sheridan, "but it is most important that the dispatches should go through; so, if you are willing to risk it, take the best horse you can find, and the sooner you start the better.''

Within an hour the scout was in the saddle. At the outset Will permitted his horse to set his own pace, for in case of pursuit he should want the animal fresh enough to at least hold his own. But no pursuit materialized, and when the dawn came up he had covered seventy miles, and reached a station on Coon Creek, manned by colored troops. Here he delivered a letter to Major Cox, the officer in command, and after eating breakfast, took a fresh horse, and resumed his journey before the sun was above the plain.

Fort Dodge was reached, the dispatches delivered by nine o'clock, and Will turned in for a needed sleep. When he awoke, he was assured by John Austin, chief of the scouts at Dodge, that his coming through unharmed from Fort Hayes was little short of a miracle. He was also assured that a journey to his own headquarters, Fort Larned, would be even more ticklish than his late ride, as the hostiles were especially thick in that direction. But the officer in command at Dodge desired to send dispatches to Larned, and as none of the other scouts were willing to take them, Will volunteered his services.

''Larned's my headquarters,'' said he, ''and I must go there anyway; so if you'll give me a good horse, I'll take your dispatches.''

''We haven't a decent horse left,'' said the officer; ''but you can take your pick of some fine government mules.''

Will made a gesture of despair. Another race on mule-back with Indians was not an inviting prospect. There were very few mules like unto his quondam mouse-colored mount. But he succumbed to the inevitable, picked out the most enterprising looking mule in the bunch, and set forth. And neither he nor the mule guessed what was in store for each of them.

At Coon Creek Will dismounted for a drink of water, and the mule embraced the opportunity to pull away, and start alone on the wagon-trail to Larned. Will did not suspect that he should have any trouble in overtaking the capricious beast, but at the end of a mile he was somewhat concerned. He had threatened and entreated, raged and cajoled. 'Twas all wasted. The mule was as deaf to prayer as to objurgation. It browsed contentedly along the even tenor of its way, so near and yet so far from the young man, who, like "panting time, toil'd after it in vain." And Larned much more than twenty miles away.

What the poet calls "the golden exhalations of the dawn" began to warm the gray of the plain. The sun was in the roots of the grass. Four miles away the lights of Larned twinkled. The only blot on a fair landscape was the mule—in the middle distance. But there was a wicked gleam in the eye of the footsore young man in the foreground.

Boom! The sunrise gun at the fort. The mule threw back its head, waved its ears, and poured forth a song of triumph, a loud, exultant bray.

Crack! Will's rifle. Down went the mule. It had made the fatal mistake of gloating over its villainy. Never again would it jeopardize the life of a rider.

It had been a thirty-five-mile walk, and every bone in Will's body ached. His shot alarmed the garrison, but he was soon on the ground with the explanation; and after turning over his dispatches, he sought his bed.

During the day General Hazen returned, under escort, from Fort Harker, with dispatches for Sheridan, and Will offered to be the bearer of them.   An army mule was suggested, but he declined to again put his life in the keeping of such an animal.   A good horse was selected, and the journey made without incident.

General Sheridan was roused at daylight to receive the scout's report, and praised Will warmly for having undertaken and safely accomplished three such long and dangerous rides.

"In all," says General Sheridan, in his Memoirs, "Cody rode three hundred and fifty miles in less than sixty hours, and such an exhibition of endurance and courage was more than enough to convince me that his services would be extremely valuable in the campaign; so I retained him at Fort Hayes until the battalion of Fifth Cavalry arrived, and then made him chief of scouts for that regiment."

CHAPTER XVII.

SATANTA, CHIEF OF THE KIOWAS.

WITHIN plain view of Fort Larned lay a large camp of Kiowas and Comanches. They were not yet bedaubed with war paint, but they were as restless as panthers in a cage, and it was only a matter of days when they would whoop and howl with the loudest.

The principal chief of the Kiowas was Satanta, a powerful and resourceful warrior, who, because of remarkable talents for speech-making, was called "The Orator of the Plains." Satanta was short and bullet-headed. Hatred for the whites swelled every square inch of his breast, but he had the deep cunning of his people, with some especially fine points of treachery learned from dealings with dishonest agents and traders. There probably never was an Indian so depraved that he could not be corrupted further by association with a rascally white man.

When the Kiowas were friendly with the government, Satanta received a guest with all the magnificence the tribe afforded. A carpet was spread for the white man to sit upon, and a folding board was set up for a table. The question of expense never intruded.

Individually, too, Satanta put on a great deal of style. Had the opportunity come to him, he would have worn a silk hat with a sack-coat, or a dress suit in the afternoon. As it was, he produced some startling effects with blankets and feathers.

It was part of General Hazen's mission to Fort Larned
to patch up a treaty with the outraged Kiowas and
Comanches, if it could be brought about.   On one warm
August morning, the general set out for Fort Zarah, on a
tour of inspection.   Zarah was on the Arkansas, in what is
now Barton County, Kansas.   An early start was made, as
it was desired to cover the thirty miles by noon.   The
general rode in a four-mule army ambulance, with an escort
of ten foot soldiers, in a four-mule escort wagon.

After dinner at Zarah the general went on to Fort
Harker, leaving orders for the scout and soldiers to return
to Larned on the following day.   But as there was nothing
to do at Fort Zarah, Will determined to return at once; so
he trimmed the sails of his mule-ship, and squared away
for Larned.

The first half of the journey was without incident, but
when Pawnee Rock was reached, events began to crowd
one another.   Some forty Indians rode out from behind the
rock and surrounded the scout.

"How? How?" they cried, as they drew near, and
offered their hands for the white man's salutation.

The braves were in war paint, and intended mischief;
but there was nothing to be lost by returning their greeting, so Will extended his hand.

One warrior seized it and gave it a violent jerk; another
caught the mule's bridle; a third pulled the revolvers from
the holsters; a fourth snatched the rifle from across the
saddle; while a fifth, for a climax, dealt Will a blow on the
head with a tomahawk that nearly stunned him.

Then the band started for the Arkansas River, lashing
the mule, singing, yelling, and whooping.   For one supposed to be stolid and taciturn, the Indian makes a good
deal of noise at times.

Across the river was a vast throng of warriors, who had finally decided to go on the war-path. Will and his captors forded the shallow stream, and the prisoner was conducted before the chiefs of the tribe, with some of whom he was acquainted.

His head throbbed from the tomahawking, but his wits were still in working order, and when asked by Satanta where he had been, he replied that he had been out searching for "whoa-haws."

He knew that the Indians had been promised a herd of "whoa-haws," as they termed cattle, and he knew, too, that the herd had not arrived, and that the Indians had been out of meat for several weeks; hence he hoped to enlist Satanta's sympathetic interest.

He succeeded. Satanta was vastly interested. Where were the cattle? Oh, a few miles back. Will had been sent forward to notify the Indians that an army of sirloin steaks was advancing upon them.

Satanta was much pleased, and the other chiefs were likewise interested. Did General Hazen say the cattle were for them? Was there a chance that the scout was mistaken?

Not a chance; and with becoming dignity Will demanded a reason for the rough treament he had received.

Oh, that was all a joke, Satanta explained. The Indians who had captured the white chief were young and frisky. They wished to see whether he was brave. They were simply testing him. It was sport—just a joke.

Will did not offer to argue the matter. No doubt an excellent test of a man's courage is to hit him over the head with a tomahawk. If he lives through it, he is brave as Agamemnon. But Will insisted mildly that it was a rough way to treat friends; whereupon Satanta read the riot act to his high-spirited young men, and bade them return the captured weapons to the scout.

The next question was, were there soldiers with the cattle? Certainly, replied Will; a large party of soldiers were escorting the succulent sirloins. This intelligence necessitated another consultation. Evidently hostilities must be postponed until after the cattle had arrived. Would Will drive the cattle to them? He would be delighted to. Did he desire that the chief's young men should accompany him? No, indeed. The soldiers, also, were high-spirited, and they migh test the bravery of the chief's young men by shooting large holes in them. It would be much better if the scout returned alone.

Satanta agreed with him, and Will recrossed the river without molestation; but, glancing over his shoulder, he noted a party of ten or fifteen young braves slowly following him. Satanta was an extremely cautious chieftain.

Will rode leisurely up the gentle slope of the river's bank, but when he had put the ridge between him and the Indian camp he pointed his mule westward, toward Fort Larned, and set it going at its best pace. When the Indians reached the top of the ridge, from where they could scan the valley, in which the advancing cattle were supposed to be, there was not a horn to be seen, and the scout was flying in an opposite direction.

They gave chase, but the mule had a good start, and when it got its second wind—always necessary in a mule—the Indian ponies gained but slowly. When Ash Creek, six miles from Larned, was reached, the race was about even, but two miles farther on, the Indians were uncomfortably close behind. The sunset gun at the fort boomed a cynical welcome to the man four miles away, flying toward it for his life.

At Pawnee Fork, two miles from the fort, the Indians had crept up to within five hundred yards. But here, on the farther bank of the stream, Will came upon a government wagon containing half a dozen soldiers and Denver Jim, a well-known scout.

The team was driven among the trees, and the men hid themselves in the bushes, and when the Indians came along they were warmly received. Two of the reds were killed; the others wheeled and rode back in safety.

In 1868 General Sheridan had taken command of all the troops in the field. He arranged what is known as the winter expeditions against the Kiowas, Comanches, Southern Cheyennes, and Arapahoes. He personally commanded the expedition which left Fort Dodge, with General Custer as chief of cavalry. General Penrose started for Fort Lyon, Colorado, and General Eugene A. Carr was ordered from the Republican River country, with the Fifth Cavalry, to Fort Wallace, Kansas. Will at this time had a company of forty scouts with General Carr's command. He was ordered by General Sheridan, when leaving Fort Lyon, to follow the trail of General Penrose's command until it was overtaken. General Carr was to proceed to Fort Lyon, and follow on the trail of General Penrose, who had started from there three weeks before, when, as Carr ranked Penrose, he would then take command of both expeditions. It was the 21st of November when Carr's expedition left Fort Lyon. The second day out they encountered a terrible snow-storm and blizzard in a place they christened "Freeze Out Cañon," by which name it is still known. As Penrose had only a pack-train and no heavy wagons, and the ground was covered with snow, it was a very difficult matter to follow his trail. But taking his general course, they finally came up with him on the south fork of the Canadian River, where they found him and his soldiers in a sorry plight, subsisting wholly on buffalo-meat. Their animals had all frozen to death.

General Carr made what is known as a supply camp, leaving Penrose's command and some of his own disabled stock therein. Taking with him the Fifth Cavalry and the best horses and pack-mules, he started south toward the main fork of the Canadian River, looking for the Indians. He was gone from the supply camp thirty days, but could not locate the main band of Indians, as they were farther to the east, where General Sheridan had located them, and had sent General Custer in to fight them, which he did, in what is known as the great battle of Wichita.

They had a very severe winter, and returned in March to Fort Lyon, Colorado.

In the spring of 1869, the Fifth Cavalry, ordered to the Department of the Platte, took up the line of march for Fort McPherson, Nebraska.

It was a large command, including seventy-six wagons for stores, ambulance wagons, and pack-mules. Those chief in authority were Colonel Royal (afterward superseded by General Carr), Major Brown, and Captain Sweetman.

The average distance covered daily was only ten miles, and when the troops reached the Solomon River there was no fresh meat in camp. Colonel Royal asked Will to look up some game.

"All right, sir," said Will. "Will you send a couple of wagons along to fetch in the meat?"

"We'll send for the game, Cody, when there's some game to send for," curtly replied the colonel.

That settled the matter, surely, and Will rode away, a trifle ruffled in temper.

He was not long in rounding up a herd of seven buffaloes, and he headed them straight for camp. As he drew
near the lines, he rode alongside his game, and brought
down one after another, until only an old bull remained.
This he killed in almost the center of the camp.

The charge of the buffaloes had nearly stampeded the
picketed horses, and Colonel Royal, who, with the other
officers, had watched the hunt, demanded, somewhat
angrily:

"What does this mean, Cody?"

"Why," said Will, "I thought, sir, I'd save you the
trouble of sending after the game."

The colonel smiled, though perhaps the other officers
enjoyed the joke more than he.

At the north fork of the Beaver, Will discovered a large
and fresh Indian trail. The tracks were scattered all over
the valley, showing that a large village had recently passed
that way. Will estimated that at least four hundred
lodges were represented; that would mean from twenty-
five hundred to three thousand warriors, squaws, and
children.

When General Carr (who had taken the command) got
the news, he followed down a ravine to Beaver Creek, and
here the regiment went into camp. Lieutenant Ward and
a dozen men were detailed to accompany Will on a reconnoissance. They followed Beaver Creek for twelve miles,
and then the lieutenant and the scout climbed a knoll for a
survey of the country. One glance took in a large Indian
village some three miles distant. Thousands of ponies were
picketed out, and small bands of warriors were seen returning from the hunt, laden with buffalo-meat.

"I think, Lieutenant," said Will, "that we have
important business at camp."

"I agree with you," said Ward. "The quicker we get out of here, the better."

When they rejoined the men at the foot of the hill, Ward dispatched a courier to General Carr, the purpose of the lieutenant being to follow slowly and meet the troops which he knew would be sent forward.

The courier rode away at a gallop, but in a few moments came riding back, with three Indians at his horse's heels. The little company charged the warriors, who turned and fled for the village.

"Lieutenant," said Will, "give me that note." And as it was passed over, he clapped spurs to his horse and started for the camp.

He had proceeded but a short distance when he came upon another party of Indians, returning to the village with buffalo-meat. Without stopping, he fired a long-range shot at them, and while they hesitated, puzzled by the action, he galloped past. The warriors were not long in recovering from their surprise, and cutting loose their meat, followed; but their ponies were tired from a long hunt, and Will's fresh horse ran away from them.

When General Carr received the lieutenant's dispatch, he ordered the bugler to sound the inspiring "Boots and Saddles," and, while two companies remained to guard the wagons, the rest of the troops hastened against the Indians.

Three miles out they were joined by Lieutenant Ward's company, and five miles more brought them within sight of a huge mass of mounted Indians advancing up the creek. These warriors were covering the retreat of their squaws, who were packing up and getting ready for hasty flight.

General Carr ordered a charge on the red line. If it were broken, the cavalry was to continue, and surround the village. The movement was successfully executed, but one officer misunderstood the order, and, charging on the left wing of the hostiles, was speedily hemmed in by some three hundred redskins. Reinforcements were dispatched to his relief, but the plan of battle was spoiled, and the remainder of the afternoon was spent in contesting the ground with the Indians, who fought for their lodges, squaws, and children with desperate and dogged courage. When night came on, the wagon-trains, which had been ordered to follow, had not put in an appearance, and, though the regiment went back to look for them, it was nine o'clock before they were reached.

Camp was broken at daybreak, and the pursuit began, but not an Indian was in sight. All the day the trail was followed. There was evidence that the Indians had abandoned everything that might hinder their flight. That night the regiment camped on the banks of the Republican, and the next morning caught a distant glimpse of the foe.

About eleven o'clock a charge was made by three hundred mounted warriors, but they were repulsed with considerable loss, and when they discovered that defeat was certain, they evaded further pursuit by breaking up into companies and scattering to all points of the compass. A large number of ponies were collected as trophies of this expedition.

BUFFALO BILL'S
Wild West Show

The show on parade, Union Square, New York City, 1884.

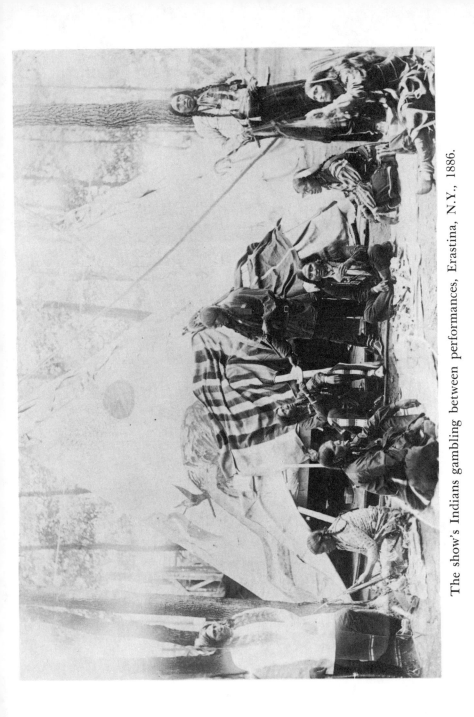

The show's Indians gambling between performances, Erastina, N.Y., 1886.

Royalty graces the Deadwood stage in London, 1887. John Nelson is on top of the coach, and Cody is standing.

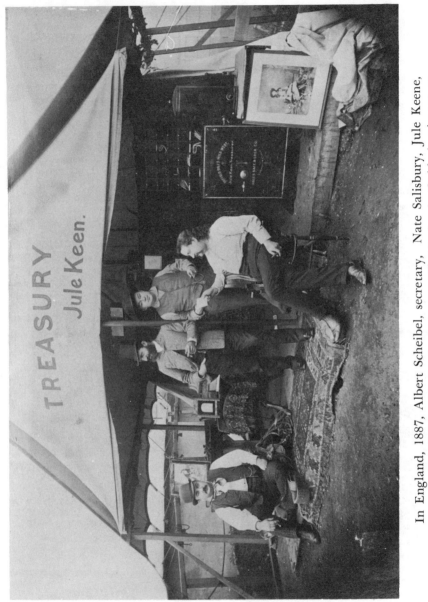

In England, 1887, Albert Scheibel, secretary, Nate Salisbury, Jule Keene, treasurer, and John Burke, press agent. That's Annie Oakley's picture at the far right.

Touring Venice, Italy in a gondola in 1887.

A group from the show photographed in Mannheim, Germany, 1890.

Unloading freight cars for another performance, 1901.

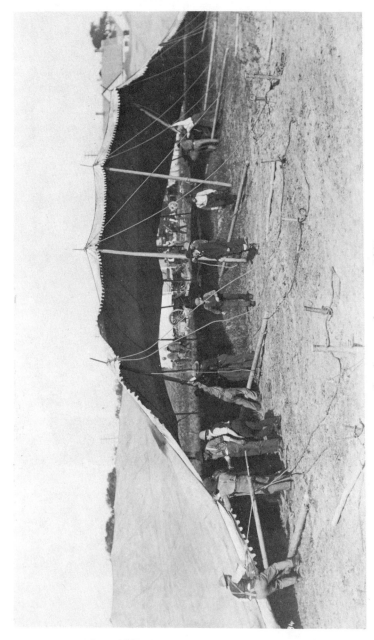

Setting up the tents, 1901.

The crowds throng to the performance, 1901.

Peeking under the tent, 1901.

Johnny Baker shows them how to hit the bullseye, upside down, 1901.

William F. Cody in 1915 with his Arabian horses, later killed by ligthning in France.

CHAPTER XVIII.

WILL MADE CHIEF OF SCOUTS.

In due time the Fifth Cavalry reached Fort McPherson, which became its headquarters while they were fitting out a new expedition to go into the Republican River country. At this time General Carr recommended to General Augur, who was in command of the Department, that Will be made chief of scouts in the Department of the Platte.

Will's fancy had been so taken by the scenery along the line of march that he proceeded to explore the country around McPherson, the result being a determination to make his future home in the Platte Valley.

Shortly after reaching the fort, the scouts' division of the Fifth Cavalry was reinforced by Major Frank North and three companies of the celebrated Pawnee scouts. These became the most interesting and amusing objects in camp, partly on account of their race, but mainly because of the bizarre dress fashions they affected. My brother, in his autobiography, describes the appearance presented by these scouts during a review of the command by Brigadier-General Duncan.

The regiment made a fine showing, the men being well drilled and thoroughly versed in tactics. The Pawnees also showed up well on drill, but their full-dress uniforms were calculated to excite even the army horses to laughter. Regular cavalry suits had been furnished them, but no two of the Pawnees seemed to agree as to the correct manner in which the various articles should be worn. As they lined up for dress parade, some of them wore heavy overcoats, others discarded even pantaloons, content with a breech-clout. Some wore large black hats, with brass accouterments, others were bareheaded. Many wore the pantaloons, but declined the shirts, while a few of the more original cut the seats from the pantaloons, leaving only leggings. Half of them were without boots or moccasins, but wore the clinking spurs with manifest pride.

They were a quaint and curious lot, but drilled remarkably well for Indians, and obeyed orders. They were devoted to their white chief, Major North, who spoke Pawnee like a native, and they were very proud of their position in the United States army. Good soldiers they made, too—hard riders, crack shots, and desperate fighters.

At the close of the parade and review referred to, the officers and the ladies attended an Indian dance, given by the Pawnees, which climaxed a rather exciting day.

The following morning an expedition moved back to the Republican River, to curb the high spirits of a band of Sioux, who had grown boldly troublesome. This was the sort of service the Pawnees welcomed, as they and the Sioux were hereditary enemies.

At the journey's end, camp was made at the mouth of the Beaver, and the Sioux were heard from within the hour. A party of them raided the mules that had been taken to the river, and the alarm was given by a herder, who dashed into camp with an arrow sticking in his shoulder.

Will did not wait to saddle his horse, but the Pawnees were as quick as he, and both of them rather surprised the Sioux, who did not expect such a swift response. Especially were they surprised to find themselves confronted by their tribal foe, the Pawnee, and they fell back hastily, closely pressed by Will and his red allies. A running fight was kept up for fifteen miles, and when many of the Sioux had been stretched upon the plain and the others scattered, the pursuing party returned to camp.

Will himself, on a fine horse, had been somewhat chagrined at being passed in the chase by a Pawnee on an inferior-looking steed. Upon inquiring of Major North, he found that the swifter horse was, like his own, government property. The Pawnee was much attached to his mount, but he was also fond of tobacco, and a few pieces of that commodity, supplemented by some other articles, induced him to exchange horses. Will named his new charge "Buckskin Joe," and rode him for four years. Joe proved a worthy successor to Brigham for speed, endurance, and intelligence.

This was the first adventure that Will and the Pawnees had pursued together, and they emerged with an increased esteem for each other. Not long afterward, Will's skill as a buffalo-hunter raised the admiration of the Indians to enthusiasm.

Twenty Pawnees that circled around one herd of buffaloes killed only twenty-two, and when the next herd came in view Will asked Major North to keep the Indians in the background while he showed them a thing or two. Buckskin Joe was a capital buffalo-hunter, and so well did he perform his part that Will brought down thirty-six, about one at every shot.

The Pawnees were delighted. They held it considerable of an achievement to kill two or three of the monarchs of the plains at a single run, and Will's feat dazzled them. He was at once pronounced a great chief, and ever after occupied a high place in their regard.

Moving up the Republican River, the troops went into camp on Black Tail Deer Fork. Scarcely were the tents pitched when a band of Indians were seen sweeping toward them at full speed, singing, yelling, and waving lances. The camp was alive in an instant, but the Pawnees, instead of preparing for defense, began to sing and yell in unison with the advancing braves. "Those are some of our own Indians," said Major North; "they've had a fight, and are bringing in the scalps."

And so it proved. The Pawnees reported a skirmish with the Sioux, in which a few of the latter had been killed.

The next day the regiment set forth upon the trail of the Sioux. They traveled rapidly, and plainly gained ground.

At every camp the print of a woman's shoe was noted among the tracks of moccasined feet. The band evidently had a white captive in tow, and General Carr, selecting the best horses, ordered a forced march, the wagon-trains to follow as rapidly as possible. Will, with six Pawnees, was to go ahead and locate the hostiles, and send back word, so that a plan of attack might be arranged before the Indian village was reached.

This village the scouts discovered among the sand-hills at Summit Springs, a few miles from the South Platte River; and while the Pawnees remained to watch, Will returned to General Carr with the news.

There was suppressed excitement all along the line, as officers and men prepared for what promised to be a lively scrimmage. The troops moved forward by a circuitous route, and reached a hill overlooking the hostile camp without their presence being dreamed of by the red men.

The bugler was ordered to sound the charge, but he was trembling with excitement, and unable to blow a note.

"Sound the charge, man!" ordered General Carr a second time; but the unhappy wight could scarcely hold his horn, much less blow it. Quartermaster Hays snatched the instrument from the flustered man's hands, and as the call rang out loud and clear the troops rushed to the attack.

Taken wholly by surprise, the Indian village went to pieces in a twinkling. A few of the Sioux mounted and rode forward to repel the assault, but they turned back in half a minute, while those that were not mounted scattered for the foothills hard by. The cavalry swept through the village like a prairie fire, and pursued the flying Indians until darkness put an end to the chase.

By the next morning the bugler had grown calm enough to sound "Boots and Saddles!" and General Carr split his force into companies, as it was discovered that the Indians had divided. Each company was to follow a separate trail.

Will made one of a band of two hundred, and for two days they dogged the red man's footsteps. At sunrise of the third day the trail ran into another, showing that the Sioux had reunited their forces. This was serious for the little company of regulars, but they went ahead, eager for a meeting with the savages.

They had not long to wait. The sun was scarcely an hour high when some six hundred Sioux were espied riding in close ranks along the bank of the Platte. The Indians discovered the troops at the same moment, and at once gave battle. The Indian is not a coward, though he frequently declines combat if the odds are not largely in his favor.

In this engagement the Sioux outnumbered the soldiers three to one, and the latter fell back slowly until they reached a ravine. Here they tethered their horses and waited the course of Indian events, which, as usual, came in circular form. The Sioux surrounded the regulars, and finding them comparatively few in number, made a gallant charge.

But bows and arrows are futile against powder and ball, and the warriors reeled back from a scathing fire, leaving a score of their number dead.

Another charge, another repulse; and then a council of war. This lasted an hour, and evidently evolved a brilliant stratagem, for the Sioux divided into two bands, and while one made a show of withdrawing, the other circled around and around the position where the soldiers lay.

At a point in this revolving belt of redskins rode a well-mounted, hadsome warrior, plainly a chief. It had been Will's experience that to lay low a chief was half the battle when fighting Indians, but this particular mogul kept just out of rifle-shot. There are, however, as many ways of killing an Indian as of killing a cat; so Will crawled on hands and knees along the ravine to a point which he thought would be within range of the chief when next he swung around the circle.

The calculation was close enough, and when the warrior came loping along, slacking his pace to cross the ravine, Will rose and fired.

It was a good four hundred yards, but the warrior pitched from his seat, and his pony ran down the ravine into the ranks of the soldiers, who were so elated over the success of the shot that they voted the animal to Will as a trophy.

The fallen warrior was Tall Bull, one of the ablest chiefs the Sioux ever had. His death so disheartened his braves that they at once retreated.

A union of General Carr's scattered forces followed, and a few days later an engagement took place in which three hundred warriors and a large number of ponies were captured. Some white captives were released, and several hundred squaws made prisoners.

Among these latter was the amiable widow of Tall Bull, who, far from cherishing animosity against Will as the slayer of her spouse, took pride in the fact that he had fallen under the fire of so great a warrior as "Pahaska," Long-haired Chief, by which name our scout was known among the Indians.

CHAPTER XIX.

ARMY LIFE AT FORT M'PHERSON.

IN the spring of 1870 Will proceeded to put into effect the determination of the previous year—to establish a home in the lovely country of the westerly Platte. After preparing quarters wherein his family might be comfortable, he obtained a leave of absence and departed for St. Louis to fetch his wife and daughter Arta, now a beautiful child of three.

The fame of "Buffalo Bill" had extended far beyond the plains, and during his month's sojourn in St. Louis he was the object of a great deal of attention. When the family prepared to depart for the frontier home, my sister-in-law wrote to me to ask if I did not wish to accompany them. I should have been delighted to accept the invitation, but at that especial time there were strong attractions for me in my childhood's home; besides, I felt that sister May, who had not enjoyed the pleasure of the St. Louis trip, was entitled to the Western jaunt.

So May made a visit to McPherson, and a delightful time she had, though she was at first inclined to quarrel with the severe discipline of army life. Will ranked with the officers, and as a result May's social companions were limited to the two daughters of General Augur, who were also on a visit to the fort. To compensate for the shortage of feminine society, however, there were a number of young unmarried officers.

Every day had its curious or enlivening incident, and May's letters to me were filled with accounts of the gayety of life at an army post. After several months I was invited to join her. She was enthusiastic over a proposed buffalo-hunt, as she desired to take part in one before her return to Leavenworth, and wished me to enjoy the sport with her.

In accepting the invitation I fixed a certain day for my arrival at McPherson, but I was delayed in my journey, and did not reach the fort until three days after the date set. May was much disturbed. She had allowed me three days for recuperation from the journey, and I had arrived on the eve of the buffalo-hunt. Naturally, I was too fatigued to rave over buffaloes, and I objected to joining the hunt; and I was encouraged in my objecting by the discovery that my brother was away on a scouting trip.

"You don't think of going buffalo-hunting without Will, do you?" I asked May.

"Why," said she, "we can never tell when he will be in camp and when away; he's off scouting nearly all the time. And we can't get up a buffalo-hunt on five minutes' notice; we must plan ahead. Our party is all ready to start, and there's a reporter here from an Omaha paper to write it up. We can't put it off, and you must go."

After that, of course, there was nothing more to be said, and when the hunting-party set forth I made one of it.

A gay party it was. For men, there were a number of officers, and the newspaper man, Dr. Frank Powell, now of La Crosse; for women, the wives of two of the officers, the daughters of General Augur, May, and myself. There was sunshine, laughter, and incessant chatter, and when one is young and fond of horseback-riding, and a handsome young officer rides by one's side, physical fatigue is apt to vanish for a time.

The fort was soon nothing but a break in the sky-line, and with a sense almost of awe I looked for the first time upon the great American Desert.   To our left, as we rode eastward, ran the swift and shallow Platte, dotted with green-garbed islands.   This river Washington Irving called "the most magnificent and the most useless of streams." "The islands," he wrote, "have the appearance of a labyrinth of groves floating on the waters.   Their extraordinary position gives an air of youth and loveliness to the whole scene.   If to this be added the undulations of the river, the waving of the verdure, the alternations of light and shade, and the purity of the atmosphere, some idea may be formed of the pleasing sensations which the traveler experiences on beholding a scene that seems to have started fresh from the hands of the Creator."

In sharp contrast was the sandy plain over which we rode.   On this grew the short, stubby buffalo-grass, the dust-colored sage-brush, and cactus in rank profusion. Over to the right, perhaps a mile away, a long range of foothills ran down to the horizon, with here and there the great cañons, through which entrance was effected to the upland country, each cañon bearing a historical or legendary name.

To my eyes the picture was as beautiful as it was novel. As far as one could see there was no sign of human habitation.   It was one vast, untenanted waste, with the touch of infinity the ocean wears.

As we began to get into the foothills, one of our equestriennes narrowly escaped a fall.   Her horse dropped a foot into a prairie-dog's hole, and came to an abrupt stop. The foot was extricated, and I was instructed in the dangers that beset the prairie voyager in these blind traps of the plain.

The trail had been ascending at a gentle grade, and we had a slight change of scene—desert hill instead of desert plain. The sand-hills rose in tiers before us, and I was informed that they were formed ages ago by the action of water. What was hard, dry ground to our horses' hoofs was once the bottom of the sea.

I was much interested in the geology of my environments; much more so than I should have been had I been told that those strange, weird hills were the haunt of the red man, who was on the war-path, and looking constantly for scalps. But these unpleasant facts were not touched upon by the officers, and in blissful ignorance we pursued the tenor of our way.

We were obliged to ride a great distance before we sighted any game, and after twenty miles had been gone over, my temporarily forgotten weariness began to reassert itself. Dr. Powell proposed that the ladies should do the shooting, but my interest in the hunt had waned. It had been several years since I had ridden a horse, and after the first few miles I was not in a suitable frame of mind or body to enjoy the most exciting hunt.

A herd of buffaloes finally came into view, and the party was instantly alive. One old bull was a little apart from the others of the herd, and was singled out for the first attack. As we drew within range, a rifle was given to May, with explicit directions as to its handling. The buffalo has but one vulnerable spot, and it is next to impossible for a novice to make a fatal shot. May fired, and perhaps her shot might be called a good one, for the animal was struck; but it was only wounded and infuriated, and dropping its shaggy head, it rushed toward us. The officers fusilladed the mountain of flesh, succeeding only in rousing it to added fury. Another rifle was handed to May, and Dr. Powell directed its aim; but terrified by the near presence of the charging bull, May discharged it at random.

Although this is strictly a narrative of facts, exercising the privilege of the novelist, we leave our present heroine in her perilous position, and return, for a space, to the fort.

Will returned from his scouting trip shortly after the departure of the hunting party, and his first query was:

"Is Nellie here?"

"Come and gone," replied his wife; and she informed him of the manner in which I had been carried off on the long-talked-of buffalo-hunt. Whereupon Will gave way to one of his rare fits of passion. The scouting trip had been long and arduous, he was tired and hungry, but also keenly anxious for our safety. He knew what we were ignorant of—that should we come clear of the not insignificant dangers attendant upon a buffalo-hunt, there remained the possibility of capture by Indians.

"I must go after them at once," said he; and off he went, without thought of rest or food. He did take time, however, to visit the officers' quarters and pour a vial of wrath upon the bewildered head of the inferior who occupied the place of the absent commandant.

"Didn't you know," cried Will, "that my continued absence meant danger in the air? Fine idea, to let a party of ladies go beyond the fort on such a foolhardy expedition before I had assured you it was safe to do so! Understand, if any harm comes to my sisters, I'll hold the government responsible!"

With which tremendous threat he mounted the swiftest

horse in camp and rode away before the astonished officer had recovered from his surprise.

He was able to track us over the sand-hills, and reached us, in accepted hero fashion, in the very nick of time. The maddened bull buffalo was charging on May, unchecked by a peppering fire from the guns of the officers. All hands were so absorbed by the intense excitement of the moment that the sound of approaching hoof-beats was unnoted. But I heard, from behind us, the crack of a rifle, and saw the buffalo fall dead almost at our feet.

The ill-humor of our rescuer dampened the ardor of the welcome we gave him. The long ride on an empty stomach had not smoothed a ripple of his ruffled temper, and we were all properly lectured. We were ordered back to the fort at once, and the command was of such a nature that no one thought of disputing it. The only question was, whether we could make the fort before being cut off by Indians. There was no time to be wasted, even in cutting meat from the tongue of the fallen buffalo. Will showed us the shortest cut for home, and himself zigzagged ahead of us, on the watch for a danger signal.

For my part, I was so worn out that I would as soon be captured by Indians, if they would agree to provide me with a wigwam wherein I might lie down and rest; but no Indians appeared. Five miles from the fort was the ranch of a wealthy bachelor, and at May's request a halt was here called. It was thought that the owner of the ranch might take pity upon my deplorable condition, and provide some sort of vehicle to convey the ladies the remainder of the journey.

We were heartily welcomed, and our bachelor host made us extremely comfortable in his cozy apartments, while he ordered supper for the party. Will considered that we were within the safety zone, so he continued on to the fort to obtain his postponed rest; and after supper the ladies rode to the fort in a carriage.

The next day's Omaha paper contained an account of the hunt from Dr. Powell's graphic pen, and in it May Cody received all the glory of the shot that laid the buffalo low. Newspaper men are usually ready to sacrifice exact facts to an innate sense of the picturesque.

At this time the fort was somewhat concerned over numerous petty crimes among the civilians, and General Emory, now chief in authority at the post, requested the county commissioners to appoint Will a justice of the peace. This was done, much to the dismay of the new justice, who, as he phrased it, "knew no more of law than a mule knows of singing." But he was compelled to bear the blushing honors thrust upon him, and his sign was posted in a conspicuous place:

WILLIAM F. CODY,

JUSTICE OF THE PEACE.

Almost the first thing he was called upon to do in his new capacity was to perform a wedding ceremony. Cold sweat stood upon his brow as he implored our aid in this desperate emergency. The big law book with which he had been equipped at his installation was ransacked in vain for the needed information. The Bible was examined more diligently, perhaps, than it had ever been by him before, but the Good Book was as unresponsive as the legal tome. "Remember your own wedding ceremony," was our advice. "Follow that as nearly as possible." But he shook his head despondently. The cool-headed scout and Indian fighter was dismayed, and the dignity of the law trembled in the balance.

To put an edge on the crisis, nearly the entire fort attended the wedding. All is well, said we, as we watched the justice take his place before the bridal pair with not a sign of trepidation. At the outset his conducting of the ceremony was irreproachable, and we were secretly con‑gratulating ourselves upon his success, when our ears were startled by the announcement:

"Whom God and Buffalo Bill hath joined together, let no man put asunder."

So far as I am informed, no man has attempted it.

Before May returned home, Will became the very proud father of a son. He had now three children, a second daughter, Orra, having been born two years before. The first boy of the family was the object of the undivided interest of the post for a time, and names by the dozen were suggested. Major North offered Kit Carson as an appropriate name for the son of a great scout and buffalo‑hunter, and this was finally settled on.

My first touch of real anxiety came with an order to Will to report at headquarters for assignment to duty. The country was alive with Indians, the officer in command informed him, and this intelligence filled me with dread. My sister-in-law had grown accustomed to her husband's excursions into danger-land, and accepted such sallies as incidents of his position. Later, I, too, learned this stoical philosophy, but at first my anxiety was so keen that Will laughed at me.

"Don't worry," said he; "the Indians won't visit the fort to-night. There's no danger of them scalping you."

"But," said I, "it is for you, not for myself, that I am

afraid. It is horrible to think of you going out alone among those foothills, which swarm with Indians."

The fort was on the prairie, but the distant foothills stretched away interminably, and these furnished favorite lurking-places for the redskins. Will drew me to a window, and pointed out the third tier of hills, some twelve or fifteen miles away.

"I would advise you," said he, "to go to bed and sleep, but if you insist on keeping awake and worrying, I will kindle a blaze on top of that hill at midnight. Watch closely. I can send up only one flash, for there will be Indian eyes unclosed as well as yours."

One may imagine with what a beating heart I stared into the darkness when the hour of twelve drew on. The night was a veil that hid a thousand terrors, but a gauzy veil, to my excited fancy, behind which passed a host of shadowy horsemen with uptossing lances. How could a man ride alone into such a gloomy, terror-haunted domain? The knights of old, who sallied forth in search of dismal ogres and noxious dragons, were not of stouter heart, and they breasted only fancied perils.

Twelve o'clock! The night had a thousand eyes, but they did not pierce the darkness of the foothills.

Ah! A thin ribbon of light curled upward for an instant, then vanished. Will was safe thus far. But there were many hours—and the darkest—before the dawn, and I carried to my bed the larger share of my forebodings.

Next day the scout came home to report the exact location of the hostile Sioux. The troops, ready for instant action, were hurled against them, and the Indians were thoroughly thrashed. A large number of chiefs were captured, among them "Red Shirt," an interesting redskin, who afterward traveled with the "Wild West."

Captive chiefs were always esteemed of great interest by the ladies of the fort. To me the braves taken in the last raid were remarkable mainly for economy of apparel and sulkiness of demeanor.

This same fall the fort was visited by a gentleman introduced as Colonel Judson, though the public knows him better as "Ned Buntline," the story-writer. He desired to accompany the scouts on a certain proposed trip, and Major Brown informed Will that the ulterior motive of the author was to project Buffalo Bill into a novel as hero.

"Now, I'd look pretty in a novel, wouldn't I?" said Will, sarcastically and blushingly.

"Yes, I think you would," returned the major, eying the other's splendid proportions critically.

Whereupon the scout blushed again, and doffed his sombrero in acknowledgment of the compliment, for—

> "'Tis pleasant, sure, to see one's name in print ;
> A book's a book, although there's nothing in't."

A retired naval officer, Ned Buntline wore a black undress military suit. His face was bronzed and rugged, determined yet kindly; he walked with a slight limp, and carried a cane. He shook Will's hand cordially when they were introduced, and expressed great pleasure in the meeting. This was the genesis of a friendship destined to work great changes in Buffalo Bill's career.

During the scouting expedition that followed, the party chanced upon an enormous bone, which the surgeon pronounced the femur of a human body. Will understood the Indian tongues well enough to be in part possession of their traditions, and he related the Sioux legend of the flood.

It was taught by the wise men of this tribe that the

earth was originally peopled by giants, who were fully three times the size of modern men. They were so swift and powerful that they could run alongside a buffalo, take the animal under one arm, and tear off a leg, and eat it as they ran. So vainglorious were they because of their own size and strength that they denied the existence of a Creator. When it lightened, they proclaimed their superiority to the lightning; when it thundered, they laughed.

This displeased the Great Spirit, and to rebuke their arrogance he sent a great rain upon the earth. The valleys filled with water, and the giants retreated to the hills. The water crept up the hills, and the giants sought safety on the highest mountains. Still the rain continued, the waters rose, and the giants, having no other refuge, were drowned.

The Great Spirit profited by his former mistake. When the waters subsided, he made a new race of men, but he made them smaller and less strong.

This tradition has been handed down from Sioux father to Sioux son since earliest ages. It shows, at least, as the legends of all races do, that the story of the Deluge is history common to all the world.

Another interesting Indian tradition bears evidence of a later origin. The Great Spirit, they say, once formed a man of clay, and he was placed in the furnace to bake, but he was subjected to the heat too long a time, and came out burnt. Of him came the negro race. At another trial the Great Spirit feared the second clay man might also burn, and he was not left in the furnace long enough. Of him came the paleface man. The Great Spirit was now in a position to do perfect work, and the third clay man was left in the furnace neither too long nor too short a time; he emerged a masterpiece, the *ne plus ultra* of creation—the noble red man.

CHAPTER XX.

ALTHOUGH the glory of killing the buffalo on our hunt was accredited to sister May, to me the episode proved of much more moment. In the spring of 1871 I was married to Mr. Jester, the bachelor ranchman at whose place we had tarried on our hurried return to the fort. His house had a rough exterior, but was substantial and commodious, and before I entered it, a bride, it was refitted in a style almost luxurious. I returned to Leavenworth to prepare for the wedding, which took place at the home of an old friend, Thomas Plowman, his daughter Emma having been my chum in girlhood.

In our home near McPherson we were five miles "in the country." Nature in primitive wildness encompassed us, but life's song never ran into a monotone. The prairie is never dull when one watches it from day to day for signs of Indians. Yet we were not especially concerned, as we were near enough to the fort to reach it on short notice, and besides our home there was another house where the ranchmen lived. With these I had little to do. My especial factotum was a negro boy, whose chief duty was to saddle my horse and bring it to the door, attend me upon my rides, and minister to my comfort generally. Poor little chap! He was one of the first of the Indians' victims.

Early one morning John, as he was called, was sent out

alone to look after the cattle.   During breakfast the clatter
of hoofs was heard, and Will rode up to inform us that the
Indians were on the war-path and massed in force just
beyond our ranch.   Back of Will were the troops, and
we were advised to ride at once to the fort.   Hastily packing a few valuables, we took refuge at McPherson, and
remained there until the troops returned with the news that
all danger was over.

Upon our return to the ranch we found that the cattle
had been driven away, and poor little John was picked up
dead on the skirts of the foothills.   The redskins had
apparently started to scalp him, but had desisted.   Perhaps they thought his wool would not make a desirable
trophy, perhaps they were frightened away.   At all events,
the poor child's scalp was left to him, though the mark of
the knife was plain.

Shortly after this episode, some capitalists from the
East visited my husband.   One of them, Mr. Bent, owned
a large share in the cattle-ranches.   He desired to visit
this ranch, and the whole party planned a hunt at the same
time.   As there were no banking facilities on the frontier,
drafts or bills of exchange would have been of no use; so
the money designed for Western investment had been
brought along in cash.   To carry this on the proposed trip
was too great a risk, and I was asked banteringly to act as
banker.   I consented readily, but imagine my perturbation
when twenty-five thousand dollars in bank-notes were
counted out and left in my care.   I had never had the
responsibility of so large a sum of money before, and com-
pared to me the man with the elephant on his hands had a
tranquil time of it.   After considering various methods for
secreting the money, I decided for the hair mattress on
my bed.   This I ripped open, inserted the envelope con-

taining the bank-notes, and sewed up the slit.   No one was aware of my trust, and I regarded it safe.

A few mornings later I ordered my pony and rode away to visit my nearest neighbor; a Mrs. Erickson, purposing later to ride to the fort and spend the day with Lou, my sister-in-law.   When I reached Mrs. Erickson's house, that good woman came out in great excitement to greet me.

"You must come right in, Mrs. Jester!" said she. "The foothills are filled with Indians on the war-path."

She handed me her field-glasses, and directed my gaze to the trail below our ranch, over which buffaloes, cattle, and Indians passed down to the Platte.   I could plainly see the warriors tramping along Indian-file, their head-feathers waving in the breeze and their blankets flapping about them as they walked.   Instantly the thought of the twenty-five thousand dollars intrusted to my care flashed across my mind.

"Oh, Mrs. Erickson," I exclaimed, "I must return to the ranch immediately!"

"You must not do so, Mrs. Jester; it's as much as your life is worth to attempt it," said she.

But I thought only of the money, and notwithstanding warning and entreaty, mounted my horse and flew back on the homeward path, not even daring to look once toward the foothills.   When I reached the house, I called to the overseer:

"The Indians are on the war-path, and the foothills are full of them!   Have two or three men ready to escort me to the fort by the time I have my valise packed."

"Why, Mrs. Jester," was the reply, "there are no Indians in sight."

"But there are," said I. "I saw them as plainly as I see you, and the Ericksons saw them, too."

"You have been the victim of a mirage," said the overseer. "Look! there are no Indians now in view."

I scanned the foothills closely, but there was no sign of a warrior. With my field-glasses I searched the entire rim of the horizon; it was tranquillity itself. I experienced a great relief, nevertheless. My nerves were so shaken that I could not remain at home; so I packed a valise, taking along the package of bank-notes, and visited another neighbor, a Mrs. McDonald, a dear friend of many years' standing, who lived nearer the fort.

This excellent woman was an old resident of the frontier. After she had heard my story, she related some of her own Indian experiences. When she first settled in her present home, there was no fort to which she could flee from Indian molestation, and she was often compelled to rely upon her wits to extricate her from dangerous situations. The story that especially impressed me was the following:

"One evening when I was alone," said Mrs. McDonald, "I became conscious that eyes were peering at me from the darkness outside my window. Flight was impossible, and my husband would not likely reach home for an hour or more. What should I do? A happy thought came to me. You know, perhaps, that Indians, for some reason, have a strange fear of a drunken woman, and will not molest one. I took from a closet a bottle filled with a dark-colored liquid, poured out a glassful and drank it. In a few minutes I repeated the dose, and then seemingly it began to take effect. I would try to walk across the room, staggering and nearly falling. I became uproariously 'happy.' I flung my arms above my head, lurched from side to side, sang a maudlin song, and laughed loudly and foolishly. The stratagem succeeded. One by one the shadowy faces at the window disappeared, and by the time my husband and the men returned there was not an Indian in the neighborhood. I became sober immediately. Molasses and water is not a very intoxicating beverage.''

I plucked up courage to return to the ranch that evening, and shortly afterward the hunting-party rode up. When I related the story of my fright, Mr. Bent complimented me upon what he was pleased to call my courage.

"You are your brother's own sister," said he. "We'll make you banker again."

"Thank you, but I do not believe you will," said I. "I have had all the experience I wish for in the banking business in this Indian country."

Upon another occasion Indians were approaching the fort from the farther side, but as we were not regarded as in danger, no warning was sent to us. The troops sallied out after the redskins, and the cunning warriors described a circle. To hide their trail they set fire to the prairie, and the hills about us were soon ablaze. The flames spread swiftly, and the smoke rolled upon us in suffocating volume. We retreated to the river, and managed to exist by dashing water upon our faces. Here we were found by soldiers sent from the fort to warn settlers of their peril, and at their suggestion we returned to the ranch, saddled horses, and rode through the dense smoke five miles to the fort. It was the most unpleasant ride of my life.

In the preceding chapter mention was made of the finding of a remarkable bone. It became famous, and in the summer of 1871 Professor Marsh, of Yale College, brought out a party of students to search for fossils. They found a number, but were not rewarded by anything the most credulous could torture into a human relic.

This summer also witnessed an Indian campaign somewhat out of the common in several of its details. More than one volume would be required to record all the adventures Scout Cody had with the Children of the Plains, most of which had so many points in common that it is necessary to touch upon only those containing incidents out of the ordinary.

An expedition, under command of General Duncan, was fitted out for the Republican River country. Duncan was a jolly officer and a born fighter. His brother officers had a story that once on a time he had been shot in the head by a cannon-ball, and that while he was not hurt a particle, the ball glanced off and killed one of the toughest mules in the army.

Perhaps it was because the Pawnees spoke so little English, and spoke that little so badly, that General Duncan insisted upon their repeating the English call, which would be something like this: "Post Number One. Nine o'clock. All's well." The Pawnee effort to obey was so ludicrous, and provocative of such profanity (which they could express passing well), that the order was countermanded.

One afternoon Major North and Will rode ahead of the command to select a site for the night's camp. They ran into a band of some fifty Indians, and were obliged to take the back track as fast as their horses could travel. Will's whip was shot from his hand and a hole put through his hat. As they sighted the advance-guard of the command, Major North rode around in a circle—a signal to the Pawnees that hostiles were near. Instantly the Pawnees broke ranks and dashed pell-mell to the relief of their white chief.

The hostiles now took a turn at retreating, and kept it up for several miles.

The troops took up the trail on the following day, and a stern chase set in. In passing through a deserted camp the troops found an aged squaw, who had been left to die. The soldiers built a lodge for her, and she was provided with sufficient rations to last her until she reached the Indian heaven, the happy hunting-grounds. She was in no haste, however, to get to her destination, and on their return the troops took her to the fort with them. Later she was sent to the Spotted Tail agency.

In September of 1871 General Sheridan and a party of friends arrived at the post for a grand hunt. Between him and Will existed a warm friendship, which continued to the close of the general's life. Great preparations were made for the hunt. General Emory, now commander of the fort, sent a troop of cavalry to meet the distinguished visitors at the station and escort them to the fort. Besides General Sheridan, there were in the party Leonard and Lawrence Jerome, Carroll Livingstone, James Gordon Bennett, J. G. Heckscher, General Fitzhugh, Schuyler Crosby, Dr. Asch, Mr. McCarthy, and other well-known men. When they reached the post they found the regiment drawn up on dress parade; the band struck up a martial air, the cavalry were reviewed by General Sheridan, and the formalities of the occasion were regarded as over.

It was Sheridan's request that Will should act as guide and scout for the hunting-party. One hundred troopers under Major Brown were detailed as escort, and the commissary department fairly bulged. Several ambulances were also taken along, for the comfort of those who might weary of the saddle.

Game was abundant, and rare sport was had. Buffalo,

elk, and deer were everywhere, and to those of the party who were new to Western life the prairie-dog villages were objects of much interest.   These villages are often of great extent.   They are made up of countless burrows, and so honeycombed is the country infested by the little animals that travel after nightfall is perilous for horses.   The dirt is heaped around the entrance to the burrows a foot high, and here the prairie-dogs, who are sociability itself, sit on their hind legs and gossip with one another.   Owls and rattlesnakes share the underground homes with the rightful owners, and all get along together famously.

When the hunting-party returned to McPherson its members voted Will a veritable Nimrod—a mighty hunter, and he was abundantly thanked for his masterly guidance of the expedition.

That winter a still more distinguished party visited the post—the Grand Duke Alexis and his friends.   As many of my readers will recall, the nobleman's visit aroused much enthusiasm in this country.   The East had wined and dined him to satiety, but wining and dining are common to all nations, and the Grand Duke desired to see the wild life of America—the Indian in his tepee and the prairie monarch in his domain, as well as the hardy frontiersman, who feared neither savage warrior nor savage beast.

The Grand Duke had hunted big game in Eastern lands, and he was a capital shot.   General ,Sheridan engineered this expedition also, and, as on the previous occasion, he relied upon Will to make it a success.   The latter received word to select a good camp on Red Willow Creek, where game was plentiful, and to make all needed arrangements for the comfort and entertainment of the noble party.   A special feature suggested by Sheridan for the amusement and instruction of the continental guests

was an Indian war-dance and Indian buffalo-hunt.   To
procure this entertainment it was necessary to visit Spotted
Tail, chief of the Sioux, and persuade him to bring over a
hundred warriors.   At this time there was peace between
the Sioux and the government, and the dance idea was
feasible; nevertheless, a visit to the Sioux camp was not
without its dangers.   Spotted Tail himself was seemingly
sincere in a desire to observe the terms of the ostensible
peace between his people and the authorities, but many of
the other Indians would rather have had the scalp of the
Long-haired Chief than a century of peace.

Will so timed his trip as to reach the Indian camp at
dusk, and hitching his horse in the timber, he wrapped his
blanket closely about him, so that in the gathering darkness he might easily pass for a warrior.   Thus invested, he
entered the village, and proceeded to the lodge of Spotted
Tail.

The conference with the distinguished redskin was made
smooth sailing by Agent Todd Randall, who happened to
be on hand, and who acted as interpreter.   The old chief
felt honored by the invitation extended to him, and readily
promised that in "ten sleeps" from that night he, with a
hundred warriors, would be present at the white man's
camp, which was to be pitched at the point where the government trail crossed Red Willow Creek.

As Spotted Tail did not repose a great amount of confidence in his high-spirited young men, he kept Will in his
own lodge through the night.   In the morning the chief
assembled the camp, and presenting his guest, asked if his
warriors knew him.

"It is Pa-has-ka, the Long-haired Chief!" they
answered.

Whereupon Spotted Tail informed them that he had

eaten bread with the Long-haired Chief, thus establishing a bond of friendship, against violating which the warriors were properly warned.

After that Will was entirely at his ease, although there were many sullen faces about him. They had long yearned for his scalp, and it was slightly irritating to find it so near and yet so far.

CHAPTER XXI.

THE HUNT OF THE GRAND DUKE ALEXIS.

A SPECIAL train brought the Grand Duke Alexis and party to North Platte on January 12, 1872. Will was presented to the illustrious visitor by General Sheridan, and was much interested in him. He was also pleased to note that General Custer made one of the party.

Will had made all the arrangements, and had everything complete when the train pulled in. As soon as the Grand Duke and party had breakfasted, they filed out to get their horses or to find seats in the ambulances. All who were mounted were arranged according to rank. Will had sent one of his guides ahead, while he was to remain behind to see that nothing was left undone. Just as they were to start, the conductor of the Grand Duke's train came up to Will and said that Mr. Thompson had not received a horse. "What Thompson?" asked Will. "Why, Mr. Frank Thompson, who has charge of the Grand Duke's train." Will looked over the list of names sent him by General Sheridan of those who would require saddle-horses, but failed to find that of Mr. Thompson. However, he did not wish to have Mr. Thompson or any one else left out. He had following him, as he always did, his celebrated war-horse, "Buckskin Joe." This horse was not a very prepossessing "insect." He was buckskin in color, and rather a sorry-looking animal, but he was known all over the frontier as the greatest long-distance and best

buffalo-horse living.   Will had never allowed any one but
himself to ride this horse, but as he had no other there at
the time, he got a saddle and bridle, had it put on old
Buckskin Joe, and told Mr. Thompson he could ride him
until he got where he could get him another.   This horse
looked so different from the beautiful animals the rest of
the party were supplied with that Mr. Thompson thought
it rather discourteous to mount him in such fashion.
However, he got on, and Will told him to follow up, as he
wanted to go ahead to where the general was.   As Mr.
Thompson rode past the wagons and ambulances he
noticed the teamsters pointing at him, and thinking the
men were guying him, rode up to one of them, and said,
"Am I not riding this horse all right?"   Mr. Thompson
felt some personal pride in his horsemanship, as he was a
Pennsylvania fox-hunter.

The driver replied, "Yes, sir; you ride all right."

"Well, then," said Thompson, "it must be this horse
you are guying."

The teamster replied:

"Guying that horse?   Not in a thousand years!'

"Well, then, why am I such a conspicuous object?"

"Why, sir, are you not the king?"

"The king?   Why did you take me for the king?'

"Because you are riding that horse.   I guess you don't
know what horse you are riding, do you?   Nobody gets to
ride that horse but Buffalo Bill.   So when we all saw you
riding him we supposed that of course you were the king,
for that horse, sir, is Buckskin Joe."

Thompson had heard General Sheridan telling about
Buckskin Joe on the way out, and how Buffalo Bill had
once run him eighty miles when the Indians were after
him.   Thompson told Will afterward that he grew about

four feet when he found out that he was riding that most celebrated horse of the plains. He at once galloped ahead to overtake Will and thank him most heartily for allowing him the honor of such a mount. Will told him that he was going to let the Grand Duke kill his first buffalo on Buckskin Joe. "Well," replied Thompson, "I want to ask one favor of you. Let me also kill a buffalo on this horse." Will replied that nothing would afford him greater pleasure. Buckskin Joe was covered with glory on this memorable hunt, as both the Grand Duke of Russia and Mr. Frank Thompson, later president of the Pennsylvania Railroad, killed their first buffalo mounted on his back, and my brother ascribes to old Joe the acquisition of Mr. Frank Thompson's name to his list of life friendships. This hunt was an unqualified success, nothing occurring to mar one day of it.

Spotted Tail was true to his promise. He and his hundred braves were on hand, shining in the full glory of war paint and feathers, and the war-dance they perfomed was of extraordinary interest to the Grand Duke and his friends. The outlandish contortions and grimaces of the Indians, their leaps and crouchings, their fiendish yells and whoops, made up a barbaric jangle of picture and sound not soon to be forgotten. To the European visitors the scene was picturesque rather than ghastly, but it was not a pleasing spectacle to the old Indian fighters looking on. There were too many suggestions of bloodshed and massacre in the past, and of bloodshed and massacre yet to come.

The Indian buffalo-hunt followed the Terpsichorean revelry, and all could enjoy the skill and strength displayed by the red huntsmen. One warrior, Two-Lance by name, performed a feat that no other living Indian could do; he sent an arrow entirely through the body of a bull running at full speed.

General Sheridan desired that the Grand Duke should carry away with him a knowledge of every phase of life on the frontier, and when the visitors were ready to drive to the railroad station, Will was requested to illustrate, for their edification, the manner in which a stagecoach and six were driven over the Rocky Mountains.

Will was delighted at the idea; so was Alexis at the outset, as he had little idea of what was in store for him. The Grand Duke and the general were seated in a closed carriage drawn by six horses, and were cautioned to fasten their hats securely on their heads, and to hang onto the carriage; then Will climbed to the driver's seat.

"Just imagine," said he to his passengers, "that fifty Indians are after us." And off went the horses, with a jump that nearly spilled the occupants of the coach into the road.

The three miles to the station were covered in just ten minutes, and the Grand Duke had the ride of his life. The carriage tossed like a ship in a gale, and no crew ever clung to a life-line with more desperate grip than did Will's passengers to their seats. Had the fifty Indians of the driver's fancy been whooping behind, he would not have plied the whip more industriously, or been deafer to the groans and ejaculations of his fares. When the carriage finally drew up with another teeth-shaking jerk, and Will, sombrero in hand, opened the coach door to inquire of his Highness how he had enjoyed the ride, the Grand Duke replied, with suspicious enthusiasm:

"I would not have missed it for a large sum of money; but rather than repeat it, I would return to Russia via

Alaska, swim Bering Strait, and finish my journey on one of your government mules."

This ride completed a trip which the noble party pronounced satisfactory in every detail. The Grand Duke invited Will into his private car, where he received the thanks of the company for his zeal and skill as pilot of a hunting-party. He was also invited by Alexis to visit him at his palace should he ever make a journey to Russia, and was, moreover, the recipient of a number of valuable souvenirs.

At that time Will had very little thought of crossing the seas, but he did decide to visit the East, whither he had more than once journeyed in fancy. The Indians were comparatively quiet, and he readily obtained a leave of absence.

The first stopping-place was Chicago, where he was entertained by General Sheridan; thence he went to New York, to be kindly received by James Gordon Bennett, Leonard and Lawrence Jerome, J. G. Heckscher, and others, who, it will be recalled, were members of the hunting-party of the preceding year. Ned Buntline also rendered his sojourn in the metropolis pleasant in many ways. The author had carried out his intention of writing a story of Western life with Scout Cody for the hero, and the result, having been dramatized, was doing a flourishing business at one of the great city's theaters. Will made one of a party that attended a performance of the play one evening, and it was shortly whispered about the house that "Buffalo Bill" himself was in the audience. It is customary to call for the author of a play, and no doubt the author of this play had been summoned before the footlights in due course, but on this night the audience demanded the hero. To respond to the call was an ordeal for which

Will was unprepared; but there was no getting out of it, and he faced a storm of applause. The manager of the performance, enterprising like all of his profession, offered Will five hundred dollars a week to remain in New York and play the part of "Buffalo Bill," but the offer was declined with thanks.

During his stay in the city Will was made the guest of honor at sundry luncheons and dinners given by his wealthy entertainers. He found considerable trouble in keeping his appointments at first, but soon caught on to the to him unreasonable hours at which New Yorkers dined, supped, and breakfasted. The sense of his social obligations lay so heavily on his mind that he resolved to balance accounts with a dinner at which he should be the host. An inventory of cash on hand discovered the sum of fifty dollars that might be devoted to playing Lucullus. Surely that would more than pay for all that ten or a dozen men could eat at one meal. "However," he said to himself, "I don't care if it takes the whole fifty. It's all in a lifetime, anyway."

In all confidence he hied him to Delmonico's, at which famous restaurant he had incurred a large share of his social obligations. He ordered the finest dinner that could be prepared for a party of twelve, and set as date the night preceding his departure for the West. The guests were invited with genuine Western hospitality. His friends had been kind to him, and he desired to show them that a man of the West could not only appreciate such things, but return them.

The dinner was a thorough success. Not an invited guest was absent. The conversation sparkled. Quip and repartee shot across the "festive board," and all went merry as a dinner-bell. The host was satisfied, and proud withal.   The next morning he approached Delmonico's cashier with an air of reckless prodigality.

"My bill, please," said he, and when he got it, he looked hard at it for several minutes.   It dawned on him gradually that his fifty dollars would about pay for one plate.   As he confided to us afterward, that little slip of paper frightened him more than could the prospect of a combat single-handed with a whole tribe of Sioux Indians.

Unsophisticated Will!   There was, as he discovered, a wonderful difference between a dinner at Delmonico's and a dinner on the plains.   For the one, the four corners of the earth are drawn upon to provide the bill of fare; for the other, all one needs is an ounce of lead and a charge of powder, a bundle of fagots and a match.

But it would never do to permit the restaurant cashier to suspect that the royal entertainer of the night before was astonished at his bill; so he requested that the account be forwarded to his hotel, and sought the open air, where he might breathe more freely.

There was but one man in New York to whom he felt he could turn in his dilemma, and that was Ned Buntline. One who could invent plots for stories, and extricate his characters from all sorts of embarrassing situations, should be able to invent a method of escape from so comparatively simple a perplexity as a tavern bill.   Will's confidence in the wits of his friend was not unfounded.   His first great financial panic was safely weathered, but how it was done I do not know to this day.

One of Will's main reasons for visiting the East was to look up our only living relatives on mother's side—Colonel Henry R. Guss and family, of Westchester, Pennsylvania. Mother's sister, who had married this gentleman, was not living, and we had never met him or any of his family.

Ned Buntline accompanied Will on his trip to West-chester.

To those who have passed through the experience of waiting in a strange drawing-room for the coming of relatives one has never seen, and of whose personality one has but the vaguest idea, there is the uncertainty of the reception. Will it be frank and hearty, or reserved and doubtful? During the few minutes succeeding the giving of his and Buntline's cards to the servant, Will rather wished that the elegant reception-room might be meta-morphosed into the Western prairie. But presently the entrance to the parlor was brightened by the loveliest girl he had ever looked upon, and following her walked a courtly, elegant gentleman. These were Cousin Lizzie and Uncle Henry. There was no doubt of the quality of the welcome; it was most cordial, and Will enjoyed a delightful visit with his relatives. For his cousin he con-ceived an instant affection. The love he had held for his mother—the purest and strongest of his affections—became the heritage of this beautiful girl.

CHAPTER XXII.

THEATRICAL EXPERIENCES.

THE Fifth Cavalry at Fort McPherson had been ordered to Arizona, and was replaced by the Third Cavalry under command of General Reynolds. Upon Will's return to McPherson he was at once obliged to take the field to look for Indians that had raided the station during his absence and carried off a considerable number of horses. Captain Meinhold and Lieutenant Lawson commanded the company dispatched to recover the stolen property. Will acted as guide, and had as an assistant T. B. Omohundro, better known by his frontier name of "Texas Jack."

Will was not long in finding Indian tracks, and accompanied by six men, he went forward to locate the redskin camp. They had proceeded but a short distance when they sighted a small party of Indians, with horses grazing. There were just thirteen Indians—an unlucky number—and Will feared that they might discover the scouting party should it attempt to return to the main command. He had but to question his companions to find them ready to follow wheresoever he might lead, and they moved cautiously toward the Indian camp.

At the proper moment the seven rushed upon the unsuspecting warriors, who sprang for their horses and gave battle. But the rattle of the rifles brought Captain Meinhold to the scene, and when the Indians saw the reinforcements coming up they turned and fled. Six of their

number were dead on the plain, and nearly all of the stolen
horses were recovered. One soldier was killed, and this
was one of the few occasions when Will received a
wound.

And now once more was the versatile plainsman called
upon to enact a new rôle. Returning from a long scout in
the fall of 1872, he found that his friends had made him a
candidate for the Nebraska legislature from the twenty-
sixth district. He had never thought seriously of politics,
and had a well-defined doubt of his fitness as a law-maker.
He made no campaign, but was elected by a flattering
majority. He was now privileged to prefix the title
"Honorable" to his name, and later this was supplanted
by "Colonel"—a title won in the Nebraska National
Guard, and which he claims is much better suited to his
attainments.

Will, unlike his father, had no taste for politics or for
political honors. I recall one answer—so characteristic of
the man—to some friends who were urging him to enter
the political arena. "No," said he, "politics are by far
too deep for me. I think I can hold my own in any fair
and no foul fight; but politics seem to me all foul and no
fair. I thank you, my friends, but I must decline to set
out on this trail, which I know has more cactus burs
to the square inch than any I ever followed on the
plains."

Meantime Ned Buntline had been nurturing an ambitious project. He had been much impressed by the fine
appearance made by Will in the New York theater, and
was confident that a fortune awaited the scout if he would
consent to enter the theatrical profession. He conceived
the idea of writing a drama entitled "The Scout of the
Plains," in which Will was to assume the title rôle and

shine as a star of the first magnitude. The bait he dangled was that the play should be made up entirely of frontier scenes, which would not only entertain the public, but instruct it.

The bait was nibbled at, and finally swallowed, but there was a proviso that Wild Bill and Texas Jack must first be won over to act as "pards" in the enterprise. He telegraphed his two friends that he needed their aid in an important business matter, and went to Chicago to meet them. He was well assured that if he had given them an inkling of the nature of the "business matter," neither would put in an appearance; but he relied on Ned Buntline's persuasive powers, which were well developed.

There had never been a time when Wild Bill and Texas Jack declined to follow Will's lead, and on a certain morning the trio presented themselves at the Palmer House in Chicago for an interview with Colonel Judson.

The author could scarcely restrain his delight. All three of the scouts were men of fine physique and dashing appearance. It was very possible that they had one or two things to learn about acting, but their inexperience would be more than balanced by their reputation and personal appearance, and the knowledge that they were enacting on the stage mock scenes of what to them had oft been stern reality.

"Don't shoot, pards!" began Will, when the conference opened. "I guess, Judson," he continued, after vainly trying to find a diplomatic explanation, "you'd better tell them what we want."

Buntline opened with enthusiasm, but he did not kindle Wild Bill and Texas Jack, who looked as if they might at any moment grab their sombreros and stampede for the frontier. Will turned the scale.

"We're bound to make a fortune at it," said he. "Try it for a while, anyway."

The upshot of a long discussion was that the scouts gave a reluctant consent to a much-dreaded venture. Will made one stipulation.

"If the Indians get on the rampage," said he, "we must be allowed leave of absence to go back and settle them."

"All right, boys," said Buntline; "that shall be put in the contract. And if you're called back into the army to fight redskins, I'll go with you."

This reply established the author firmly in the esteem of the scouts. The play was written in four hours (most playwrights allow themselves at least a week), and the actor-scouts received their "parts." Buntline engaged a company to support the stellar trio, and the play was widely advertised.

When the critical "first night" arrived, none of the scouts knew a line of his part, but each had acquired all the varieties of stage fright known to the profession. Buntline had hinted to them the possibility of something of the sort, but they had not realized to what a condition of abject dismay a man may be reduced by the sight of a few hundred inoffensive people in front of a theater curtain. It would have done them no good to have told them (as is the truth) that many experienced actors have touches of stage fright, as well as the unfortunate novice. All three declared that they would rather face a band of war-painted Indians, or undertake to check a herd of stampeding buffaloes, than face the peaceful-looking audience that was waiting to criticise their Thespian efforts.

Like almost all amateurs, they insisted on peering through the peep-holes in the curtain, which augmented their nervousness, and if the persuasive Colonel Judson had not been at their elbows, reminding them that he, also, was to take part in the play, it is more than likely they would have slipped quietly out at the stage door and bought railway passage to the West.

Presently the curtain rolled up, and the audience applauded encouragingly as three quaking six-footers, clad in buckskin, made their first bow before the footlights.

I have said that Will did not know a line of his part, nor did he when the time to make his opening speech arrived. It had been faithfully memorized, but oozed from his mind like the courage from Bob Acres's finger-tips. "Evidently," thought Buntline, who was on the stage with him, "he needs time to recover." So he asked carelessly:

"What have you been about lately, Bill?"

This gave "The Scout of the Plains" an inspiration. In glancing over the audience, he had recognized in one of the boxes a wealthy gentleman named Milligan, whom he had once guided on a big hunt near McPherson. The expedition had been written up by the Chicago papers, and the incidents of it were well known.

"I've been out on a hunt with Milligan," replied Will, and the house came down. Milligan was quite popular, but had been the butt of innumerable jokes because of his alleged scare over the Indians. The applause and laughter that greeted the sally stocked the scout with confidence, but confidence is of no use if one has forgotten his part. It became manifest to the playwright-actor that he would have to prepare another play in place of the one he had expected to perform, and that he must prepare it on the spot.

"Tell us about it, Bill," said he, and the prompter groaned.

One of the pleasures of frontier life consists in telling stories around the camp-fire. A man who ranks as a good frontiersman is pretty sure to be a good raconteur. Will was at ease immediately, and proceeded to relate the story of Milligan's hunt in his own words. That it was amusing was attested by the frequent rounds of applause. The prompter, with a commendable desire to get things running smoothly, tried again and again to give Will his cue, but even cues had been forgotten.

The dialogue of that performance must have been delightfully absurd. Neither Texas Jack nor Wild Bill was able to utter a line of his part during the entire evening. In the Indian scenes, however, they scored a great success; here was work that did not need to be painfully memorized, and the mock red men were slain at an astonishing rate.

Financially the play proved all that its projectors could ask for. Artistically—well, the critics had a great deal of fun with the hapless dramatist. The professionals in the company had played their parts acceptably, and, oddly enough, the scouts were let down gently in the criticisms; but the critics had no means of knowing that the stars of the piece had provided their own dialogue, and poor Ned Buntline was plastered with ridicule. It had got out that the play was written in four hours, and in mentioning this fact, one paper wondered, with delicate sarcasm, what the dramatist had been doing all that time. Buntline had played the part of "Gale Durg," who met death in the second act, and a second paper, commenting on this, suggested that it would have been a happy consummation had the death occurred before the play was written. A third critic pronounced it a drama that might be begun in the middle and played both ways, or played backward, quite as well as the way in which it had been written.

However, nothing succeeds like success. A number of

managers offered to take hold of the company, and others asked for entrance to the enterprise as partners. Ned Buntline took his medicine from the critics with a smiling face, for "let him laugh who wins."

The scouts soon got over their stage fright, in the course of time were able to remember their parts, and did fully their share toward making the play as much of a success artistically as it was financially. From Chicago the company went to St. Louis, thence to Cincinnati and other large cities, and everywhere drew large and appreciative houses.

When the season closed, in Boston, and Will had made his preparations to return to Nebraska, an English gentleman named Medley, presented himself, with a request that the scout act as guide on a big hunt and camping trip through Western territory. The pay offered was liberal— a thousand dollars a month and expenses—and Will accepted the offer. He spent that summer in his old occupation, and the ensuing winter continued his tour as a star of the drama. Wild Bill and Texas Jack consented again to "support" him, but the second season proved too much for the patience of the former, and he attempted to break through the contract he had signed for the season. The manager, of course, refused to release him, but Wild Bill conceived the notion that under certain circumstances the company would be glad to get rid of him.

That night he put his plan into execution by discharging his blank cartridges so near the legs of the dead Indians on the stage that the startled "supers" came to life with more realistic yells than had accompanied their deaths. This was a bit of "business" not called for in the playbook, and while the audience was vastly entertained, the management withheld its approval.

Will was delegated to expostulate with the reckless Indian-slayer; but Wild Bill remarked calmly that he "hadn't hurt the fellows any," and he continued to indulge in his innocent pastime.

Severe measures were next resorted to. He was informed that he must stop shooting the Indians after they were dead, or leave the company. This was what Wild Bill had hoped for, and when the curtain went up on the next performance he was to be seen in the audience, enjoying the play for the first time since he had been mixed up with it.

Will sympathized with his former "support," but he had a duty to perform, and faithfully endeavored to persuade the recreant actor to return to the company. Persuasion went for nothing, so the contract was annulled, and Wild Bill returned to his beloved plains.

The next season Will removed his family to Rochester, and organized a theatrical company of his own. There was too much artificiality about stage life to suit one that had been accustomed to stern reality, and he sought to do away with this as much as possible by introducing into his own company a band of real Indians. The season of 1875-76 opened brilliantly; the company played to crowded houses, and Will made a large financial success.

One night in April, when the season was nearing its close, a telegram was handed to him, just as he was about to step upon the stage. It was from his wife, and summoned him to Rochester, to the bedside of his only son, Kit Carson Cody. He consulted with his manager, and it was arranged that after the first act he should be excused, that he might catch the train.

That first act was a miserable experience, though the audience did not suspect that the actor's heart was almost stopped by fear and anxiety. He caught his train, and the manager, John Burke, an actor of much experience, played out the part.

It was, too, a miserable ride to Rochester, filled up with the gloomiest of forebodings, heightened by memories of every incident in the precious little life now in danger.

Kit was a handsome child, with striking features and curly hair. His mother always dressed him in the finest clothes, and tempted by these combined attractions, gypsies had carried him away the previous summer. But Kit was the son of a scout, and his young eyes were sharp. He marked the trail followed by his captors, and at the first opportunity gave them the slip and got safely home, exclaiming as he toddled into the sobbing family circle, "I tumed back adain, mama; don't cry." Despite his anxiety, Will smiled at the recollection of the season when his little son had been a regular visitor at the theater. The little fellow knew that the most important feature of a dramatic performance, from a management's point of view, is a large audience. He watched the seats fill in keen anxiety, and the moment the curtain rose and his father appeared on the stage, he would make a trumpet of his little hands, and shout from his box, "Good house, papa!" The audience learned to expect and enjoy this bit of by-play between father and son. His duty performed, Kit settled himself in his seat, and gave himself up to undisturbed enjoyment of the play.

When Will reached Rochester he found his son still alive, though beyond the reach of medical aid. He was burning up with fever, but still conscious, and the little arms were joyfully lifted to clasp around his father's neck. He lingered during the next day and into the night, but the end came, and Will faced a great sorrow of his life.

He had built fond hopes for his son, and in a breath they had been swept away. His boyhood musings over the prophecy of the fortune-teller had taken a turn when his own boy was born. It might be Kit's destiny to become President of the United States; it was not his own. Now, hope and fear had vanished together, the fabric of the dream had dissolved, and left "not a rack behind."

Little Kit was laid to rest in Mount Hope Cemetery, April 24, 1876. He is not dead, but sleeping; not lost, but gone before. He has joined the innumerable company of the white-souled throng in the regions of the blest. He has gone to aid my mother in her mission unfulfilled—that of turning heavenward the eyes of those that loved them so dearly here on earth.

CHAPTER XXIII.

THE GOVERNMENT'S INDIAN POLICY.

VERY glad was the sad-hearted father that the theatrical season was so nearly over. The mummeries of stage life were more distasteful to him than ever when he returned to his company with his crushing grief fresh upon him. He played nightly to crowded houses, but it was plain that his heart was not in his work. A letter from Colonel Mills, informing him that his services were needed in the army, came as a welcome relief. He canceled his few remaining dates, and disbanded his company with a substantial remuneration.

This was the spring of the Centennial year. It has also been called the "Custer year," for during that summer the gallant general and his heroic Three Hundred fell in their unequal contest with Sitting Bull and his warriors.

Sitting Bull was one of the ablest chiefs and fighters the Sioux nation ever produced. He got his name from the fact that once when he had shot a buffalo he sprang astride of it to skin it, and the wounded bull rose on its haunches with the Indian on its back. He combined native Indian cunning with the strategy and finesse needed to make a great general, and his ability as a leader was conceded alike by red and white man. A dangerous man at best, the wrongs his people had suffered roused all his Indian cruelty, vindictiveness, hatred, and thirst for revenge.

The Sioux war of 1876 had its origin, like most of its predecessors and successors, in an act of injustice on the part of the United States government and a violation of treaty rights.

In 1868 a treaty had been made with the Sioux, by which the Black Hills country was reserved for their exclusive use, no settling by white men to be allowed. In 1874 gold was discovered, and the usual gold fever was followed by a rush of whites into the Indian country. The Sioux naturally resented the intrusion, and instead of attempting to placate them, to the end that the treaty might be revised, the government sent General Custer into the Black Hills with instructions to intimidate the Indians into submission. But Custer was too wise, too familar with Indian nature, to adhere to his instructions to the letter. Under cover of a flag of truce a council was arranged. At this gathering coffee, sugar, and bacon were distributed among the Indians, and along with those commodities Custer handed around some advice. This was to the effect that it would be to the advantage of the Sioux if they permitted the miners to occupy the gold country. The coffee, sugar, and bacon were accepted thankfully by Lo, but no nation, tribe, or individual since the world began has ever welcomed advice. It was thrown away on Lo. He received it with such an air of indifference and in such a stoical silence that General Custer had no hope his mission had succeeded.

In 1875 General Crook was sent into the Hills to make a farcical demonstration of the government's desire to maintain good faith, but no one was deceived, the Indians least of all. In August Custer City was laid out, and in two weeks its population numbered six hundred. General Crook drove out the inhabitants, and as he marched tri-

umphantly out of one end of the village the people marched
in again at the other.

The result of this continued bad faith was inevitable;
everywhere the Sioux rose in arms.   Strange as it might
seem to one who has not followed the government's remarkable Indian policy, it had dispensed firearms to the Indians with a generous hand.   The government's Indian
policy, condensed, was to stock the red man with rifles
and cartridges, and then provide him with a first-class
reason for using them against the whites.   During May,
June, and July of that year the Sioux had received 1,120
Remington and Winchester rifles and 13,000 rounds of
patent ammunition.   During that year they received several thousand stands of arms and more than a million
rounds of ammunition, and for three years before that they
had been regularly supplied with weapons.   The Sioux
uprising of 1876 was expensive for the government.   One
does not have to go far to find the explanation.

Will expected to join General Crook, but on reaching
Chicago he found that General Carr was still in command
of the Fifth Cavalry, and had sent a request that Will
return to his old regiment.   Carr was at Cheyenne; thither
Will hastened at once.   He was met at the station by Captain Charles King, the well-known author, and later serving
as brigadier-general at Manila, then adjutant of the regiment.
As the pair rode into camp the cry went up, "Here comes
Buffalo Bill!"   Three ringing cheers expressed the delight
of the troopers over his return to his old command, and
Will was equally delighted to meet his quondam companions.   He was appointed guide and chief of scouts, and
the regiment proceeded to Laramie.   From there they
were ordered into the Black Hills country, and Colonel
Merritt replaced General Carr.

The incidents of Custer's fight and fall are so well known that it is not necessary to repeat them here. It was a better fight than the famous charge of the Light Brigade at Balaklava, for not one of the three hundred came forth from the "jaws of death." As at Balaklava, "some one had blundered," not once, but many times, and Custer's command discharged the entire debt with their lifeblood.

When the news of the tragedy reached the main army, preparations were made to move against the Indians in force. The Fifth Cavalry was instructed to cut off, if possible, eight hundred Cheyenne warriors on their way to join the Sioux, and Colonel Wesley Merritt, with five hundred men, hastened to Hat, or War-Bonnet, Creek, purposing to reach the trail before the Indians could do so. The creek was reached on the 17th of July, and at daylight the following morning Will rode forth to ascertain whether the Cheyennes had crossed the trail. They had not, but that very day the scout discerned the warriors coming up from the south.

Colonel Merritt ordered his men to mount their horses, but to remain out of sight, while he, with his adjutant, Charles King, accompanied Will on a tour of observation. The Cheyennes came directly toward the troops, and presently fifteen or twenty of them dashed off to the west along the trail the army had followed the night before. Through his glass Colonel Merritt remarked two soldiers on the trail, doubtless couriers with dispatches, and these the Indians manifestly designed to cut off. Will suggested that it would be well to wait until the warriors were on the point of charging the couriers, when, if the colonel were willing, he would take a party of picked men and cut off the hostile delegation from the main body, which was just coming over the divide.

The colonel acquiesced, and Will, galloping back to

camp, returned with fifteen men.   The couriers were some
four hundred yards away, and their Indian pursuers two
hundred behind them.   Colonel Merritt gave the word to
charge, and Will and his men skurried toward the redskins.

In the skirmish that ensued three Indians were killed.
The rest started for the main band of warriors, who had
halted to watch the fight, but they were so hotly pursued
by the soldiers that they turned at a point half a mile distant from Colonel Merritt, and another skirmish took place.

Here something a little out of the usual occurred—a
challenge to a duel.   A warrior, whose decorations and
war-bonnet proclaimed him a chief, rode out in front of his
men, and called out in his own tongue, which Will could
understand:

"I know you, Pa-has-ka! Come and fight me, if you
want to fight!"

Will rode forward fifty yards, and the warrior advanced
a like distance.   The two rifles spoke, and the Indian's
horse fell; but at the same moment Will's horse stumbled
into a gopher-hole and threw its rider.   Both duelists were
instantly on their feet, confronting each other across a
space of not more than twenty paces.   They fired again
simultaneously, and though Will was unhurt, the Indian
fell dead.

The duel over, some two hundred warriors dashed up
to recover the chieftain's body and to avenge his death.
It was now Colonel Merritt's turn to move.   He dispatched
a company of soldiers to Will's aid, and then ordered the
whole regiment to the charge.   As the soldiers advanced,
Will swung the Indian's topknot and war-bonnet which he
had secured, and shouted, "The first scalp for Custer!"

The Indians made a stubborn resistance, but as they
found this useless, began a retreat toward Red Cloud

agency, whence they had come.   The retreat continued
for thirty-five miles, the troops following into the agency.
The fighting blood of the Fifth was at fever heat, and they
were ready to encounter the thousands of warriors at the
agency should they exhibit a desire for battle.   But they
manifested no such desire.

Will learned that the name of the chief he had killed
that morning was "Yellow Hand."   He was the son of
"Cut Nose," a leading spirit among the Cheyennes.   This
old chieftain offered Will four mules if he would return the
war-bonnet and accouterments worn by the young warrior
and captured in the fight, but Will did not grant the
request, much as he pitied Cut Nose in his grief.

The Fifth Cavalry on the following morning started on
its march to join General Crook's command in the Big
Horn Mountains.   The two commands united forces on
the 3d of August, and marched to the confluence of the
Powder River with the Yellowstone.   Here General Miles
met them, to report that no Indians had crossed the stream.

No other fight occurred; but Will made himself useful
in his capacity of scout.   There were many long, hard
rides, carrying dispatches that no one else would volunteer
to bear.   When he was assured that the fighting was all
over, he took passage, in September, on the steamer "Far
West," and sailed down the Missouri.

People in the Eastern States were wonderfully interested in the stirring events on the frontier, and Will conceived the idea of putting the incidents of the Sioux war
upon the stage.   Upon his return to Rochester he had a
play written for his purpose, organized a company, and
opened his season.   Previously he had paid a flying visit
to Red Cloud agency, and induced a number of Sioux
Indians to take part in his drama.

The red men had no such painful experience as Wild Bill and Texas Jack. All they were expected to do in the way of acting was what came natural to them. Their part was to introduce a bit of "local color," to give a war-dance, take part in a skirmish, or exhibit themselves in some typical Indian fashion.

At the close of this season Will bought a large tract of land near North Platte, and started a cattle-ranch. He already owned one some distance to the northward, in partnership with Major North, the leader of the Pawnee scouts. Their friendship had strengthened since their first meeting, ten years before.

In this new ranch Will takes great pride. He has added to its area until it now covers seven thousand acres, and he has developed its resources to the utmost. Twenty-five hundred acres are devoted to alfalfa and twenty-five hundred sown to corn. One of the features of interest to visitors is a wooded park, containing a number of deer and young buffaloes. Near the park is a beautiful lake. In the center of the broad tract of land stands the picturesque building known as "Scout's Rest Ranch," which, seen from the foothills, has the appearance of an old castle.

The ranch is one of the most beautiful spots that one can imagine, and is, besides, an object-lesson in the value of scientific investigation and experiment joined with persistence and perseverance. When Will bought the property he was an enthusiastic believer in the possibilities of Nebraska development. His brother-in-law, Mr. Goodman, was put in charge of the place.

The whole Platte Valley formed part of the district once miscalled the Great American Desert. It was an idea commonly accepted, but, as the sequel proved, erroneous, that lack of moisture was the cause of lack of vegetation.

An irrigating ditch was constructed on the ranch, trees were planted, and it was hoped that with such an abundance of moisture they would spring up like weeds. Vain hope! There was "water, water everywhere," but not a tree would grow.

Will visited his old Kansas home, and the sight of tall and stately trees filled him with a desire to transport some of this beauty to his Nebraska ranch.

"I'd give five hundred dollars," said he, "for every tree I had like that in Nebraska!"

Impressed by the proprietor's enthusiasm for arboreal development, Mr. Goodman began investigation and experiment. It took him but a short time to acquire a knowledge of the deficiencies of the soil, and this done, the bigger half of the problem was solved.

Indian legend tells us that this part of our country was once an inland sea. There is authority for the statement that to-day it is a vast subterranean reservoir, and the conditions warrant the assertion. The soil in all the region has a depth only of from one to three feet, while underlying the shallow arable deposit is one immense bedrock, varying in thickness, the average being from three to six feet. Everywhere water may be tapped by digging through the thin soil and boring through the rock formation. The country gained its reputation as a desert, not from lack of moisture, but from lack of soil. In the pockets of the foothills, where a greater depth of soil had accumulated from the washings of the slopes above, beautiful little groves of trees might be found, and the islands of the Platte River were heavily wooded. Everywhere else was a treeless waste.

The philosophy of the transformation from sea to plain is not fully understood. The most tenable theory yet advanced is that the bedrock is an alkaline deposit, left by the waters in a gradually widening and deepening margin. On this the prairie wind sifted its accumulation of dust, and the rain washed down its quota from the bank above. In the slow process of countless years the rock formation extended over the whole sea; the alluvial deposit deepened; seeds lodged in it, and the buffalo-grass and sage-brush began to grow, their yearly decay adding to the ever-thickening layer of soil.

Having learned the secret of the earth, Mr. Goodman devoted himself to the study of the trees. He investigated those varieties having lateral roots, to determine which would flourish best in a shallow soil. He experimented, he failed, and he tried again. All things come round to him who will but work. Many experiments succeeded the first, and many failures followed in their train. But at last, like Archimedes, he could cry "Eureka! I have found it!" In a very short time he had the ranch charmingly laid out with rows of cottonwoods, box-elder, and other members of the tree family. The ranch looked like an oasis in the desert, and neighbors inquired into the secret of the magic that had worked so marvelous a transformation. The streets of North Platte are now beautiful with trees, and adjoining farms grow many more. It is "Scout's Rest Ranch," however, that is pointed out with pride to travelers on the Union Pacific Railroad.

Mindful of his resolve to one day have a residence in North Platte, Will purchased the site on which his first residence was erected. His family had sojourned in Rochester for several years, and when they returned to the West the new home was built according to the wishes and under the supervision of the wife and mother. To the dwelling was given the name "Welcome Wigwam,"

CHAPTER XXIV.

LITERARY WORK.

IT was during this period of his life that my brother's first literary venture was made. As the reader has seen, his school-days were few in number, and as he told Mr. Majors, in signing his first contract with him, he could use a rifle better than a pen. A life of constant action on the frontier does not leave a man much time for acquiring an education; so it is no great wonder that the first sketch Will wrote for publication was destitute of punctuation and short of capitals in many places. His attention was directed to these shortcomings, but Western life had cultivated a disdain for petty things.

"Life is too short," said he, "to make big letters when small ones will do; and as for punctuation, if my readers don't know enough to take their breath without those little marks, they'll have to lose it, that's all."

But in spite of his jesting, it was characteristic of him that when he undertook anything he wished to do it well. He now had leisure for study, and he used it to such good advantage that he was soon able to send to the publishers a clean manuscript, grammatical, and well spelled, capitalized, and punctuated. The publishers appreciated the improvement, though they had sought after his work in its crude state, and paid good prices for it.

Our author would never consent to write anything except actual scenes from border life. As a sop to the

Cerberus of sensationalism, he did occasionally condescend to heighten his effects by exaggeration. In sending one story to the publisher he wrote:

"I am sorry to have to lie so outrageously in this yarn. My hero has killed more Indians on one war-trail than I have killed in all my life. But I understand this is what is expected in border tales. If you think the revolver and bowie-knife are used too freely, you may cut out a fatal shot or stab wherever you deem it wise."

Even this story, which one accustomed to border life confessed to be exaggerated, fell far short of the sensational and blood-curdling tales usually written, and was published exactly as the author wrote it.

During the summer of 1877 I paid a visit to our relatives in Westchester, Pennsylvania. My husband had lost all his wealth before his death, and I was obliged to rely upon my brother for support. To meet a widespread demand, Will this summer wrote his autobiography. It was published at Hartford, Connecticut, and I, anxious to do something for myself, took the general agency of the book for the state of Ohio, spending a part of the summer there in pushing its sale. But I soon tired of a business life, and turning over the agency to other hands, went from Cleveland to visit Will at his new home in North Platte, where there were a number of other guests at the time.

Besides his cattle-ranch in the vicinity of North Platte, Will had another ranch on the Dismal River, sixty-five miles north, touching the Dakota line. One day he remarked to us:

"I'm sorry to leave you to your own resources for a few days, but I must take a run up to my ranch on Dismal River."

Not since our early Kansas trip had I had an experience

in camping out, and in those days I was almost too young to appreciate it; but it had left me with a keen desire to try it again.

"Let us all go with you, Will," I exclaimed. "We can camp out on the road."

Our friends added their approval, and Will fell in with the suggestion at once.

"There's no reason why you can't go if you wish to," said he. Will owned numerous conveyances, and was able to provide ways and means to carry us all comfortably. Lou and the two little girls, Arta and Orra, rode in an open phaëton. There were covered carriages, surreys, and a variety of turn-outs to transport the invited guests. Several prominent citizens of North Platte were invited to join the party, and when our arrangements were completed we numbered twenty-five.

Will took a caterer along, and made ample provisions for the inner man and woman. He knew, from long experience, that a camping trip without an abundance of food is rather a dreary affair.

All of us except Will were out for pleasure solely, and we found time to enjoy ourselves even during the first day's ride of twenty-five miles. As we looked around at the new and wild scenes while the tents were pitched for the night, Will led the ladies of the party to a tree, saying:

"You are the first white women whose feet have trod this region. Carve your names here, and celebrate the event."

After a good night's rest and a bounteous breakfast, we set out in high spirits, and were soon far out in the foot-hills.

One who has never seen these peculiar formations can have but little idea of them. On every side, as far as the

eye can see, undulations of earth stretch away like the
waves of the ocean, and on them no vegetation flourishes
save buffalo-grass, sage-brush, and the cactus, blooming
but thorny.

The second day I rode horseback, in company with
Will and one or two others of the party, over a constant
succession of hill and vale; we mounted an elevation and
descended its farther side, only to be confronted by another
hill. The horseback party was somewhat in advance of
those in carriages.

From the top of one hill Will scanned the country with
his field-glass, and remarked that some deer were headed
our way, and that we should have fresh venison for dinner.
He directed us to ride down into the valley and tarry
there, so that we might not startle the timid animals, while
he continued part way up the hill and halted in position to
get a good shot at the first one that came over the knoll.
A fawn presently bounded into view, and Will brought his
rifle to his shoulder; but much to our surprise, instead of
firing, dropped the weapon to his side. Another fawn
passed him before he fired, and as the little creature
fell we rode up to Will and began chaffing him unmercifully,
one gentleman remarking:

"It is difficult to believe we are in the presence of the
crack shot of America, when we see him allow two deer to
pass by before he brings one down."

But to the laughing and chaffing Will answered not a
word, and recalling the childish story I had heard of his
buck fever, I wondered if, at this late date, it were possible for him to have another attack of that kind. The
deer was handed over to the commissary department, and
we rode on.

"Will, what was the matter with you just now?" I

asked him, privately. "Why didn't you shoot that first deer; did you have another attack like you had when you were a little boy?"

He rode along in silence for a few moments, and then turned to me with the query:

"Did you ever look into a deer's eyes?" And as I replied that I had not, he continued:

"Every one has his little weakness; mine is a deer's eye. I don't want you to say anything about it to your friends, for they would laugh more than ever, but the fact is I have never yet been able to shoot a deer if it looked me in the eye. With a buffalo, or a bear, or an Indian, it is different. But a deer has the eye of a trusting child, soft, gentle, and confiding. No one but a brute could shoot a deer if he caught that look. The first that came over the knoll looked straight at me; I let it go by, and did not look at the second until I was sure it had passed me."

He seemed somewhat ashamed of his soft-heartedness; yet to me it was but one of many little incidents that revealed a side of his nature the rough life of the frontier had not corrupted.

Will expected to reach the Dismal River on the third day, and at noon of it he remarked that he had better ride ahead and give notice of our coming, for the man who looked after the ranch had his wife with him, and she would likely be dismayed at the thought of preparing supper for so large a crowd on a minute's notice.

Sister Julia's son, Will Goodman, a lad of fifteen, was of our party, and he offered to be the courier.

"Are you sure you know the way?" asked his uncle.

"Oh, yes," was the confident response; "you know I have been over the road with you before, and I know just how to go."

"Well, tell me how you would go."

Young Will described the trail so accurately that his uncle concluded it would be safe for him to undertake the trip, and the lad rode ahead, happy and important.

It was late in the afternoon when we reached the ranch, and the greeting of the overseer was:

"Well, well; what's all this?"

"Didn't you know we were coming?" asked Will, quickly. "Hasn't Will Goodman been here?" The ranchman shook his head.

"Haven't seen him, sir," he replied, "since he was here with you before."

"Well, he'll be along," said Will, quietly; but I detected a ring of anxiety in his voice. "Go into the house and make yourselves comfortable," he added. "It will be some time before a meal can be prepared for such a supper party." We entered the house, but he remained outside, and mounting the stile that served as a gate, examined the nearer hills with his glass. There was no sign of Will, Jr.; so the ranchman was directed to dispatch five or six men in as many directions to search for the boy, and as they hastened away on their mission Will remained on the stile, running his fingers every few minutes through the hair over his forehead—a characteristic action with him when worried. Thinking I might reassure him, I came out and chided him gently for what I was pleased to regard as his needless anxiety. It was impossible for Willie to lose his way very long, I explained, without knowing anything about my subject. "See how far you can look over these hills. It is not as if he were in the woods," said I.

Will looked at me steadily and pityingly for a moment. "Go back in the house, Nell," said he, with a touch of impatience; "you don't know what you are talking about."

That was true enough, but when I returned obediently to the house I repeated my opinion that worry over the absent boy was needless, for it would be difficult, I declared, for one to lose himself where the range of vision was so extensive as it was from the top of one of these foothills.

"But suppose," said one of the party, "that you were in the valley behind one of the foothills—what then?"

This led to an animated discussion as to the danger of getting lost in this long-range locality, and in the midst of it Will walked in, his equanimity quite restored.

"It's all right," said he; "I can see the youngster coming along."

We flocked to the stile, and discovered a moving speck in the distance. Looked at through the field-glasses, it proved to be the belated courier. Then we appealed to Will to settle the question that had been under discussion.

"Ladies and gentlemen," he answered, impressively, "if one of you were lost among these foothills, and a whole regiment started out in search of you, the chances are ten to one that you would starve to death, to say the least, before you could be found."

To find the way with ease and locate the trail unerringly over an endless and monotonous succession of hills identical in appearance is an ability the Indian possesses, but few are the white men that can imitate the aborigine. I learned afterward that it was accounted one of Will's great accomplishments as a scout that he was perfectly at home among the frozen waves of the prairie ocean.

When the laggard arrived, and was pressed for particulars, he declared he had traveled eight or ten miles when he found that he was off the trail. "I thought I was lost," said he; "but after considering the matter I decided that I had one chance—that was to go back over my own tracks. The marks of my horse's hoofs led me out on the main trail, and your tracks were so fresh that I had no further trouble.''

"Pretty good," said Will, patting the boy's shoulder. "Pretty good. You have some of the Cody blood in you, that's plain.''

The next day was passed in looking over the ranch, and the day following we visited, at Will's solicitation, a spot that he had named "The Garden of the Gods." Our thoughtful host had sent ranchmen ahead to prepare the place for our reception, and we were as surprised and delighted as he could desire. A patch on the river's brink was filled with tall and stately trees and luxuriant shrubs, laden with fruits and flowers, while birds of every hue nested and sang about us. It was a miniature paradise in the midst of a desert of sage-brush and buffalo-grass. The interspaces of the grove were covered with rich green grass, and in one of these nature-carpeted nooks the workmen, under Will's direction, had put up an arbor, with rustic seats and table. Herein we ate our luncheon, and every sense was pleasured.

As it was not likely that the women of the party would ever see the place again, so remote was it from civilization, belonging to the as yet uninhabited part of the Western plains, we decided to explore it, in the hope of finding something that would serve as a souvenir. We had not gone far when we found ourselves out of Eden and in the desert that surrounded it, but it was the desert that held our great discovery. On an isolated elevation stood a lone, tall tree, in the topmost branches of which reposed what seemed to be a large package. As soon as our imaginations got fairly to work the package became the hidden treasure of some prairie bandit, and while two of the party returned for our masculine forces the rest of us kept guard over the cachet in the treetop. Will came up with the others, and when we pointed out to him the supposed chest of gold he smiled, saying that he was sorry to dissipate the hopes which the ladies had built in the tree, but that they were not gazing upon anything of intrinsic value, but on the open sepulcher of some departed brave. "It is a wonder," he remarked, laughingly, "you women didn't catch on to the skeleton in that closet."

As we retraced our steps, somewhat crestfallen, we listened to the tale of another of the red man's superstitions.

When some great chief, who particularly distinguishes himself on the war-path, loses his life on the battle-field without losing his scalp, he is regarded as especially favored by the Great Spirit. A more exalted sepulcher than mother earth is deemed fitting for such a warrior. Accordingly he is wrapped in his blanket-shroud, and, in his war paint and feathers and with his weapons by his side, he is placed in the top of the highest tree in the neighborhood, the spot thenceforth being sacred against intrusion for a certain number of moons. At the end of that period messengers are dispatched to ascertain if the remains have been disturbed. If they have not, the departed is esteemed a spirit chief, who, in the happy hunting-grounds, intercedes for and leads on to sure victory the warriors who trusted to his leadership in the material world.

We bade a reluctant adieu to the idyllic retreat, and threw it many a backward glance as we took our way over the desert that stretched between us and the ranch. Here another night was passed, and then we set out for home. The brief sojourn "near to Nature's heart" had been a delightful experience, holding for many of us the charm of novelty, and for all recreation and pleasant comradeship.

With the opening of the theatrical season Will returned to the stage, and his histrionic career continued for five years longer. As an actor he achieved a certain kind of success. He played in every large city of the United States, always to crowded houses, and was everywhere received with enthusiasm. There was no doubt of his financial success, whatever criticisms might be passed on the artistic side of his performance. It was his personality and reputation that interested his audiences. They did not expect the art of Sir Henry Irving, and you may be sure that they did not receive it.

Will never enjoyed this part of his career; he endured it simply because it was the means to an end. He had not forgotten his boyish dream—his resolve that he would one day present to the world an exhibition that would give a realistic picture of life in the Far West, depicting its dangers and privations, as well as its picturesque phases. His first theatrical season had shown him how favorably such an exhibition would be received, and his long-cherished ambition began to take shape. He knew that an enormous amount of money would be needed, and to acquire such a sum he lived for many years behind the footlights.

I was present in a Leavenworth theater during one of his last performances—one in which he played the part of a loving swain to a would-be charming lassie. When the curtain fell on the last act I went behind the scenes, in company with a party of friends, and congratulated the star upon his excellent acting.

"Oh, Nellie," he groaned, "don't say anything about

it. If heaven will forgive me this foolishness, I promise to quit it forever when this season is over.''

That was the way he felt about the stage, so far as his part in it was concerned. He was a fish out of water. The feeble pretensions to a stern reality, and the mock dangers exploited, could not but fail to seem trivial to one who had lived the very scenes depicted.

CHAPTER XXV.

FIRST VISIT TO THE VALLEY OF THE BIG HORN.

MY brother was again bereaved in 1880 by the death of his little daughter Orra. At her own request, Orra's body was interred in Rochester, in beautiful Mount Hope Cemetery, by the side of little Kit Carson.

But joy follows upon sadness, and the summer before Will spent his last season on the stage was a memorable one for him. It marked the birth of another daughter, who was christened Irma. This daughter is the very apple of her father's eye; to her he gives the affection that is her due, and round her clings the halo of the tender memories of the other two that have departed this life.

This year, 1882, was also the one in which Will paid his first visit to the valley of the Big Horn. He had often traversed the outskirts of that region, and heard incredible tales from Indians and trappers of its wonders and beauties, but he had yet to explore it himself. In his early experience as Pony Express rider, California Joe had related to him the first story he had heard of the enchanted basin, and in 1875, when he was in charge of a large body of Arapahoe Indians that had been permitted to leave their reservation for a big hunt, he obtained more details.

The agent warned Will that some of the Indians were dissatisfied, and might attempt to escape, but to all appearances, though he watched them sharply, they were entirely content. Game was plentiful, the weather fine,

233

and nothing seemed omitted from the red man's happiness.

One night about twelve o'clock Will was aroused by an Indian guide, who informed him that a party of some two hundred Arapahoes had started away some two hours before, and were on a journey northward. The red man does not wear his heart upon his sleeve for government daws to peck at. One knows what he proposes to do after he has done it. The red man is conspicuously among the things that are not always what they seem.

Pursuit was immediately set on foot, and the entire body of truant warriors were brought back without bloodshed. One of them, a young warrior, came to Will's tent to beg for tobacco. The Indian—as all know who have made his acquaintance—has no difficulty in reconciling begging with his native dignity. To work may be beneath him, to beg is a different matter, and there is frequently a delightful hauteur about his mendicancy. In this respect he is not unlike some of his white brothers. Will gave the young chief the desired tobacco, and then questioned him closely concerning the attempted escape.

"Surely," said he, "you cannot find a more beautiful spot than this. The streams are full of fish, the grazing is good, the game is plentiful, and the weather is fine. What more could you desire?"

The Indian drew himself up. His face grew eager, and his eyes were full of longing as he answered, by the interpreter:

"The land to the north and west is the land of plenty. There the buffalo grows larger, and his coat is darker. There the bu-yu (antelope) comes in droves, while here there are but few. There the whole region is covered with the short, curly grass our ponies like. There grow the wild plums that are good for my people in summer and winter.   There are the springs of the Great Medicine Man, Tel-ya-ki-y. To bathe in them gives new life; to drink them cures every bodily ill.

"In the mountains beyond the river of the blue water there is gold and silver, the metals that the white man loves.   There lives the eagle, whose feathers the Indian must have to make his war-bonnet.   There, too, the sun shines always.

"It is the Ijis (heaven) of the red man.   My heart cries for it.   The hearts of my people are not happy when away from the Eithity Tugala."

The Indian folded his arms across his breast, and his eyes looked yearningly toward the country whose delights he had so vividly pictured; then he turned and walked sorrowfully away.   The white man's government shut him out from the possession of his earthly paradise.   Will learned upon further inquiry that Eithity Tugala was the Indian name of the Big Horn Basin.

In the summer of 1882 Will's party of exploration left the cars at Cheyenne, and struck out from this point with horses and pack-mules.   Will's eyes becoming inflamed, he was obliged to bandage them, and turn the guidance of the party over to a man known as "Reddy."   For days he traveled in a blinded state, and though his eyes slowly bettered, he did not remove the bandage until the Big Horn Basin was reached.   They had paused for the midday siesta, and Reddy inquired whether it would not be safe to uncover the afflicted eyes, adding that he thought Will "would enjoy looking around a bit."

Off came the bandage, and I shall quote Will's own words to describe the scene that met his delighted gaze:

"To my right stretched a towering range of snow-capped

mountains, broken here and there into minarets, obelisks, and spires. Between me and this range of lofty peaks a long irregular line of stately cottonwoods told me a stream wound its way beneath. The rainbow-tinted carpet under me was formed of innumerable brilliant-hued wild flowers; it spread about me in every direction, and sloped gracefully to the stream. Game of every kind played on the turf, and bright-hued birds flitted over it. It was a scene no mortal can satisfactorily describe. At such a moment a man, no matter what his creed, sees the hand of the mighty Maker of the universe majestically displayed in the beauty of nature; he becomes sensibly conscious, too, of his own littleness. I uttered no word for very awe; I looked upon one of nature's masterpieces.

"Instantly my heart went out to my sorrowful Arapahoe friend of 1875. He had not exaggerated; he had scarcely done the scene justice. He spoke of it as the Ijis, the heaven of the red man. I regarded it then, and still regard it, as the Mecca of all appreciative humanity."

To the west of the Big Horn Basin, Hart Mountain rises abruptly from the Shoshone River. It is covered with grassy slopes and deep ravines; perpendicular rocks of every hue rise in various places and are fringed with ever-greens. Beyond this mountain, in the distance, towers the hoary head of Table Mountain. Five miles to the southwest the mountains recede some distance from the river, and from its bank Castle Rock rises in solitary gran-deur. As its name indicates, it has the appearance of a castle, with towers, turrets, bastions, and balconies.

Grand as is the western view, the chief beauty lies in the south. Here the Carter Mountain lies along the entire distance, and the grassy spaces on its side furnish pastur-age for the deer, antelope, and mountain sheep that abound in this favored region. Fine timber, too, grows on its rugged slopes; jagged, picturesque rock-forms are seen in all directions, and numerous cold springs send up their welcome nectar.

It is among the foothills nestling at the base of this mountain that Will has chosen the site of his future permanent residence. Here there are many little lakes, two of which are named Irma and Arta, in honor of his daughters. Here he owns a ranch of forty thousand acres, but the home proper will comprise a tract of four hundred and eighty acres. The two lakes referred to are in this tract, and near them Will proposes to erect a palatial residence. To him, as he has said, it is the Mecca of earth, and thither he hastens the moment he is free from duty and obligation. In that enchanted region he forgets for a little season the cares and responsibilities of life.

A curious legend is told of one of the lakes that lie on the border of this valley. It is small—half a mile long and a quarter wide—but its depth is fathomless. It is bordered and shadowed by tall and stately pines, quaking-asp and birch trees, and its waters are pure and ice-cold the year round. They are medicinal, too, and as yet almost unknown to white men. Will heard the legend of the lake from the lips of an old Cheyenne warrior.

"It was the custom of my tribe," said the Indian, "to assemble around this lake once every month, at the hour of midnight, when the moon is at its full. Soon after midnight a canoe filled with the specters of departed Cheyenne warriors shot out from the eastern side of the lake and crossed rapidly to the western border; there it suddenly disappeared.

"Never a word or sound escaped from the specters in the canoe. They sat rigid and silent, and swiftly plied their oars.   All attempts to get a word from them were in vain.

"So plainly were the canoe and its occupants seen that the features of the warriors were readily distinguished, and relatives and friends were recognized."

For years, according to the legend, the regular monthly trip was made, and always from the eastern to the western border of the lake.   In 1876 it suddenly ceased, and the Indians were much alarmed.   A party of them camped on the bank of the lake, and watchers were appointed for every night.   It was fancied that the ghostly boatmen had changed the date of their excursion.   But in three months there was no sign of canoe or canoeists, and this was regarded as an omen of evil.

At a council of the medicine men, chiefs, and wiseacres of the tribe it was decided that the canoeing trip had been a signal from the Great Spirit—the canoe had proceeded from east to west, the course always followed by the red man.   The specters had been sent from the Happy Hunting-Grounds to indicate that the tribe should move farther west, and the sudden disappearance of the monthly signal was augured to mean the extinction of the race.

Once when Will was standing on the border of this lake a Sioux warrior came up to him.   This man was unusually intelligent, and desired that his children should be educated.   He sent his two sons to Carlisle, and himself took great pains to learn the white man's religious beliefs, though he still clung to his old savage customs and superstitions.   A short time before he talked with Will large companies of Indians had made pilgrimages to join one large conclave, for the purpose of celebrating the Messiah, or "Ghost Dance."   Like all religious celebrations among savage people, it was accompanied by the grossest

excesses and most revolting immoralities. As it was not
known what serious happening these large gatherings might
portend, the President, at the request of many people, sent
troops to disperse the Indians. The Indians resisted, and
blood was spilled, among the slain being the sons of the
Indian who stood by the side of the haunted lake.

"It is written in the Great Book of the white man,"
said the old chief to Will, "that the Great Spirit—the
Nan-tan-in-chor—is to come to him again on earth. The
white men in the big villages go to their council-lodges
(churches) and talk about the time of his coming. Some
say one time, some say another, but they all know the time
will come, for it is written in the Great Book. It is the
great and good among the white men that go to these
council-lodges, and those that do not go say, 'It is well;
we believe as they believe; He will come.' It is written
in the Great Book of the white man that all the human
beings on earth are the children of the one Great Spirit.
He provides and cares for them. All he asks in return is
that his children obey him, that they be good to one
another, that they judge not one another, and that they
do not kill or steal. Have I spoken truly the words of the
white man's Book?"

Will bowed his head, somewhat surprised at the tone of
the old chief's conversation. The other continued:

"The red man, too, has a Great Book. You have never
seen it; no white man has ever seen it; it is hidden here."
He pressed his hand against his heart. "The teachings of
the two books are the same. What the Great Spirit says
to the white man, the Nan-tan-in-chor says to the red
man. We, too, go to our council-lodges to talk of the
second coming. We have our ceremony, as the white
man has his. The white man is solemn, sorrowful; the

red man is happy and glad.   We dance and are joyful, and
the white man sends soldiers to shoot us down.   Does
their Great Spirit tell them to do this?

"In the big city (Washington) where I have been, there
is another big book (the Federal Constitution), which says
the white man shall not interfere with the religious liberty
of another.   And yet they come out to our country and
kill us when we show our joy to Nan-tan-in-chor.

"We rejoice over his second coming; the white man
mourns, but he sends his soldiers to kill us in our rejoicing.
Bah!   The white man is false.   I return to my people, and
to the customs and habits of my forefathers.   I am an
Indian!"

The old chief strode away with the dignity of a red
Cæsar, and Will, alone by the lake, reflected that every
question has two sides to it.   The one the red man has
held in the case of the commonwealth versus the Indian has
ever been the tragic side.

CHAPTER XXVI.

TOUR OF GREAT BRITAIN.

IT was not until the spring of 1883 that Will was able to put into execution his long-cherished plan—to present to the public an exhibition which should delineate in throbbing and realistic color, not only the wild life of America, but the actual history of the West, as it was lived for, fought for, died for, by Indians, pioneers, and soldiers.

The wigwam village; the Indian war-dance; the chant to the Great Spirit as it was sung over the plains; the rise and fall of the famous tribes; the "Forward, march!" of soldiers, and the building of frontier posts; the life of scouts and trappers; the hunt of the buffalo; the coming of the first settlers; their slow, perilous progress in the prairie schooners over the vast and desolate plains; the period of the Deadwood stage and the Pony Express; the making of homes in the face of fire and Indian massacre; United States cavalry on the firing-line, "Death to the Sioux!"—these are the great historic pictures of the Wild West, stirring, genuine, heroic.

It was a magnificent plan on a magnificent scale, and it achieved instant success. The adventurous phases of Western life never fail to quicken the pulse of the East.

An exhibition which embodied so much of the historic and picturesque, which resurrected a whole half-century of dead and dying events, events the most thrilling and dramatic in American history, naturally stirred up the interest of the entire country. The actors, too, were historic characters—no weakling imitators, but men of sand and grit, who had lived every inch of the life they pictured.

The first presentation was given in May, 1883, at Omaha, Nebraska, the state Will had chosen for his home. Since then it has visited nearly every large city on the civilized globe, and has been viewed by countless thousands—men, women, and children of every nationality. It will long hold a place in history.

The "grand entrance" alone has never failed to chain the interest of the onlooker. The furious galloping of the Indian braves—Sioux, Arapahoe, Brulé, and Cheyenne, all in war paint and feathers; the free dash of the Mexicans and cowboys, as they follow the Indians into line at breakneck speed; the black-bearded Cossacks of the Czar's light cavalry; the Riffian Arabs on their desert thoroughbreds; a cohort from the "Queen's Own" Lancers; troopers from the German Emperor's bodyguard; chasseurs and cuirassiers from the crack cavalry regiments of European standing armies; detachments from the United States cavalry and artillery; South American gauchos; Cuban veterans; Porto Ricans; Hawaiians; again frontiersmen, rough riders, Texas rangers—all plunging with dash and spirit into the open, each company followed by its chieftain and its flag; forming into a solid square, tremulous with color; then a quicker note to the music; the galloping hoofs of another horse, the finest of them all, and "Buffalo Bill," riding with the wonderful ease and stately grace which only he who is "born to the saddle" can ever attain, enters under the flash of the lime-light, and sweeping off his sombrero, holds his head high, and with a ring of pride in his voice, advances before his great audience and exclaims:

UNDER THE LIME LIGHT.

"Ladies and gentlemen, permit me to introduce to you a congress of the rough riders of the world."

As a child I wept over his disregard of the larger sphere predicted by the soothsayer; as a woman, I rejoice that he was true to his own ideals, for he sits his horse with a natural grace much better suited to the saddle than to the Presidential chair.

From the very beginning the "Wild West" was an immense success.   Three years were spent in traveling over the United States; then Will conceived the idea of visiting England, and exhibiting to the mother race the wild side of the child's life.   This plan entailed enormous expense, but it was carried out successfully.

Still true to the state of his adoption, Will chartered the steamer "State of Nebraska," and on March 31, 1886 a living freight from the picturesque New World began its voyage to the Old.

At Gravesend, England, the first sight to meet the eyes of the watchers on the steamer was a tug flying American colors.   Three ringing cheers saluted the beautiful emblem, and the band on the tug responded with "The Star-Spangled Banner."   Not to be outdone, the cowboy band on the "State of Nebraska" struck up "Yankee Doodle."   The tug had been chartered by a company of Englishmen for the purpose of welcoming the novel American combination to British soil.

When the landing was made, the members of the Wild West company entered special coaches and were whirled toward London.   Then even the stolidity of the Indians was not proof against sights so little resembling those to which they had been accustomed, and they showed their pleasure and appreciation by frequent repetition of the red man's characteristic grunt.

Major John M. Burke had made the needed arrangements for housing the big show, and preparations on a gigantic scale were rapidly pushed to please an impatient London public. More effort was made to produce spectacular effects in the London amphitheater than is possible where a merely temporary staging is erected for one day's exhibition. The arena was a third of a mile in circumference, and provided accommodation for forty thousand spectators. Here, as at Manchester, where another great amphitheater was erected in the fall, to serve as winter quarters, the artist's brush was called on to furnish illusions.

The English exhibited an eager interest in every feature of the exhibition — the Indian war-dances, the bucking broncho, speedily subjected by the valorous cowboy, and the stagecoach attacked by Indians and rescued by United States troops. The Indian village on the plains was also an object of dramatic interest to the English public. The artist had counterfeited the plains successfully.

It is the hour of dawn. Scattered about the plains are various wild animals. Within their tents the Indians are sleeping. Sunrise, and a friendly Indian tribe comes to visit the wakening warriors. A friendly dance is executed, at the close of which a courier rushes in to announce the approach of a hostile tribe. These follow almost at the courier's heels, and a sham battle occurs, which affords a good idea of the barbarity of Indian warfare. The victors celebrate their triumph with a wild war-dance.

A Puritan scene follows. The landing of the Pilgrims is shown, and the rescue of John Smith by Pocahontas. This affords opportunity for delineating many interesting Indian customs on festive celebrations, such as weddings and feast-days.

Again the prairie. A buffalo-lick is shown. The shaggy monsters come down to drink, and in pursuit of them is "Buffalo Bill," mounted on his good horse "Charlie." He has been acting as guide for an emigrant party, which soon appears. Camp-fires are lighted, supper is eaten, and the camp sinks into slumber with the dwindling of the fires. Then comes a fine bit of stage illusion. A red glow is seen in the distance, faint at first, but slowly deepening and broadening. It creeps along the whole horizon, and the camp is awakened by the alarming intelligence that the prairie is on fire. The emigrants rush out, and heroically seek to fight back the rushing, roaring flames. Wild animals, driven by the flames, dash through the camp, and a stampede follows. This scene was extremely realistic.

A cyclone was also simulated, and a whole village blown out of existence.

The "Wild West" was received with enthusiasm, not only by the general public, but by royalty. Gladstone made a call upon Will, in company with the Marquis of Lorne, and in return a lunch was tendered to the "Grand Old Man" by the American visitors. In an after-dinner speech, the English statesman spoke in the warmest terms of America. He thanked Will for the good he was doing in presenting to the English public a picture of the wild life of the Western continent, which served to illustrate the difficulties encountered by a sister nation in its onward march of civilization.

The initial performance was before a royal party comprising the Prince and Princess of Wales and suite. At the close of the exhibition the royal guests, at their own request, were presented to the members of the company. Unprepared for this contingency, Will had forgotten to coach the performers in the correct method of saluting royalty, and when the girl shots of the company were presented to the Princess of Wales, they stepped forward in true democratic fashion and cordially offered their hands to the lovely woman who had honored them.

According to English usage, the Princess extends the hand, palm down, to favored guests, and these reverently touch the finger-tips and lift the hand to their lips. Perhaps the spontaneity of the American girls' welcome was esteemed a pleasing variety to the established custom. At all events, her Highness, true to her breeding, appeared not to notice any breach of etiquette, but took the proffered hands and shook them cordially.

The Indian camp was also visited, and Red Shirt, the great chief, was, like every one else, delighted with the Princess. Through an interpreter the Prince expressed his pleasure over the performance of the braves, headed by their great chief, and the Princess bade him welcome to England. Red Shirt had the Indian gift of oratory, and he replied, in the unimpassioned speech for which the race is noted, that it made his heart glad to hear such kind words from the Great White Chief and his beautiful squaw.

During the round the Prince stopped in at Will's private quarters, and took much interest in his souvenirs, being especially pleased with a magnificent gold-hilted sword, presented to Will by officers of the United States army in recognition of his services as scout.

This was not the only time the exhibition was honored by the visit of royalty. That the Prince of Wales was sincere in his expression of enjoyment of the exhibition was evidenced by the report that he carried to his mother, and shortly afterward a command came from Queen Victoria that the big show appear before her. It was plainly impossible to take the ''Wild West'' to court; the next best thing was to construct a special box for the use of her Majesty. This box was placed upon a dais covered with crimson velvet trimmings, and was superbly decorated. When the Queen arrived and was driven around to the royal box, Will stepped forward as she dismounted, and doffing his sombrero, made a low courtesy to the sovereign lady of Great Britain. ''Welcome, your Majesty,'' said he, ''to the Wild West of America!''

One of the first acts in the performance is to carry the flag to the front. This is done by a soldier, and is introduced to the spectators as an emblem of a nation desirous of peace and friendship with all the world. On this occasion it was borne directly before the Queen's box, and dipped three times in honor of her Majesty. The action of the Queen surprised the company and the vast throng of spectators. Rising, she saluted the American flag with a bow, and her suite followed her example, the gentlemen removing their hats. Will acknowledged the courtesy by waving his sombrero about his head, and his delighted company with one accord gave three ringing cheers that made the arena echo, assuring the spectators of the healthy condition of the lungs of the American visitors.

The Queen's complaisance put the entire company on their mettle, and the performance was given magnificently. At the close Queen Victoria asked to have Will presented to her, and paid him so many compliments as almost to bring a blush to his bronzed cheek. Red Shirt was also presented, and informed her Majesty that he had come across the Great Water solely to see her, and his heart was glad. This polite speech discovered a streak in Indian nature that, properly cultivated, would fit the red man to shine as a courtier or politician. Red Shirt walked away with the insouciance of a king dismissing an audience, and some of the squaws came to display papooses to the Great White Lady. These children of nature were not the least awed by the honor done them. They blinked at her Majesty as if the presence of queens was an incident of their everyday existence.

A second command from the Queen resulted in another exhibition before a number of her royal guests. The kings of Saxony, Denmark, and Greece, the Queen of the Belgians, and the Crown Prince of Austria, with others of lesser rank, illumined this occasion.

The Deadwood coach was peculiarly honored. This is a coach with a history. It was built in Concord, New Hampshire, and sent to the Pacific Coast to run over a trail infested by road agents. A number of times was it held up and the passengers robbed, and finally both driver and passengers were killed and the coach abandoned on the trail, as no one could be found who would undertake to drive it. It remained derelict for a long time, but was at last brought into San Francisco by an old stage-driver and placed on the Overland trail. It gradually worked its way eastward to the Deadwood route, and on this line figured in a number of encounters with Indians. Again were driver and passengers massacred, and again was the coach abandoned. Will ran across it on one of his scouting expeditions, and recognizing its value as an adjunct to his exhibition, purchased it. Thereafter the tragedies it figured in were of the mock variety.

One of the incidents of the Wild West, as all remember, is an Indian attack on the Deadwood coach. The royal visitors wished to put themselves in the place of the traveling public in the Western regions of America;

so the four potentates of Denmark, Saxony, Greece, and Austria became the passengers, and the Prince of Wales sat on the box with Will. The Indians had been secretly instructed to "whoop 'em up" on this interesting occasion, and they followed energetically the letter of their instructions. The coach was surrounded by a demoniac band, and the blank cartridges were discharged in such close proximity to the coach windows that the passengers could easily imagine themselves to be actual Western travelers. Rumor hath it that they sought refuge under the seats, and probably no one would blame them if they did; but it is only rumor, and not history.

When the wild ride was over, the Prince of Wales, who admires the American national game of poker, turned to the driver with the remark:

"Colonel, did you ever hold four kings like that before?"

"I have held four kings more than once," was the prompt reply; "but, your Highness, I never held four kings and the royal joker before."

The Prince laughed heartily; but Will's sympathy went out to him when he found that he was obliged to explain his joke in four different languages to the passengers.

In recognition of this performance, the Prince of Wales sent Will a handsome souvenir. It consisted of his feathered crest, outlined in diamonds, and bearing the motto "*Ich dien*" worked in jewels underneath. An accompanying note expressed the pleasure of the royal visitors over the novel exhibition.

Upon another occasion the Princess of Wales visited the show incognito, first advising Will of her intention; and at the close of the performance assured him that she had spent a delightful evening.

The set performances of the "Wild West" were punctuated by social entertainments. James G. Blaine, Chauncey M. Depew, Murat Halstead, and other prominent Americans were in London at the time, and in their honor Will issued invitations to a rib-roast breakfast prepared in Indian style. Fully one hundred guests gathered in the "Wild West's" dining-tent at nine o'clock of June 10, 1887. Besides the novel decorations of the tent, it was interesting to watch the Indian cooks putting the finishing touches to their roasts. A hole had been dug in the ground, a large tripod erected over it, and upon this the ribs of beef were suspended. The fire was of logs, burned down to a bed of glowing coals, and over these the meat was turned around and around until it was cooked to a nicety. This method of open-air cooking over wood imparts to the meat a flavor that can be given to it in no other way.

The breakfast was unconventional. Part of the bill of fare was hominy, "Wild West" pudding, popcorn, and peanuts. The Indians squatted on the straw at the end of the dining-tables, and ate from their fingers or speared the meat with long white sticks. The striking contrast of table manners was an interesting object-lesson in the progress of civilization.

The breakfast was a novelty to the Americans who partook of it, and they enjoyed it thoroughly.

Will was made a social lion during his stay in London, being dined and fêted upon various occasions. Only a man of the most rugged health could have endured the strain of his daily performances united with his social obligations.

The London season was triumphantly closed with a meeting for the establishing of a court of arbitration to settle disputes between America and England.

After leaving the English metropolis the exhibition visited Birmingham, and thence proceeded to its winter headquarters in Manchester. Arta, Will's elder daughter, accompanied him to England, and made a Continental tour during the winter.

The sojourn in Manchester was another ovation. The prominent men of the city proposed to present to Will a fine rifle, and when the news of the plan was carried to London, a company of noblemen, statesmen, and journalists ran down to Manchester by special car. In acknowledgment of the honor done him, Will issued invitations for another of his unique American entertainments. Boston pork and beans, Maryland fried chicken, hominy, and popcorn were served, and there were other distinctly American dishes. An Indian rib-roast was served on tin plates, and the distinguished guests enjoyed—or said they did—the novelty of eating it from their fingers, in true aboriginal fashion. This remarkable meal evoked the heartiest of toasts to the American flag, and a poem, a parody on "Hiawatha," added luster to the occasion.

The Prince of Wales was Grand Master of the Free Masons of England, which order presented a gold watch to Will during his stay in Manchester. The last performance in this city was given on May 1, 1887, and as a good by to Will the spectators united in a rousing chorus of "For he's a jolly good fellow!" The closing exhibition of the English season occurred at Hull, and immediately afterward the company sailed for home on the "Persian Monarch." An immense crowd gathered on the quay, and shouted a cordial "bon voyage."

One sad event occurred on the homeward voyage, the death of "Old Charlie," Will's gallant and faithful horse. He was a half-blood Kentucky horse, and had been Will's constant and unfailing companion for many years on the plains and in the "Wild West."

He was an animal of almost human intelligence, extraordinary speed, endurance, and fidelity. When he was quite young Will rode him on a hunt for wild horses, which he ran down after a chase of fifteen miles. At another time, on a wager of five hundred dollars that he could ride him over the prairie one hundred miles in ten hours, he went the distance in nine hours and forty-five minutes.

When the "Wild West" was opened at Omaha, Charlie was the star horse, and held that position at all the exhibitions in this country and in Europe. In London the horse attracted a full share of attention, and many scions of royalty solicited the favor of riding him. Grand Duke Michael of Russia rode Charlie several times in chase of the herd of buffaloes in the "Wild West," and became quite attached to him.

On the morning of the 14th Will made his usual visit to Charlie, between decks. Shortly after the groom reported him sick. He grew rapidly worse, in spite of all the care he received, and at two o'clock on the morning of the 17th he died. His death cast an air of sadness over the whole ship, and no human being could have had more sincere mourners than the faithful and sagacious old horse. He was brought on deck wrapped in canvas and covered with the American flag. When the hour for the ocean burial arrived, the members of the company and others assembled on deck. Standing alone with uncovered head beside the dead was the one whose life the noble animal had shared so long. At length, with choking utterance, Will spoke, and Charlie for the first time failed to hear the familiar voice he had always been so prompt to obey:

"Old fellow, your journeys are over. Here in the ocean

you must rest.   Would that I could take you back and lay you down beneath the billows of that prairie you and I have loved so well and roamed so freely; but it cannot be. How often at break of day, the glorious sun rising on the horizon has found us far from human habitation! Yet, obedient to my call, gladly you bore your burden on, little heeding what the day might bring, so that you and I but shared its sorrows and pleasures alike.   You have never failed me.   Ah, Charlie, old fellow, I have had many friends, but few of whom I could say that.   Rest entombed in the deep bosom of the ocean!   I'll never forget you.   I loved you as you loved me, my dear old Charlie.   Men tell me you have no soul; but if there be a heaven, and scouts can enter there, I'll wait at the gate for you, old friend.''

On this homeward trip Will made the acquaintance of a clergyman returning from a vacation spent in Europe. When they neared the American coast this gentleman prepared a telegram to send to his congregation.   It read simply: ''2 John i. 12.''   Chancing to see it, Will's interest was aroused, and he asked the clergyman to explain the significance of the reference, and when this was done he said: ''I have a religious sister at home who knows the Bible so well that I will wire her that message and she will not need to look up the meaning.''

He duplicated to me, as his return greeting, the minister's telegram to his congregation, but I did not justify his high opinion of my Biblical knowledge.   I was obliged to search the Scriptures to unravel the enigma.   As there may be others like me, but who have not the incentive I had to look up the reference, I quote from God's word the message I received: ''Having many things to write unto you, I would not write with paper and ink; but I trust to come unto you, and speak face to face, that our joy may be full.''

CHAPTER XXVII.

RETURN OF THE "WILD WEST" TO AMERICA.

WHEN the "Wild West" returned to America from its first venture across seas, the sail up the harbor was described by the New York *World* in the following words:

"The harbor probably has never witnessed a more picturesque scene than that of yesterday, when the 'Persian Monarch' steamed up from quarantine. Buffalo Bill stood on the captain's bridge, his tall and striking figure clearly outlined, and his long hair waving in the wind; the gayly painted and blanketed Indians leaned over the ship's rail; the flags of all nations fluttered from the masts and connecting cables. The cowboy band played 'Yankee Doodle' with a vim and enthusiasm which faintly indicated the joy felt by everybody connected with the 'Wild West' over the sight of home."

Will had been cordially welcomed by our English cousins, and had been the recipient of many social favors, but no amount of foreign flattery could change him one hair from an "American of the Americans," and he experienced a thrill of delight as he again stepped foot upon his native land. Shortly afterward he was much pleased by a letter from William T. Sherman—so greatly prized that it was framed, and now hangs on the wall of his Nebraska home. Following is a copy:

"FIFTH AVENUE HOTEL, NEW YORK.
"COLONEL WM. F. CODY:
"*Dear Sir :* In common with all your countrymen, I want to let you know that I am not only gratified but proud of your management and success. So far as I can make out, you have been modest, graceful, and dignified in all you have done to illustrate the history of civilization

on this continent during the past century. I am especially pleased with the compliment paid you by the Prince of Wales, who rode with you in the Deadwood coach while it was attacked by Indians and rescued by cowboys. Such things did occur in our days, but they never will again.

"As nearly as I can estimate, there were in 1865 about nine and one-half million of buffaloes on the plains between the Missouri River and the Rocky Mountains; all are now gone, killed for their meat, their skins, and their bones. This seems like desecration, cruelty, and murder, yet they have been replaced by twice as many cattle. At that date there were about 165,000 Pawnees, Sioux, Cheyennes, and Arapahoes, who depended upon these buffaloes for their yearly food. They, too, have gone, but they have been replaced by twice or thrice as many white men and women, who have made the earth to blossom as the rose, and who can be counted, taxed, and governed by the laws of nature and civilization. This change has been salutary, and will go on to the end. You have caught one epoch of this country's history, and have illustrated it in the very heart of the modern world—London, and I want you to feel that on this side of the water we appreciate it.

"This drama must end; days, years, and centuries follow fast; even the drama of civilization must have an end. All I aim to accomplish on this sheet of paper is to assure you that I fully recognize your work. The presence of the Queen, the beautiful Princess of Wales, the Prince, and the British public are marks of favor which reflect back on America sparks of light which illuminate many a house and cabin in the land where once you guided me honestly and faithfully, in 1865-66, from Fort Riley to Kearny, in Kansas and Nebraska.

Sincerely your friend,
W. T. SHERMAN."

Having demonstrated to his satisfaction that the largest measure of success lay in a stationary exhibition of his show, where the population was large enough to warrant it, Will purchased a tract of land on Staten Island, and here he landed on his return from England. Teamsters for miles around had been engaged to transport the outfit across the island to Erastina, the site chosen for the exhibition. And you may be certain that Cut Meat, American Bear, Flat Iron, and the other Indians furnished unlimited joy to the ubiquitous small boy, who was present by the hundreds to watch the unloading scenes.

The summer season at this point was a great success. One incident connected with it may be worth the relating.

Teachers everywhere have recognized the value of the "Wild West" exhibition as an educator, and in a number of instances public schools have been dismissed to afford the children an opportunity of attending the entertainment. It has not, however, been generally recognized as a spur to religious progress, yet, while at Staten Island, Will was invited to exhibit a band of his Indians at a missionary meeting given under the auspices of a large mission Sunday-school. He appeared with his warriors, who were expected to give one of their religious dances as an object-lesson in devotional ceremonials.

The meeting was largely attended, and every one, children especially, waited for the exercises in excited curiosity and interest. Will sat on the platform with the superintendent, pastor, and others in authority, and close by sat the band of stolid-faced Indians.

The service began with a hymn and the reading of the Scriptures; then, to Will's horror, the superintendent requested him to lead the meeting in prayer. Perhaps the good man fancied that Will for a score of years had fought Indians with a rifle in one hand and a prayer-book in the other, and was as prepared to pray as to shoot. At least he surely did not make his request with the thought of embarrassing Will, though that was the natural result. However, Will held holy things in deepest reverence; he had the spirit of Gospel if not the letter; so, rising, he quietly and simply, with bowed head, repeated the Lord's Prayer.

A winter exhibition under roof was given in New York, after which the show made a tour of the principal cities of the United States. Thus passed several years, and then arrangements were made for a grand Continental trip. A plan had been maturing in Will's mind ever since the British season, and in the spring of 1889 it was carried into effect.

The steamer "Persian Monarch" was again chartered, and this time its prow was turned toward the shores of France. Paris was the destination, and seven months were passed in the gay capital. The Parisians received the show with as much enthusiasm as did the Londoners, and in Paris as well as in the English metropolis everything American became a fad during the stay of the "Wild West." Even American books were read—a crucial test of faddism; and American curios were displayed in all the shops. Relics from American plain and mountain—buffalo-robes, bearskins, buckskin suits embroidered with porcupine quills, Indian blankets, woven mats, bows and arrows, bead-mats, Mexican bridles and saddles—sold like the proverbial hot cakes.

In Paris, also, Will became a social favorite, and had he accepted a tenth of the invitations to receptions, dinners, and balls showered upon him, he would have been obliged to close his show.

While in this city Will accepted an invitation from Rosa Bonheur to visit her at her superb château, and in return for the honor he extended to her the freedom of his stables, which contained magnificent horses used for transportation purposes, and which never appeared in the public perform-ance—Percherons, of the breed depicted by the famous artist in her well-known painting of "The Horse Fair." Day upon day she visited the camp and made studies, and as a token of her appreciation of the courtesy, painted a picture of Will mounted on his favorite horse, both horse and rider bedecked with frontier paraphernalia. This sou-

venir, which holds the place of honor in his collection, he
immediately shipped home.

The wife of a London embassy attaché relates the following story:

"During the time that Colonel Cody was making his
triumphant tour of Europe, I was one night seated at a
banquet next to the Belgian Consul.   Early in the course
of the conversation he asked:

" 'Madame, you haf undoubted been to see ze gr-rand
Bouf-falo Beel?'

"Puzzled by the apparently unfamiliar name, I asked:

" 'Pardon me, but whom did you say?'

" 'Vy, Bouf-falo Beel, ze famous Bouf-falo Beel, zat
gr-reat countryman of yours.   You must know him.'

"After a moment's thought, I recognized the well-
known showman's name in its disguise.   I comprehended
that the good Belgian thought his to be one of America's
most eminent names, to be mentioned in the same breath
with Washington and Lincoln."

After leaving Paris, a short tour of Southern France was
made, and at Marseilles a vessel was chartered to transport
the company to Spain.   The Spanish grandees eschewed
their favorite amusement—the bull-fight—long enough to
give a hearty welcome to the "Wild West."   Next followed a tour of Italy; and the visit to Rome was the most
interesting of the experiences in this country.

The Americans reached the Eternal City at the time of
Pope Leo's anniversary celebration, and, on the Pope's
invitation, Will visited the Vatican.   Its historic walls have
rarely, if ever, looked upon a more curious sight than was
presented when Will walked in, followed by the cowboys
in their buckskins and sombreros and the Indians in war

paint and feathers. Around them crowded a motley throng of Italians, clad in the brilliant colors so loved by these children of the South, and nearly every nationality was represented in the assemblage.

Some of the cowboys and Indians had been reared in the Catholic faith, and when the Pope appeared they knelt for his blessing. He seemed touched by this action on the part of those whom he might be disposed to regard as savages, and bending forward, extended his hands and pronounced a benediction; then he passed on, and it was with the greatest difficulty that the Indians were restrained from expressing their emotions in a wild whoop. This, no doubt, would have relieved them, but it would, in all probability, have stampeded the crowd.

When the Pope reached Will he looked admiringly upon the frontiersman. The world-known scout bent his head before the aged "Medicine Man," as the Indians call his reverence, the Papal blessing was again bestowed, and the procession passed on. The Thanksgiving Mass, with its fine choral accompaniment, was given, and the vast concourse of people poured out of the building.

This visit attracted much attention.

> "I'll take my stalwart Indian braves
>   Down to the Coliseum,
> And the old Romans from their graves
>   Will all arise to see 'em.
> Prætors and censors will return
>   And hasten through the Forum;
> The ghostly Senate will adjourn,
>   Because it lacks a quorum.
>
> "And up the ancient Appian Way
>   Will flock the ghostly legions,
> From Gaul unto Calabria,
>   And from remoter regions;

From British bay and wild lagoon,
　　And Libyan desert sandy,
They'll all come marching to the tune
　　Of ' Yankee Doodle Dandy.'

" Prepare triumphal cars for me,
　　And purple thrones to sit on,
For I've done more than Julius C.—
　　He could not down the Briton !
Cæsar and Cicero shall bow,
　　And ancient warriors famous,
Before the myrtle-wreathed brow
　　Of Buffalo Williamus.

" We march, unwhipped, through history—
　　No bulwark can detain us—
And link the age of Grover C.
　　And Scipio Africanus.
I'll take my stalwart Indian braves
　　Down to the Coliseum,
And the old Romans from their graves
　　Will all arise to see 'em."

It may be mentioned in passing that Will had visited the
Coliseum with an eye to securing it as an amphitheater for
the "Wild West" exhibition, but the historic ruin was too
dilapidated to be a safe arena for such a purpose, and the
idea was abandoned.

The sojourn in Rome was enlivened by an incident that
created much interest among the natives. The Italians
were somewhat skeptical as to the abilities of the cowboys
to tame wild horses, believing the bronchos in the show
were specially trained for their work, and that the horse-
breaking was a mock exhibition.

The Prince of Sermonetta declared that he had some
wild horses in his stud which no cowboys in the world could
ride. The challenge was promptly taken up by the daring
riders of the plains, and the Prince sent for his wild steeds.
That they might not run amuck and injure the specta-

tors, specially prepared booths of great strength were erected.

The greatest interest and enthusiasm were manifested by the populace, and the death of two or three members of the company was as confidently looked for as was the demise of sundry gladiators in the "brave days of old."

But the cowboys laughed at so great a fuss over so small a matter, and when the horses were driven into the arena, and the spectators held their breath, the cowboys, lassos in hand, awaited the work with the utmost nonchalance.

The wild equines sprang into the air, darted hither and thither, and fought hard against their certain fate, but in less time than would be required to give the details, the cowboys had flung their lassos, caught the horses, and saddled and mounted them. The spirited beasts still resisted, and sought in every way to throw their riders, but the experienced plainsmen had them under control in a very short time; and as they rode them around the arena, the spectators rose and howled with delight. The display of horsemanship effectually silenced the skeptics; it captured the Roman heart, and the remainder of the stay in the city was attended by unusual enthusiasm.

Beautiful Florence, practical Bologna, and stately Milan, with its many-spired cathedral, were next on the list for the triumphal march. For the Venetian public the exhibition had to be given at Verona, in the historic amphitheater built by Diocletian, A. D. 290. This is the largest building in the world, and within the walls of this representative of Old World civilization the difficulties over which New World civilization had triumphed were portrayed. Here met the old and new; hoary antiquity and bounding youth kissed each other under the sunny Italian skies.

The "Wild West" now moved northward, through the Tyrol, to Munich, and from here the Americans digressed for an excursion on the "beautiful blue Danube." Then followed a successful tour of Germany.

During this Continental circuit Will's elder daughter, Arta, who had accompanied him on his British expedition, was married. It was impossible for the father to be present, but by cablegram he sent his congratulations and check.

CHAPTER XXVIII.

A TRIBUTE TO GENERAL MILES.

IN view of the success achieved by my brother, it is remarkable that he excited so little envy. Now for the first time in his life he felt the breath of slander on his cheek, and it flushed hotly. From an idle remark that the Indians in the "Wild West" exhibition were not properly treated, the idle gossip grew to the proportion of malicious and insistent slander. The Indians being government wards, such a charge might easily become a serious matter; for, like the man who beat his wife, the government believes it has the right to maltreat the red man to the top of its bent, but that no one else shall be allowed to do so.

A winter campaign of the "Wild West" had been contemplated, but the project was abandoned and winter quarters decided on. In the quaint little village of Benfield was an ancient nunnery and a castle, with good stables. Here Will left the company in charge of his partner, Mr. Nate Salisbury, and, accompanied by the Indians for whose welfare he was responsible, set sail for America, to silence his calumniators.

The testimony of the red men themselves was all that was required to refute the notorious untruths. Few had placed any belief in the reports, and friendly commenters were also active.

As the sequel proved, Will came home very opportunely. The Sioux in Dakota were again on the war-path, and his help was needed to subdue the uprising. He disbanded the warriors he had brought back from Europe, and each returned to his own tribe and people, to narrate around the camp-fire the wonders of the life abroad, while Will reported at headquarters to offer his services for the war. Two years previously he had been honored by the commission of Brigadier-General of the Nebraska National Guard, which rank and title were given to him by Governor Thayer.

The officer in command of the Indian campaign was General Nelson A. Miles, who has rendered so many important services to his country, and who, as Commander-in-Chief of our army, played so large a part in the recent war with Spain. At the time of the Indian uprising he held the rank of Brigadier-General.

This brilliant and able officer was much pleased when he learned that he would have Will's assistance in conducting the campaign, for he knew the value of his good judgment, cool head, and executive ability, and of his large experience in dealing with Indians.

The "Wild West," which had served as an educator to the people of Europe in presenting the frontier life of America, had quietly worked as important educational influences in the minds of the Indians connected with the exhibition. They had seen for themselves the wonders of the world's civilization; they realized how futile were the efforts of the children of the plains to stem the resistless tide of progress flowing westward. Potentates had delighted to do honor to Pa-has-ka, the Long-haired Chief, and in the eyes of the simple savage he was as powerful as any of the great ones of earth. To him his word was law; it seemed worse than folly for their brethren to attempt to cope with so mighty a chief, therefore their influence was all for peace; and the fact that so many tribes did not join in the uprising may be attributed, in part, to their good counsel and advice.

General Miles was both able and energetic, and managed the campaign in masterly fashion. There were one or two hard-fought battles, in one of which the great Sioux warrior, Sitting Bull, the ablest that nation ever produced, was slain. This Indian had traveled with Will for a time, but could not be weaned from his loyalty to his own tribe and a desire to avenge upon the white man the wrongs inflicted on his people.

What promised at the outset to be a long and cruel frontier war was speedily quelled. The death of Sitting Bull had something to do with the termination of hostilities. Arrangements for peace were soon perfected, and Will attributed the government's success to the energy of its officer in command, for whom he has a most enthusiastic admiration. He paid this tribute to him recently:

"I have been in many campaigns with General Miles, and a better general and more gifted warrior I have never seen. I served in the Civil War, and in any number of Indian wars; I have been under at least a dozen generals, with whom I have been thrown in close contact because of the nature of the services which I was called upon to render. General Miles is the superior of them all.

"I have known Phil Sheridan, Tecumseh Sherman, Hancock, and all of our noted Indian fighters. For cool judgment and thorough knowledge of all that pertains to military affairs, none of them, in my opinion, can be said to excel General Nelson A. Miles.

"Ah, what a man he is! I know. We have been shoulder to shoulder in many a hard march. We have been together when men find out what their comrades really are.   He is a man, every inch of him, and the best general I ever served under.''

After Miles was put in command of the forces, a dinner was given in his honor by John Chamberlin.   Will was a guest and one of the speakers, and took the opportunity to eulogize his old friend.   He dwelt at length on the respect in which the red men held the general, and in closing said:

"No foreign invader will ever set foot on these shores as long as General Miles is at the head of the army.   If they should—just call on me!''

The speaker sat down amid laughter and applause.

While Will was away at the seat of war, his beautiful home in North Platte, "Welcome Wigwam," burned to the ground.   The little city is not equipped with much of a fire department, but a volunteer brigade held the flames in check long enough to save almost the entire contents of the house, among which were many valuable and costly souvenirs that could never be replaced.

Will received a telegram announcing that his house was ablaze, and his reply was characteristic:

"Save Rosa Bonheur's picture, and the house may go to blazes.''

When the frontier war was ended and the troops disbanded, Will made application for another company of Indians to take back to Europe with him.   Permission was obtained from the government, and the contingent from the friendly tribes was headed by chiefs named Long Wolf, No Neck, Yankton Charlie, and Black Heart.   In addition to these a company was recruited from among the Indians held as hostages by General Miles at Fort Sheridan, and the leaders of these hostile braves were such noted chiefs as Short Bull, Kicking Bear, Lone Bull, Scatter, and Revenge.

To these the trip to Alsace-Lorraine was a revelation, a fairy-tale more wonderful than anything in their legendary lore. The ocean voyage, with its seasickness, put them in an ugly mood, but the sight of the encampment and the cow-boys dissipated their sullenness, and they shortly felt at home. The hospitality extended to all the members of the company by the inhabitants of the village in which they wintered was most cordial, and left them the pleasantest of memories.

An extended tour of Europe was fittingly closed by a brief visit to England. The Britons gave the "Wild West" as hearty a welcome as if it were native to their heath. A number of the larger cities were visited, London being reserved for the last.

Royalty again honored the "Wild West" by its attendance, the Queen requesting a special performance on the grounds of Windsor Castle. The requests of the Queen are equivalent to commands, and the entertainment was duly given. As a token of her appreciation the Queen bestowed upon Will a costly and beautiful souvenir.

Not the least-esteemed remembrance of this London visit was an illuminated address presented by the English Workingman's Convention. In it the American plainsman was congratulated upon the honors he had won, the success he had achieved, and the educational worth of his great exhibition. A banquet followed, at which Will presented an autograph photograph to each member of the association.

Notwithstanding tender thoughts of home, English soil was left regretfully. To the "Wild West" the complacent Briton had extended a cordial welcome, and manifested an enthusiasm that contrasted strangely with his usual disdain for things American.

A singular coincidence of the homeward voyage was the death of Billy, another favorite horse of Will's.

CHAPTER XXIX.

THE "WILD WEST" AT THE WORLD'S FAIR.

EUROPEAN army officers of all nationalities regarded my brother with admiring interest. To German, French, Italian, or British eyes he was a commanding personality, and also the representative of a peculiar and interesting phase of New World life. Recalling their interest in his scenes from his native land, so unlike anything to be found in Europe to-day, Will invited a number of these officers to accompany him on an extended hunting-trip through Western America.

All that could possibly do so accepted the invitation. A date was set for them to reach Chicago, and from there arrangements were made for a special train to convey them to Nebraska.

When the party gathered, several prominent Americans were of the number. By General Miles's order a military escort attended them from Chicago, and the native soldiery remained with them until North Platte was reached.

Then the party proceeded to "Scout's Rest Ranch," where they were hospitably entertained for a couple of days before starting out on their long trail.

At Denver ammunition and supplies were taken on board the train. A French chef was also engaged, as Will feared his distinguished guests might not enjoy camp-fare. But a hen in water is no more out of place than a French cook on a "roughing-it" trip. Frontier cooks, who understand primitive methods, make no attempt at a fashionable cuisine, and the appetites developed by open-air life are equal to the rudest, most substantial fare.

Colorado Springs, the Garden of the Gods, and other places in Colorado were visited. The foreign visitors had heard stories of this wonderland of America, but, like all of nature's masterpieces, the rugged beauties of this magnificent region defy an adequate description. Only one who has seen a sunrise on the Alps can appreciate it. The storied Rhine is naught but a story to him who has never looked upon it. Niagara is only a waterfall until seen from various view-points, and its tremendous force and transcendent beauty are strikingly revealed. The same is true of the glorious wildness of our Western scenery; it must be seen to be appreciated.

The most beautiful thing about the Garden of the Gods is the entrance known as the Gateway. Color here runs riot. The mass of rock in the foreground is white, and stands out in sharp contrast to the rich red of the sandstone of the portals, which rise on either side to a height of three hundred feet. Through these giant portals, which in the sunlight glow with ruddy fire, is seen mass upon mass of gorgeous color, rendered more striking by the dazzling whiteness of Pike's Peak, which soars upward in the distance, a hoary sentinel of the skies. The whole picture is limned against the brilliant blue of the Colorado sky, and stands out sharp and clear, one vivid block of color distinctly defined against the other.

The name "Garden of the Gods" was doubtless applied because of the peculiar shape of the spires, needles, and basilicas of rock that rise in every direction. These have been corroded by storms and worn smooth by time, until they present the appearance of half-baked images of clay molded by human hands, instead of sandstone rocks fashioned by wind and weather. Each grotesque and fantastic shape has received a name. One is here introduced to the "Washerwoman," the "Lady of the Garden," the "Siamese Twins," and the "Ute God," and besides these may be seen the "Wreck," the "Baggage Room," the "Eagle," and the "Mushroom." The predominating tone is everywhere red, but black, brown, drab, white, yellow, buff, and pink rocks add their quota to make up a harmonious and striking color scheme, to which the gray and green of clinging mosses add a final touch of picturesqueness.

At Flagstaff, Arizona, the train was discarded for the saddle and the buckboard. And now Will felt himself quite in his element; it was a never-failing pleasure to him to guide a large party of guests over plain and mountain. From long experience he knew how to make ample provision for their comfort. There were a number of wagons filled with supplies, three buckboards, three ambulances, and a drove of ponies. Those who wished to ride horseback could do so; if they grew tired of a bucking broncho, opportunity for rest awaited them in ambulance or buckboard. The French chef found his occupation gone when it was a question of cooking over a camp-fire; so he spent his time picking himself up when dislodged by his broncho. The daintiness of his menu was not a correct gauge for the daintiness of his language on these numerous occasions.

Through the Grand Cañon of the Colorado Will led the party, and the dwellers of the Old World beheld some of the rugged magnificence of the New. Across rushing rivers, through quiet valleys, and over lofty mountains they proceeded, pausing on the borders of peaceful lakes, or looking over dizzy precipices into yawning chasms.

There was no lack of game to furnish variety to their table; mountain sheep, mountain lions, wildcats, deer, elk, antelope, and even coyotes and porcupines, were shot, while the rivers furnished an abundance of fish.

It seemed likely at one time that there might be a hunt of bigger game than any here mentioned, for in crossing the country of the Navajos the party was watched and followed by mounted Indians. An attack was feared, and had the red men opened fire, there would have been a very animated defense; but the suspicious Indians were merely on the alert to see that no trespass was committed, and when the orderly company passed out of their territory the warriors disappeared.

The visitors were much impressed with the vastness and the undeveloped resources of our country. They were also impressed with the climate, as the thermometer went down to forty degrees below zero while they were on Buckskin Mountain. Nature seemed to wish to aid Will in the effort to exhibit novelties to his foreign guests, for she tried her hand at some spectacular effects, and succeeded beyond mortal expectation. She treated them to a few blizzards; and shut in by the mass of whirling, blinding snowflakes, it is possible their thoughts reverted with a homesick longing to the sunny slopes of France, the placid vales of Germany, or the foggy mildness of Great Britain.

On the summit of San Francisco Mountain, the horse of Major St. John Mildmay lost its footing, and began to slip on the ice toward a precipice which looked down a couple of thousand feet. Will saw the danger, brought out his ever-ready lasso, and dexterously caught the animal in time to save it and its rider—a feat considered remarkable by the onlookers.

Accidents happened occasionally, many adventures

were met with, Indian alarms were given, and narrow were some of the escapes. On the whole, it was a remarkable trail, and was written about under the heading, "A Thousand Miles in the Saddle with Buffalo Bill."

At Salt Lake City the party broke up, each going his separate way. All expressed great pleasure in the trip, and united in the opinion that Buffalo Bill's reputation as guide and scout was a well-deserved one.

Will's knowledge of Indian nature stands him in good stead when he desires to select the quota of Indians for the summer season of the "Wild West." He sends word ahead to the tribe or reservation which he intends to visit. The red men have all heard of the wonders of the great show; they are more than ready to share in the delights of travel, and they gather at the appointed place in great numbers.

Will stands on a temporary platform in the center of the group. He looks around upon the swarthy faces, glowing with all the eagerness which the stolid Indian nature will permit them to display. It is not always the tallest nor the most comely men who are selected. The unerring judgment of the scout, trained in Indian warfare, tells him who may be relied upon and who are untrustworthy. A face arrests his attention—with a motion of his hand he indicates the brave whom he has selected; another wave of the hand and the fate of a second warrior is settled. Hardly a word is spoken, and it is only a matter of a few moments' time before he is ready to step down from his exalted position and walk off with his full contingent of warriors following happily in his wake.

The "Wild West" had already engaged space just outside the World's Fair grounds for an exhibit in 1893, and Will was desirous of introducing some new and striking feature. He had succeeded in presenting to the people of

Europe some new ideas, and, in return, the European trip had furnished to him the much-desired novelty. He had performed the work of an educator in showing to Old World residents the conditions of a new civilization, and the idea was now conceived of showing to the world gathered at the arena in Chicago a representation of the cosmopolitan military force. He called it "A Congress of the Rough Riders of the World." It is a combination at once ethnological and military.

To the Indians and cowboys were added Mexicans, Cossacks, and South Americans, with regular trained cavalry from Germany, France, England, and the United States. This aggregation showed for the first time in 1893, and was an instantaneous success. Of it Opie Read gives a fine description:

"Morse made the two worlds touch the tips of their fingers together. Cody has made the warriors of all nations join hands.

"In one act we see the Indian, with his origin shrouded in history's mysterious fog; the cowboy—nerve-strung product of the New World; the American soldier, the dark Mexican, the glittering soldier of Germany, the dashing cavalryman of France, the impulsive Irish dragoon, and that strange, swift spirit from the plains of Russia, the Cossack.

"Marvelous theatric display, a drama with scarcely a word—Europe, Asia, Africa, America in panoramic whirl, and yet as individualized as if they had never left their own country."

In 1893 the horizon of my brother's interests enlarged. In July of that year I was married to Mr. Hugh A. Wetmore, editor of the Duluth *Press*. My steps now turned to the North, and the enterprising young city on the shore of Lake Superior became my home. During the long years of my widowhood my brother always bore toward me the attitude of guardian and protector; I could rely upon his support in any venture I deemed a promising one, and his considerate thoughtfulness did not fail when I remarried. He wished to see me well established in my new home; he desired to insure my happiness and prosperity, and with this end in view he purchased the Duluth *Press* plant, erected a fine brick building to serve as headquarters for the newspaper venture, and we became business partners in the untried field of press work.

My brother had not yet seen the Zenith City. So in January of 1894 he arranged to make a short visit to Duluth. We issued invitations for a general reception, and the response was of the genuine Western kind— eighteen hundred guests assembling in the new Duluth *Press* Building to bid welcome and do honor to the world-famed Buffalo Bill.

His name is a household word, and there is a growing demand for anecdotes concerning him. As he does not like to talk about himself, chroniclers have been compelled to interview his associates, or are left to their own resources. Like many of the stories told about Abraham Lincoln, some of the current yarns about Buffalo Bill are of doubtful authority. Nevertheless, a collection of those that are authentic would fill a volume. Almost every plainsman or soldier who met my brother during the Indian campaigns can tell some interesting tale about him that has never been printed. During the youthful season of redundant hope and happiness many of his ebullitions of wit were lost, but he was always beloved for his good humor, which no amount of carnage could suppress. He was not averse to church-going, though he was liable even in church to be carried away by the rollicking spirit that was in him. Instance his visit to the little temple which he had helped to build at North Platte.

His wife and sister were in the congregation, and this ought not only to have kept him awake, but it should have insured perfect decorum on his part. The opening hymn commenced with the words, "Oh, for a thousand tongues to sing," etc. The organist, who played "by ear," started the tune in too high a key to be followed by the choir and congregation, and had to try again. A second attempt ended, like the first, in failure. "Oh, for a thousand tongues to sing, my blest—" came the opening words for the third time, followed by a squeak from the organ, and a relapse into painful silence. Will could contain himself no longer, and blurted out: "Start it at five hundred, and mebbe some of the rest of us can get in."

Another church episode occurred during the visit of the "Wild West" to the Atlanta Exposition. A locally celebrated colored preacher had announced that he would deliver a sermon on the subject of Abraham Lincoln. A party of white people, including my brother, was made up, and repaired to the church to listen to the eloquent address. Not wishing to make themselves conspicuous, the white visitors took a pew in the extreme rear, but one of the ushers, wishing to honor them, insisted on conducting them to a front seat. When the contribution platter came around, our hero scooped a lot of silver dollars from his pocket and deposited them upon the plate with such force that the receptacle was tilted and its contents poured in a jingling shower upon the floor. The preacher left his pulpit to assist in gathering up the scattered treasure, requesting the congregation to sing a hymn of thanksgiving while the task was being performed. At the conclusion of the hymn the sable divine returned to the pulpit and supplemented his sermon with the following remarks:

"Brudderen an' sisters: I obsahve dat Co'nel and Gen'l Buflo Bill am present. [A roar of "Amens" and "Bless God's" arose from the audience.] You will wifhold yuh Amens till I git froo. You all owes yuh freedom to

Abraham's bosom, but he couldn't hab went an' gone an' done it widout Buflo Bill, who he'ped him wid de sinnoose ob wah! Abraham Lincum was de brack man's fren'—Buflo Bill am de fren' ob us all. ["Amen!" screamed a sister.] Yes, sistah, he am vo' fren', moreova, an' de fren' ob every daughtah ob Jakup likewise. De chu'ch debt am a cross to us, an' to dat cross he bends his back as was prefigu'd in de scriptu's ob ol'. De sun may move, aw de sun mought stan' still, but Buflo Bill nebba stan's still—he's ma'ching froo Geo'gia wid his Christian cowboys to sto'm de Lookout Mountain ob Zion. Deacon Green Henry Turner will lead us in prayah fo' Buflo Bill."

The following is one of Will's own stories: During the first years of his career as an actor Will had in one of his theatrical companies a Westerner named Broncho Bill. There were Indians in the troupe, and a certain missionary had joined the aggregation to look after the morals of the Indians. Thinking that Broncho Bill would bear a little looking after also, the good man secured a seat by his side at the dinner-table, and remarked pleasantly:

"This is Mr. Broncho Bill, is it not?"

"Yaas."

"Where were you born?"

"Near Kit Bullard's mill, on Big Pigeon."

"Religious parents, I suppose?"

"Yaas."

"What is your denomination?"

"My what?"

"Your denomination?"

"O—ah—yaas. Smith & Wesson."

While on his European tour Will was entertained by a great many potentates. At a certain dinner given in his honor by a wealthy English lord, Will met for the first time socially a number of blustering British officers, fresh from India. One of them addressed himself to the scout as follows: "I understand you are a colonel. You Americans are blawsted fond of military titles, don't cherneow. By gad, sir, we'll have to come over and give you fellows a good licking!"

"What, again?" said the scout, so meekly that for an instant his assailant did not know how hard he was hit, but he realized it when the retort was wildly applauded by the company.

Before closing these pages I will give an account of an episode which occurred during the Black Hills gold excitement, and which illustrates the faculty my hero possesses of adapting himself to all emergencies. Mr. Mahan, of West Superior, Wisconsin, and a party of adventurous gold-seekers were being chased by a band of Indians, which they had succeeded in temporarily eluding. They met Buffalo Bill at the head of a squad of soldiers who were looking for redskins. The situation was explained to the scout, whereupon he said:

"I am looking for that identical crowd. Now, you draw up in line, and I will look you over and pick out the men that I want to go back with me."

Without any questioning he was able to select the men who really wanted to return and fight the Indians. He left but two behind, but they were the ones who would have been of no assistance had they been allowed to go to the front. Will rode some distance in advance of his party, and when the Indians sighted him, they thought he was alone, and made a dash for him. Will whirled about and made his horse go as if fleeing for his life. His men had been carefully ambushed. The Indians kept up a constant firing, and when he reached a certain point Will pretended to be hit, and fell from his horse. On came the Indians,

howling like a choir of maniacs.   The next moment they
were in a trap, and Will and his men opened fire on them,
literally annihilating the entire squad.   It was the Indian
style of warfare, and the ten "good Indians" left upon
the field, had they been able to complain, would have had
no right to do so.

Will continued the march, and as the day was well
advanced, began looking for a good place to camp.   Arriving at the top of a ridge overlooking a little river, Will saw
a spot where he had camped on a previous expedition; but,
to his great disappointment, the place was in possession of
a large village of hostiles, who were putting up their tepees,
building camp fires, and making themselves comfortable for
the coming night.

Quick as a flash Will decided what to do.   "There are
too many of them for us to whip in the tired condition of
ourselves and horses," said our hero.   Then he posted his
men along the top of the ridge, with instructions to show
themselves at a signal from him, and descended at once,
solitary and alone, to the encampment of hostiles.   Gliding
rapidly up to the chief, Will addressed him in his own
dialect as follows:

"I want you to leave here right away, quick!   I don't
want to kill your women and children.   A big lot of soldiers are following me, and they will destroy your whole
village if you are here when they come."

As he waved his hand in the direction of the hilltop,
brass buttons and polished gun-barrels began to glitter in
the rays of the setting sun, and the chief ordered his braves
to fold their tents and move on.

CHAPTER XXX.

CODY DAY AT THE OMAHA EXPOSITION.

SINCE 1893 the "Wild West" exhibitions have been restricted to the various cities of our own land. Life in "Buffalo Bill's Tented City," as it is called, is like life in a small village. There are some six hundred persons in the various departments. Many of the men have their families with them; the Indians have their squaws and papooses, and the variety of nationalities, dialects, and costumes makes the miniature city an interesting and entertaining one.

The Indians may be seen eating bundles of meat from their fingers and drinking tankards of iced buttermilk. The Mexicans, a shade more civilized, shovel with their knives great quantities of the same food into the capacious receptacles provided by nature. The Americans, despite what is said of their rapid eating, take time to laugh and crack jokes, and finish their repast with a product only known to the highest civilization—ice-cream.

When the "Wild West" visited Boston, one hot June day the parade passed a children's hospital on the way to the show-grounds. Many of the little invalids were unable to leave their couches. All who could do so ran to the open windows and gazed eagerly at the passing procession, and the greatest excitement prevailed. These more fortunate little ones described, as best they could, to the little sufferers who could not leave their beds the wonderful things they saw. The Indians were the special admiration

of the children.   After the procession passed, one wee lad,
bedridden by spinal trouble, cried bitterly because he had
not seen it.   A kind-hearted nurse endeavored to soothe
the child, but words proved unavailing.   Then a bright
idea struck the patient woman; she told him he might
write a letter to the great "Buffalo Bill" himself and ask
him for an Indian's picture.

The idea was taken up with delight, and the child spent
an eager hour in penning the letter.   It was pathetic in
its simplicity.   The little sufferer told the great exhibitor
that he was sick in bed, was unable to see the Indians when
they passed the hospital, and that he longed to see a
photograph of one.

The important missive was mailed, and even the impatient little invalid knew it was useless to expect an answer
that day.   The morning had hardly dawned before a child's
bright eyes were open.   Every noise was listened to, and
he wondered when the postman would bring him a letter.
The nurse hardly dared to hope that a busy man like
Buffalo Bill would take time to respond to the wish of a
sick child.

"Colonel Cody is a very busy man," she said.   "We
must be patient."

At perhaps the twentieth repetition of this remark the
door opened noiselessly.   In came a six-foot Indian, clad
in leather trousers and wrapped in a scarlet blanket.   He
wore a head-dress of tall, waving feathers, and carried his
bow in his hand.

The little invalids gasped in wonder; then they shrieked
with delight.   One by one, silent and noiseless, but smiling, six splendid warriors followed the first.   The visitors
had evidently been well trained, and had received explicit
directions as to their actions.

So unusual a sight in the orderly hospital so startled the nurse that she could not even speak. The warriors drew up in a line and saluted her. The happy children were shouting in such glee that the poor woman's fright was unnoticed.

The Indians ranged themselves in the narrow space between the cots, laid aside their gay blankets, placed their bows upon the floor, and waving their arms to and fro, executed a quiet war-dance. A sham battle was fought, followed by a song of victory. After this the blankets were again donned, the kindly red men went away, still smiling as benignly as their war paint would allow them to do. A cheer of gratitude and delight followed them down the broad corridors. The happy children talked about Buffalo Bill and the "Wild West" for weeks after this visit.

North Platte had long urged my brother to bring the exhibition there. The citizens wished to see the mammoth tents spread over the ground where the scout once followed the trail on the actual war-path; they desired that their famous fellow-citizen should thus honor his home town. A performance was finally given there on October 12, 1896, the special car bearing Will and his party arriving the preceding day, Sunday. The writer of these chronicles joined the party in Omaha, and we left that city after the Saturday night performance.

The Union Pacific Railroad had offered my brother every inducement to make this trip; among other things, the officials promised to make special time in running from Omaha to North Platte.

When we awoke Sunday morning, we found that in some way the train had been delayed, that instead of making special time we were several hours late. Will telegraphed this fact to the officials. At the next station double-headers were put on, and the gain became at once perceptible. At Grand Island a congratulatory telegram was sent, noting the gain in time. At the next station we passed the Lightning Express, the "flyer," to which usually everything gives way, and the good faith of the company was evidenced by the fact that this train was side-tracked to make way for Buffalo Bill's "Wild West" train. Another message was sent over the wires to the officials; it read as follows:

" Have just noticed that Lightning Express is side-tracked to make way for Wild West. I herewith promote you to top seat in heaven."

The trip was a continued ovation. Every station was thronged, and Will was obliged to step out on the platform and make a bow to the assembled crowds, his appearance being invariably greeted with a round of cheers. When we reached the station at North Platte, we found that the entire population had turned out to receive their fellow-townsman. The "Cody Guards," a band to which Will presented beautiful uniforms of white broadcloth trimmed with gold braid, struck up the strains of "See, the Conquering Hero Comes." The mayor attempted to do the welcoming honors of the city, but it was impossible for him to make himself heard. Cheer followed cheer from the enthusiastic crowd.

We had expected to reach the place some hours earlier, but our late arrival encroached upon the hour of church service. The ministers discovered that it was impossible to hold their congregations; so they were dismissed, and the pastors accompanied them to the station, one reverend gentleman humorously remarking:

"We shall be obliged to take for our text this morning 'Buffalo Bill and his Wild West,' and will now proceed to the station for the discourse."

Will's tally-ho coach, drawn by six horses, was in waiting for the incoming party. The members of his family seated themselves in that conveyance, and we passed through the town, preceded and followed by a band. As we arrived at the home residence, both bands united in a welcoming strain of martial music.

My oldest sister, Julia, whose husband is manager of "Scout's Rest Ranch," when informed that the "Wild West" was to visit North Platte, conceived the idea of making this visit the occasion of a family reunion. We had never met in an unbroken circle since the days of our first separation, but as a result of her efforts we sat thus that evening in my brother's home. The next day our mother-sister, as she had always been regarded, entertained us at "Scout's Rest Ranch."

The "Wild West" exhibition had visited Duluth for the first time that same year. This city has a population of 65,000. North Platte numbers 3,500. When he wrote to me of his intention to take the exhibition to Duluth, Will offered to make a wager that his own little town would furnish a bigger crowd than would the city of my residence. I could not accept any such inferred slur upon the Zenith City, so accepted the wager, a silk hat against a fur cloak.

October 12th, the date of the North Platte performance, dawned bright and cloudless. "To-day decides our wager," said Will. "I expect there will be two or three dozen people out on this prairie. Duluth turned out a good many thousands, so I suppose you think your wager as good as won."

The manager of the tents evidently thought the outlook a forlorn one. I shared his opinion, and was, in fancy, already the possessor of a fine fur cloak.

"Colonel, shall we stretch the full canvas?" asked the tentman.

"Every inch of it," was the prompt response. "We want to show North Platte the capacity of the 'Wild West,' at any rate."

As we started for the grounds Will was evidently uncertain over the outcome, in spite of his previous boast of the reception North Platte would give him. "We'll have a big tent and plenty of room to spare in it," he observed.

But as we drove to the grounds we soon began to see indications of a coming crowd. The people were pouring in from all directions; the very atmosphere seemed populated; as the dust was nearly a foot deep on the roads, the moving populace made the air almost too thick for breathing. It was during the time of the county fair, and managers of the Union Pacific road announced that excursion trains would be run from every town and hamlet, the officials and their families coming up from Omaha on a special car. Where the crowds came from it was impossible to say. It looked as if a feat of magic had been performed, and that the stones were turned into men, or, perchance, that, as in olden tales, they came up out of the earth.

Accustomed though he is to the success of the show, Will was dumfounded by this attendance. As the crowds poured in I became alarmed about my wager. I visited the ticket-seller and asked how the matter stood.

"It's pretty close," he answered. "Duluth seems to be dwindling away before the mightiness of the Great American Desert."

This section of the country, which was a wilderness only a few years ago, assembled over ten thousand people to attend a performance of the "Wild West."

Omaha, where the opening performance of this exhibi-

tion was given, honored Will last year by setting apart one
day as "Cody Day." August 31st was devoted to his
reception, and a large and enthusiastic crowd gathered to
do the Nebraska pioneer honor. The parade reached the
fair-grounds at eleven o'clock, where it was fittingly received
by one hundred and fifty mounted Indians from the
encampment. A large square space had been reserved for
the reception of the party in front of the Sherman gate.
As it filed through, great applause was sent up by the waiting multitude, and the noise became deafening when my
brother made his appearance on a magnificent chestnut
horse, the gift of General Miles. He was accompanied
by a large party of officials and Nebraska pioneers, who
dismounted to seat themselves on the grand-stand. Prominent among these were the governor of the state, Senator
Thurston, and Will's old friend and first employer, Mr.
Alexander Majors. As Will ascended the platform he was
met by General Manager Clarkson, who welcomed him in
the name of the president of the exposition, whose official
duties precluded his presence. Governor Holcomb was
then introduced, and his speech was a brief review of the
evolution of Nebraska from a wilderness of a generation
ago to the great state which produced this marvelous exposition. Manager Clarkson remarked, as he introduced Mr.
Majors: "Here is the father of them all, Alexander Majors,
a man connected with the very earliest history of Nebraska,
and the business father of Colonel Cody."

This old pioneer was accorded a reception only a shade
less enthusiastic than that which greeted the hero of the
day. He said:

" *Gentlemen, and My Boy, Colonel Cody :* [Laughter.] Can I say a
few words of welcome? Friend Creighton and I came down here together
to-day, and he thought I was not equal to the occasion. Gentlemen, I do

not know whether I am equal to the occasion at this time, but I am going to do the best for you that I can. Give me your hand, Colonel. Gentlemen, forty-three years ago this day, this fine-looking physical specimen of manhood was brought to me by his mother—a little boy nine years old—and little did I think at that time that the boy that was standing before me, asking for employment of some kind by which I could afford to pay his mother a little money for his services, was going to be a boy of such destiny as he has turned out to be. In this country we have great men, we have great men in Washington, we have men who are famous as politicians in this country; we have great statesmen, we have had Jackson and Grant, and we had Lincoln; we have men great in agriculture arid in stock-growing, and in the manufacturing business men who have made great names for themselves, who have stood high in the nation. Next, and even greater, we have a Cody. He, gentlemen, stands before you now, known the wide world over as the last of the great scouts. When the boy Cody came to me, standing straight as an arrow, and looked me in the face, I said to my partner, Mr. Russell, who was standing by my side, ' We will take this little boy, and we will pay him a man's wages, because he can ride a pony just as well as a man can.' He was lighter and could do service of that kind when he was nine years old. I remember when we paid him twenty-five dollars for the first month's work. He was paid in half-dollars, and he got fifty of them. He tied them up in his little handkerchief, and when he got home he untied the handkerchief and spread the money all over the table."

Colonel Cody—"I have been spreading it ever since."

A few remarks followed indicative of Mr. Majors's appreciation of the exhibition, and he closed with the remark, "Bless your precious heart, Colonel Cody!" and sat down, amid great applause.

Senator Thurston's remarks were equally happy. He said:

"Colonel Cody, this is your day. This is your exposition. This is your city. And we all rejoice that Nebraska is your state. You have carried the fame of our country and of our state all over the civilized world; you have been received and honored by princes, by emperors, and by kings; the titled women in the courts of the nations of the world have been captivated by your charm of manner and your splendid manhood. You are known wherever you go, abroad or in the United States, as Colonel Cody, the best representative of the great and progressive

West. You stand here to-day in the midst of a wonderful assembly. Here are representatives of the heroic and daring characters of most of the nations of the world. You are entitled to the honor paid you to-day, and especially entitled to it here. This people know you as a man who has carried this demonstration of yours to foreign lands, and exhibited it at home. You have not been a showman in the common sense of the word. You have been a great national and international educator of men. You have furnished a demonstration of the possibilities of our country that has advanced us in the opinion of all the world. But we who have been with you a third, or more than a third, of a century, we remember you more dearly and tenderly than others do. We remember that when this whole Western land was a wilderness, when these representatives of the aborigines were attempting to hold their own against the onward tide of civilization, the settler and the hardy pioneer, the women and the children, felt safe whenever Cody rode along the frontier; he was their protector and defender.

"Cody, this is your home. You live in the hearts of the people of our state. God bless you and keep you and prosper you in your splendid work."

Will was deeply touched by these strong expressions from his friends. As he moved to the front of the platform to respond, his appearance was the signal for a prolonged burst of cheers. He said:

"You cannot expect me to make adequate response for the honor which you have bestowed upon me to-day. You have overwhelmed my speaking faculties. I cannot corral enough ideas to attempt a coherent reply in response to the honor which you have accorded me. How little I dreamed in the long ago that the lonely path of the scout and the pony-express rider would lead me to the place you have assigned me to-day. Here, near the banks of the mighty Missouri, which flows unvexed to the sea, my thoughts revert to the early days of my manhood. I looked eastward across this rushing tide to the Atlantic, and dreamed that in that long-settled region all men were rich and all women happy. My friends, that day has come and gone. I stand among you a witness that nowhere in the broad universe are men richer in manly integrity, and women happier in their domestic kingdom, than here in our own Nebraska.

"I have sought fortune in many lands, but wherever I have wandered, the flag of our beloved state has been unfurled to every breeze: from the Platte to the Danube, from the Tiber to the Clyde, the emblem of our sovereign state has always floated over the 'Wild West.' Time goes on and brings with it new duties and responsibilities, but we 'old men,' we who are called old-timers, cannot forget the trials and tribulations which we had to encounter while paving the path for civilization and national prosperity.

"The whistle of the locomotive has drowned the howl of the coyote; the barb-wire fence has narrowed the range of the cow-puncher; but no material evidence of prosperity can obliterate our contribution to Nebraska's imperial progress.

"Through your kindness to-day I have tasted the sweetest fruit that grows on ambition's tree. If you extend your kindness and permit me to fall back into the ranks as a high private, my cup will be full.

"In closing, let me call upon the 'Wild West, the Congress of Rough Riders of the World,' to voice their appreciation of the kindness you have shown them to-day."

At a given signal the "Wild West" gave three ringing cheers for Nebraska and the Trans-Mississippi Exposition. The cowboy band followed with the "Red, White, and Blue," and an exposition band responded with the "Star-Spangled Banner." The company fell into line for a parade around the grounds, Colonel Cody following on his chestnut horse, Duke. After him came the officials and invited guests in carriages; then came the Cossacks, the Cubans, the German cavalry, the United States cavalry, the Mexicans, and representatives of twenty-five countries.

As the parade neared its end, my brother turned to his friends and suggested that as they had been detained long past the dinner-hour in doing him honor, he would like to compensate them by giving an informal spread. This invitation was promptly accepted, and the company adjourned to a café, where a tempting luncheon was spread before them. Never before had such a party of pioneers met around a banquet-table, and many were the reminiscences of early days brought out. Mr. Majors, the originator of the Pony Express line, was there. The two Creighton brothers, who put through the first telegraph line, and took the occupation of the express riders from them, had seats of honor.   A. D. Jones was introduced as the man who carried the first postoffice of Omaha around in his hat, and who still wore the hat.   Numbers of other pioneers were there, and each contributed his share of racy anecdotes and pleasant reminiscences.

CHAPTER XXXI.

THE LAST OF THE GREAT SCOUTS.

THE story of frontier days is a tale that is told. The "Wild West" has vanished like mist in the sun before the touch of the two great magicians of the nineteenth century—steam and electricity.

The route of the old historic Santa Fé trail is nearly followed by the Atchison, Topeka and Santa Fé Railroad, which was completed in 1880. The silence of the prairie was once broken by the wild war-whoop of the Indian as he struggled to maintain his supremacy over some adjoining tribe; the muffled roar caused by the heavy hoof-beats of thousands of buffaloes was almost the only other sound that broke the stillness. To-day the shriek of the engine, the clang of the bell, and the clatter of the car-wheels form a ceaseless accompaniment to the cheerful hum of busy life which everywhere pervades the wilderness of thirty years ago. Almost the only memorials of the struggles and privations of the hardy trappers and explorers, whose daring courage made the achievements of the present possible, are the historic landmarks which bear the names of some of these brave men. But these are very few in number. Pike's Peak lifts its snowy head to heaven in silent commemoration of the early traveler whose name it bears. Simpson's Rest, a lofty obelisk, commemorates the mountaineer whose life was for the most part passed upon its rugged slopes, and whose last request was that he should

BUFFALO BILL ON HORSEBACK.

FROM THE FAMOUS PAINTING BY ROSA BONHEUR.

be buried on its summit. Another cloud-capped moun-tain-height bears the name of Fisher's Peak, and thereby hangs a tale.

Captain Fisher commanded a battery in the army engaged in the conquest of New Mexico. His command encamped near the base of the mountain which now bears his name. Deceived by the illusive effect of the atmos-phere, he started out for a morning stroll to the supposed near-by elevation, announcing that he would return in time for breakfast. The day passed with no sign of Captain Fisher, and night lengthened into a new day. When the second day passed without his return, his command was forced to believe that he had fallen a prey to lurking In-dians, and the soldiers were sadly taking their seats for their evening meal when the haggard and wearied captain put in an appearance. His morning stroll had occupied two days and a night; but he set out to visit the mountain, and he did it.

The transcontinental line which supplanted the Old Salt Lake trail, and is now known as the Union Pacific Railroad, antedated the Atchison, Topeka and Santa Fé by eleven years. The story of the difficulties encountered, and the obstacles overcome in the building of this road, furnishes greater marvels than any narrated in the Arabian Nights' Tales.

This railroad superseded the Pony Express line, the reeking, panting horses of which used their utmost endeavor and carried their tireless riders fifteen miles an hour, cov-ering their circuit in eight days' time at their swiftest rate of speed. The iron horse gives a sniff of disdain, and easily traverses the same distance, from the Missouri line to the Pacific Coast, in three days.

Travelers who step aboard the swiftly moving, luxurious

cars of to-day give little thought to their predecessors; for the dangers the early voyagers encountered they have no sympathy. The traveler in the stagecoach was beset by perils without from the Indians and the outlaws; he faced the equally unpleasant companionship of fatigue and discomfort within. The jolting, swinging coach bounced and jounced the unhappy passengers as the reckless driver lashed the flying horses. Away they galloped over mountains and through ravines, with no cessation of speed. Even the shipper pays the low rate of transportation asked to-day with reluctance, and forgets the great debt he owes this adjunct of our civilization.

But great as are the practical benefits derived from the railways, we cannot repress a sigh as we meditate on the picturesque phases of the vanished era. Gone are the bullwhackers and the prairie-schooners! Gone are the stagecoaches and their drivers! Gone are the Pony Express riders! Gone are the trappers, the hardy pioneers, the explorers, and the scouts! Gone is the prairie monarch, the shaggy, unkempt buffalo!

In 1869, only thirty years ago, the train on the Kansas Pacific road was delayed eight hours in consequence of the passage of an enormous herd of buffaloes over the track in front of it. But the easy mode of travel introduced by the railroad brought hundreds of sportsmen to the plains, who wantonly killed this noble animal solely for sport, and thousands of buffaloes were sacrificed for their skins, for which there was a widespread demand. From 1868 to 1881, in Kansas alone, there was paid out $2,500,000 for the bones of this animal, which were gathered up on the prairie and used in the carbon works of the country. This represents a total death-rate of 31,000,000 buffaloes in one state. As far as I am able to ascertain, there remains at this writing only one herd, of less than twenty animals, out of all the countless thousands that roamed the prairie so short a time ago, and this herd is carefully preserved in a private park. There may be a few isolated specimens in menageries and shows, but this wholesale slaughter has resulted in the practical extermination of the species.

As with the animal native to our prairies, so has it been with the race native to our land. We may deplore the wrongs of the Indian, and sympathize with his efforts to wrest justice from his so-called protectors. We may admire his poetic nature, as evidenced in the myths and legends of the race. We may be impressed by the stately dignity and innate ability as orator and statesman which he displays. We may preserve the different articles of his picturesque garb as relics. But the old, old drama of history is repeating itself before the eyes of this generation; the inferior must give way to the superior civilization. The poetic, picturesque, primitive red man must inevitably succumb before the all-conquering tread of his pitiless, practical, progressive white brother.

Cooper has immortalized for us the extinction of a people in the "Last of the Mohicans." Many another tribe has passed away, unhonored and unsung. Westward the "Star of Empire" takes its way; the great domain west of the Mississippi is now peopled by the white race, while the Indians are shut up in reservations. Their doom is sealed; their sun is set. "Kismet" has been spoken of them; the total extinction of the race is only a question of time. In the words of Rudyard Kipling:

> " Take up the White Man's burden—
> Ye dare not stoop to less—
> Nor call too loud on freedom
> To cloke your weariness.

By all ye will or whisper,
   By all ye leave or do,
The silent, sullen peoples
   Shall weigh your God and you."

Of this past epoch of our national life there remains but one well-known representative. That one is my brother. He occupies a unique place in the portrait gallery of famous Americans to-day. It is not alone his commanding personality, nor the success he has achieved along various lines, which gives him the strong hold he has on the hearts of the American people, or the absorbing interest he possesses in the eyes of foreigners. The fact that in his own person he condenses a period of national history is a large factor in the fascination he exercises over others. He may fitly be named the "Last of the Great Scouts." He has had great predecessors. The mantle of Kit Carson has fallen upon his shoulders, and he wears it worthily. He has not, and never can have, a successor. He is the vanishing-point between the rugged wilderness of the past in Western life and the vast achievement in the present.

When the "Wild West" disbands, the last vestige of our frontier life passes from the scene of active realities, and becomes a matter of history.

"Life is real, life is earnest," sings the poet, and real and earnest it has been for my brother. It has been spent in others' service. I cannot recall a time when he has not thus been laden with heavy burdens. Yet for himself he has won a reputation, national and international. A naval officer visiting in China relates that as he stepped ashore he was offered two books for purchase—one the Bible, the other a "Life of Buffalo Bill."

For nearly half a century, which comprises his child-hood, youth, and manhood, my brother has been before

the public.   He can scarcely be said to have had a childhood, so early was he thrust among the rough scenes of
frontier life, therein to play a man's part at an age when
most boys think of nothing more than marbles and tops.
He enlisted in the Union army before he was of age, and
did his share in upholding the flag during the Civil War as
ably as many a veteran of forty, and since then he has
remained, for the most part, in his country's service,
always ready to go to the front in any time of danger.   He
has achieved distinction in many and various ways.   He is
president of the largest irrigation enterprise in the world,
president of a colonization company, of a town-site company, and of two transportation companies.   He is the
foremost scout and champion buffalo-hunter of America,
one of the crack shots of the world, and its greatest popular entertainer.   He is broad-minded and progressive in
his views, inheriting from both father and mother a hatred
of oppression in any form.   Taking his mother as a standard, he believes the franchise is a birthright which should
appertain to intelligence and education, rather than to sex.
It is his public career that lends an interest to his private
life, in which he has been a devoted and faithful son and
brother, a kind and considerate husband, a loving and
generous father.   "Only the names of them that are
upright, brave, and true can be honorably known," were
the mother's dying words; and honorably known has his
name become, in his own country and across the sea.

With the fondest expectation he looks forward to the
hour when he shall make his final bow to the public and
retire to private life.   It is his long-cherished desire to
devote his remaining years to the development of the Big
Horn Basin, in Wyoming.   He has visited every country
in Europe, and has looked upon the most beautiful of Old

World scenes. He is familiar with all the most splendid regions of his own land, but to him this new El Dorado of the West is the fairest spot on earth.

He has already invested thousands of dollars and given much thought and attention toward the accomplishment of his pet scheme. An irrigating ditch costing nearly a million dollars now waters this fertile region, and various other improvements are under way, to prepare a land flowing with milk and honey for the reception of thousands of homeless wanderers. Like the children of Israel, these would never reach the promised land but for the untiring efforts of a Moses to go on before; but unlike the ancient guide and scout of sacred history, my brother has been privileged to penetrate the remotest corner of this primitive land of Canaan. The log cabin he has erected there is not unlike the one of our childhood days. Here he finds his haven of rest, his health-resort, to which he hastens when the show season is over and he is free again for a space. He finds refreshment in the healthful, invigorating atmosphere of his chosen retreat; he enjoys sweet solace from the cares of life under the influence of its magnificent scenery.

And here, in the shadow of the Rockies, yet in the very "light of things," it is his wish to finish his days as he began them, in opening up for those who come after him the great regions of the still undeveloped West, and in poring over the lesson learned as a boy on the plains:

> " That nature never did betray
> The heart that loved her."

THE END.